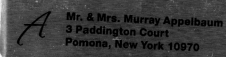

SHADOW STRIKE

Also by Yaakov Katz

*The Weapon Wizards: How Israel Became a
High-Tech Military Superpower* (with Amir Bohbot)
Israel vs. Iran: The Shadow War (with Yoaz Hendel)

SHADOW
STRIKE

Inside Israel's Secret Mission
to Eliminate Syrian Nuclear Power

YAAKOV KATZ

St. Martin's Press
New York

SHADOW STRIKE. Copyright © 2019 by Yaakov Katz. All rights reserved.
Printed in the United States of America. For information, address
St. Martin's Press, 175 Fifth Avenue, New York, N.Y. 10010.

www.stmartins.com

The Library of Congress Cataloging-in-Publication Data is available upon request.

ISBN 978-1-250-19127-4 (hardcover)
ISBN 978-1-250-19128-1 (ebook)

Our books may be purchased in bulk for promotional, educational, or business use.
Please contact your local bookseller or the Macmillan Corporate and
Premium Sales Department at 1-800-221-7945, extension 5442, or
by email at MacmillanSpecialMarkets@macmillan.com.

First Edition: May 2019

10 9 8 7 6 5 4 3 2 1

To my late grandparents—
Rene and Charles Lipshitz and
Miriam and Herman Katz—
who gifted me with a love for storytelling.

And to Chaya, Atara, Miki, Rayli
and Eli, my true heroes.

Contents

Key Characters

ISRAEL

Ehud Olmert: Prime Minister

Ehud Barak: Defense Minister

Amir Peretz: Defense Minister until June 2007

Tzipi Livni: Foreign Minister

Gabi Ashkenazi: Chief of Staff, Israel Defense Forces (IDF)

Meir Dagan: Director of the Mossad

Amos Yadlin: Commander of Military Intelligence (referred to in this book as Aman, its Hebrew acronym)

Eliezer Shkedi: Commander of the Israeli Air Force (IAF)

Ido Nehushtan: head of the IDF Planning Directorate

Ilan Mizrahi: head of National Security Council

Efraim Halevy: former head of the Mossad

UNITED STATES

George W. Bush: President

Dick Cheney: Vice President

Robert Gates: Secretary of Defense

Condoleezza Rice: Secretary of State

Michael Hayden: Director of the Central Intelligence Agency (CIA)

Stephen Hadley: National Security Adviser

Elliott Abrams: Deputy National Security Adviser

Eric Edelman: Under Secretary of Defense for Policy

Eliot Cohen: Counselor of the State Department

James Jeffrey: Deputy Assistant Secretary of State for Near Eastern Affairs

Christopher Hill: Assistant Secretary of State for East Asian and Pacific Affairs and head of the US delegation to Six Party Talks

SHADOW STRIKE

Introduction

SAVING THE COUNTRY

It was a hot summer night in 2014, and Ehud Olmert was sitting at home looking at some news sites online. The former prime minister came across a story about fighting taking place in eastern Syria near the ancient city of Deir ez-Zor, located along the banks of the mighty Euphrates River.

At first glance it didn't mean much. The civil war in Syria had erupted three years earlier and while it had long ago turned into a humanitarian disaster, the world seemed to simply not care.

It started with protests in Damascus in March 2011, as it had around the same time in other capitals throughout the Middle East and North Africa, in what was then still referred to as the Arab Spring. Ordinary Syrians took to the streets demanding democratic and economic reforms. They wanted political prisoners released from jail and an end to government corruption and draconian emergency laws that, for decades, had ruled over their lives.

Muammar Gaddafi had been captured and executed in Libya, Hosni Mubarak was dramatically overthrown in Egypt, but Bashar al-Assad, the Syrian president, was continuing to hold on and fight the rebel forces, in a deadly, bloody and controversial war that would eventually see the rise of ISIS, the Islamic State in Iraq and the Levant. Artificial border lines drawn a century earlier with a pencil and ruler were proven worthless by a force that used pickup trucks carrying five men dressed in black fatigues and armed with Kalashnikov assault rifles and rocket-propelled grenades.

By 2014, what was happening in Syria was a full-fledged war, one that had exceeded all predictions of how long it would last and whether Assad's regime would survive. With help in the beginning from Iran and Hezbollah and later from Russia, Assad was fighting back with all available means.

The regime's use of chemical weapons had passed by with little repercussion the previous summer, and while there was talk about coalition airstrikes and the global threat the Islamic State posed Europe, the West had pretty much fallen into a routine. Countries condemned Syria's leader but never took action. It was still a few months before the US would finally step up its involvement and launch airstrikes against ISIS targets throughout the country.

But that July, the Islamic State announced that it had completed its takeover of Deir ez-Zor, the primary hub of Syria's oil and natural gas industry and a place—like many in the Middle East—rich in history, blood and violence.

During Roman times, Deir ez-Zor was an important trading post. A few centuries later, it changed hands and became part of the ancient kingdom of Palmyra. But the wave of conquests didn't stop there. In the late nineteenth century, the city came under the control of the Ottoman Empire, eventually becoming the final destination point for Armenians forced on the death march during the genocide that began in 1915. Those who survived the marches were taken to a nearby desert patch where they were shot and buried in mass graves.

ISIS, Olmert read that night, was now in control of most of the Tigris-Euphrates river basin, an area similar in size to the entire United Kingdom. It reigned over the territory it conquered through a combination of terror, zealotry, a savvy use of social media and improvised battlefield tactics. It was a force that Assad's conventional military was failing to defeat.

The Israeli government was carefully tracking what was happening in Syria. From its perspective, the war there had nothing to do with Israel, and therefore there was very little it could do to make a genuine difference. Yes, it felt a moral imperative to help the people being massacred and, as a result, established a field hospital along the border to treat the wounded. But it knew that it had to be careful not to be dragged into the war over the border. If it was, Israel's involvement would be used by Assad to claim that the civil war was actually a Zionist plot, which would help him garner greater support at Israel's expense.

But that evening, Olmert was focused on Deir ez-Zor. The story he was reading was of extreme importance. It was a validation of a decision he had made seven years earlier, one that if not taken would have transformed the world and made it an even scarier place.

Olmert's three-year term as prime minister had been marked

by conflict, peace negotiations and political upheaval. In 2006, he took the country to war in Lebanon against Hezbollah and in 2008 against Hamas in the Gaza Strip. In 2009, as his term came to a premature ending, he tried to hammer out a peace deal with the Palestinians, making their leader an offer to which Olmert would never receive an answer.

But now, five years later, Olmert was still in the spotlight. A few months earlier, the Tel Aviv District Court had found him guilty of receiving bribes when he was mayor of Jerusalem, about a decade earlier, and sentenced him to six years in prison. Olmert wasn't giving up and was in the midst of finalizing his appeal to the Supreme Court.

After finishing the article, Olmert looked out the window of his home in Motza Illit, a small and sleepy suburb to the west of Jerusalem, Israel's capital city. In the distance he saw the tower of Hadassah Hospital, one of the country's leading medical institutions. To the south he could see the Har Menuchot cemetery, a place where, according to Jewish tradition, some of the first people will be resurrected when the Messiah comes. And just below was Highway 1, the country's main artery, connecting Jerusalem with Tel Aviv and beyond.

Back in 1948, when the State of Israel was first established, Highway 1 was impossible to drive on. The Jordanians had taken up positions along sections of the highway, making it dangerous for convoys to use on their way to bring supplies to the besieged Jews of Jerusalem. To get through, the newly formed Israel Defense Forces (IDF), under the direction of American-Jewish Colonel Mickey Marcus, paved the makeshift Burma Road through the mountains, bypassing the Jordanians and entering Jerusalem not far from where Olmert sat that evening. Marcus's courage cost him his life but helped breach the Jordanian siege on Jerusalem.

Israel's story, Olmert thought at the time, could have been different. As he looked out the window, he imagined what would have happened had he listened to those who had urged him not to act. He imagined how Israeli history would have been changed forever.

Israel would have found itself living under an unimaginable threat, and ISIS, he knew, would have come into possession of a nightmarish capability, morphing it from a ruthless terrorist group into an existential threat not just for Israel, but for the entire Western world.

There was no one around for Olmert to share his satisfaction with and it didn't really matter. Israel in 2014 still wasn't officially speaking about what Olmert had done back in 2007. It was an operation that would stay hidden from the public, a story that would never be told in its entirety.

Until now.

This book tells—for the first time and from the perspective of Jerusalem and Washington, DC—the full and true story behind Israel's daring operation to destroy the al-Kibar nuclear reactor, which was being built under a tight veil of secrecy in the Syrian desert, in September 2007. It is a tale of espionage, political courage, military might and psychological warfare on a national scale.

It is also a story that brings Israel's powerful military and diplomatic alliance with the United States to life. It reveals what happens behind the closed doors and heated debates in the Oval Office in Washington, the Prime Minister's Office in Jerusalem and the underground military command center beneath IDF headquarters in Tel Aviv.

It is a story of extreme importance and relevance, as these two countries remain united in a nonstop battle to prevent nuclear proliferation, to defeat Islamic terror and to curtail Iran's attempts to spread its hegemony throughout the Middle East. While this story takes place in 2007, the ramifications of what happened in Syria continue to impact the world we live in today.

The events of September 6, 2007, were, for the most part, a success. Israel discovered a threat, took action, neutralized it and avoided a larger conflict. But it could have been different. Had Israel not learned of the existence of Syria's reactor, what would the Middle East look like today? It is scary just to think about.

Despite more than 70 years of statehood, the small country of Israel still faces conflict along its borders, possibly more so today than ever before. While Israel's wars of the past—the Independence War in 1948, the Six Day War in 1967 and the Yom Kippur War in 1973—were fought against multiple enemies with conventional militaries, they were for the most part fought against adversaries that were rational and predictable.

Today, Israel is surrounded by terrorist organizations with growing weapons arsenals, in countries—like Syria, Lebanon and Egypt—whose regimes are constantly teetering on the precipice of survival. While this has an upside—Israeli territory is less at risk of being conquered—the regional situation carries with it an unprecedented sense of uncertainty and the possibility of war erupting without any warning.

When protests first broke out in Syria in 2011, Israeli and American intelligence agencies were sure that the country's president, Bashar al-Assad, would not survive: that he would meet the same fate as Mubarak or Gaddafi. Former Israeli prime minister Ehud Barak, who at the time served as defense minister, said that Assad's regime was just weeks away from falling. Others believed the same but Assad proved them all wrong, utilizing some of the most vicious military tactics available to ensure his survival, including dropping chemical weapons on his own people.

In more recent years, Israel's concern has been focused mostly on the Golan Heights, the Jewish state's version of Tuscany and home to a growing wine and beer industry, beautiful waterfalls, lush vineyards, an abundance of archeological sites, rolling mountains and wide vistas.

Conquered from Syria in 1967, the Golan was the scene of the world's last real conventional ground battle during the 1973 Yom Kippur War, when Syrian and Israeli tanks exchanged blows in a battle that ended with Israel still in control of the strategic high ground. Nowadays, old Syrian Soviet-made tanks are strewn throughout some of the Golan's uncleared minefields, a testament to the fierce battles that once raged among its hills.

Despite the countries officially being enemies, the Syrian border was, surprisingly, Israel's quietest for nearly five decades. All of that changed in the spring of 2011 when the civil war began. In the years that followed, Israel had a front-row seat to the rise of new enemies and eventually the arrival of Russia right up along its border. It was the creation of a modern Middle East mosaic.

Starting at the southern tip of the Golan near the hot springs of Hamat Gader, ISIS fighters used to roam freely. A little farther north one could encounter fighters from al Qaida affiliate Jabhat al-Nusra. A few more miles and you could meet members of Iran's Revolutionary Guard Corps as well as fighters from its Lebanese proxy, Hezbollah.

When the war first erupted, Israel's focus was on how to stay out of the fight with the exception of two red lines that, when crossed, moved the IDF into action. The first was the transfer of advanced weapons—like ballistic missiles and surface-to-air missile systems—from Syria to Hezbollah, Israel's arch nemesis in Lebanon. The second: when it identified Iranian efforts to establish bases on the Syrian side of the Golan Heights. Since 2011, over 200 such Israeli strikes have targeted these bases and convoys.

All of the strikes were carried out discreetly, with Israel maintaining a policy of ambiguity. It never confirmed responsibility for the strikes but when asked, Israel didn't deny that it had been behind them either.

"We are controlling our borders, we are protecting our country and we will continue to do so," Benjamin Netanyahu, Israel's prime minister, said in a rare public statement on Syria toward the end of 2017.[1]

One such strike took Israel and Syria to the brink of war and demonstrated how different things could have been had Israel not acted in 2007.

It was in February 2018 when Israeli Air Force radar systems detected the infiltration of an unmanned aerial vehicle, a drone, into northern Israel. The drone had taken off from T4, Syria's large airbase near the city of Homs. Time was short. While the radar system tracked the drone from the moment it left T4, Israel had no way of knowing if it was carrying explosives, missiles or was simply on a reconnaissance mission.

An Apache helicopter was scrambled from a nearby base and quickly caught up with the drone. It locked on its missiles, fired and scored a direct hit. Later, upon analyzing the wreckage, Israel discovered that the drone had been packed with explosives, and was likely on its way to crash and explode on a nearby IDF base. The drone was Iranian and was called Saegheh. It was a copy of America's RQ-170, an advanced stealth drone made by Lockheed Martin, one of which had crashed in Iran in 2011.

The infiltration was a violation of Israeli sovereignty and the first direct Iranian attack on the Jewish state. In the past, Iran used proxies like Hezbollah in Lebanon or Hamas in the Gaza Strip to attack Israel; this time Tehran was doing it all on its own. The drone was Iranian and the drone operator was Iranian.

Israel didn't waste time. Four F-16s were scrambled from the nearby Ramat David Air Force Base. As they approached the border with Syria, they dropped their GPS-guided missiles, which made their way straight to the Iranian caravan from which the drone had been operated in T4. It was a direct hit.

But then, as the F-16s began returning to base, an alarm in one of the cockpits went off. An S-200 surface-to-air missile, carrying a 200-kg warhead, was heading directly toward one of the fighter jets. It had locked on and the Israeli F-16 was about to be hit. The pilot and navigator didn't hesitate. They ejected, mere seconds before their aircraft was blown to pieces.

The country was shocked. Israel had carried out dozens of strikes against Syrian targets but had never met a response like this. Additionally, over 30 years had passed since an Israeli fighter jet was shot down by an enemy missile. This wasn't a simple matter. For the first time since the Islamic Revolution of 1979, Israel and Iran were on the brink of a direct confrontation.

Israel retaliated swiftly and aggressively. The three remaining aircraft launched the rest of their missiles at a dozen more Iranian and Syrian targets throughout the country, including the surface-to-air missile battery that had downed the F-16. Had the aircrew been killed, had they not ejected in time, Israel might have felt compelled to escalate its response.

It was an example of the volatility along Israel's northern border with Syria. Israel had operated covertly over Syria in the past. But on this day, it was all made public, showing that even small operations can sometimes have deadly consequences.

Now imagine that Syria had nuclear weapons. That it still had a nuclear reactor in northeast Syria. That in 2007, Israel had not stopped it.

Had Israel not blocked Syria's nuclear aspirations in 2007, would it have been able to take preemptive military action to stop the transfer of advanced weapons to Hezbollah, or would its hands have been tied out of fear that Assad would retaliate with nuclear weapons? What about his own people? Assad used gas against them. Would he have used nuclear weapons if he'd had them? Despite the years that have passed, even the smartest intelligence analysts cannot say for certain.

Then there is North Korea. North Korea helped Syria build its nuclear reactor. The isolated regime in Pyongyang sold nuclear technology to Damascus at the same time as it was conducting negotiations with the world to curtail its own illicit nuclear program. It proliferated and got away with it.

Was this experience what shaped North Korea's steely determination that it could do whatever it wants and get away with it? That it could test nuclear weapons and fire long-range intercontinental ballistic missiles without consequence? And what would have happened had North Korea been held accountable and made to pay a price for its proliferation and work with Syria? Would the situation in Asia look any different today?

It is impossible to know, but in this one story—seemingly just about the bombing of a nuclear reactor in Syria—we bear witness to the dangers that lurk around the globe; to how radical regimes, without ideological linkage, work closely to proliferate the most devastating weapon known to mankind. And this story shows how two countries—Israel and the United States—joined hands to stop them.

Israel, as a story, has always marveled the world. It is a tale of an ancient people who returned to their historic homeland and achieved the impossible. Israel not only survived, it persevered, succeeding in building a vibrant democracy alongside a powerful military and economy.

Since its inception, Israel has been engaged in a nonstop

battle for survival, from the conventional wars it fought with its Arab neighbors in the early years to the rockets and terror threats it faces today along its northern and southern borders.

What most people don't know is that Israel is the only country in the world to have attacked and destroyed two nuclear reactors in two different enemy countries. No other country has taken such action. It is worth keeping this in mind as the world continues to debate how to solve its current challenges.

In both cases—Iraq and Syria—Israel made use of its Top Gun–style air force to eliminate threats it viewed as existential dangers, doing, in both cases, what military planners and politicians thought wasn't humanly or technically possible.

Both attacks were executed in line with a policy that has become known in Israel as the Begin Doctrine, a reference to Menachem Begin, the Israeli prime minister who ordered the 1981 strike against the Osirak reactor in Iraq. According to the unwritten doctrine, the Jewish state will always use military force to prevent its enemies from obtaining nuclear weapons.

"Israel cannot afford the introduction of the nuclear weapon," Ariel Sharon, the former prime minister and defense minister, said after the bombing of Osirak.[2] "For us, it is not a question of balance of terror but a question of survival. We shall therefore have to prevent such a threat at its inception."

For a state built on the ashes of the Holocaust and the attempted extermination of European Jewry, it is a policy that continues to resonate as other countries in the Middle East, and particularly Iran, pursue nuclear weapons. A tiny country about the size of New Jersey, Israel lacks strategic depth. A nuclear explosion in the center of the country would have far-reaching consequences and threaten the continued viability of the Jewish state as we know it.

When Israel decided to bomb Osirak in 1981, there was little concern of a full-fledged war breaking out. Begin knew that the US would be upset and there was a possibility that Saddam Hussein would launch some long-range Scud missiles into Israel (as he would during the First Gulf War a decade later). But that was about it. A war was not a realistic scenario considering that the countries—Iraq and Israel—do not share a border.

What happened in 2007 was different. While Israel worked in the beginning with the White House—unlike in 1981—it ultimately decided to ignore the solution proposed by President George W. Bush. By doing this, Olmert ran the risk of igniting a full-blown crisis with the US, which could have undermined the strategic alliance that serves as one of the pillars of the very foundation of Israel's military and diplomatic power.

In addition, this time, the government acted while knowing that a conventional war, with dire consequences for Israel, could break out with Syria. It was just a year after the Second Lebanon War with Hezbollah, and Lieutenant General Gabi Ashkenazi, the IDF chief of staff, told the government that there was at least a 50 percent chance—and possibly even greater—that Assad and Hezbollah would retaliate with force to an Israeli bombing.

But even if the Begin Doctrine exists, it does not mean that Israel will always be able to implement it.

An attack against Iran's nuclear facilities is not comparable to the two previous strikes against the Syrian and Iraqi reactors that Israel has carried out. In those two cases, the targets consisted of one main facility, aboveground without protection by advanced air defense systems. In each case, destroying that single facility was enough to set back and delay the country's nuclear program. In Iran, though, the ayatollahs have learned lessons from Osirak and al-Kibar and have scattered their nuclear facilities throughout the country. Some are built in heavily fortified underground bunkers, making them impenetrable to conventional aerial bombings.

Will Israel continue to live by the sword that it used in 1981 and 2007, or has it reached the point when it will decide that it can preempt no more? Are there limits to even what the mighty Jewish state is capable of doing? Or is what happened in 2007 just the curtain raiser for an even bigger face-off with Iran, one that still looms on the horizon?

This book is an outline for how that might happen. As the Middle East continues to find itself in the throes of conflict and instability, it is a story people need to pay attention to.

1

A RAID IN VIENNA

In the middle of April 2007 a short, bald and burly man with a limp and a cane walked into the West Wing of the White House. He carried a small briefcase with a few folders chaotically jutting out.[1]

The man showed his diplomatic passport at the entrance. He was under the impression that he would be brought directly to the Oval Office for a private meeting with the president but, instead, the guards were under orders to keep his name off the official visitor logs and to clandestinely escort him to the office of National Security Adviser Stephen Hadley. Inside, two other men were waiting: Hadley's deputy, Elliott Abrams, and a surprise guest, the vice president of the United States, Dick Cheney.

The man the trio had gathered to meet was Meir Dagan, the renowned and feared head of the Mossad, Israel's legendary foreign spy agency and the equivalent of the CIA. A few days earlier, Prime Minister Ehud Olmert had called President

George W. Bush and told him that Dagan would be coming to Washington with some important information. "I'd appreciate if you could meet him," Olmert told Bush.

The request, phrased in a way that seemed urgent, took Bush and his staff by surprise. Heads of state—even close allies like Olmert—don't usually ask the president to meet the directors of their intelligence agencies alone. If they ever do meet them, it is almost always according to diplomatic protocol and in the presence of the foreign leader.

So, the president's aides decided to stick to protocol. They would first meet Dagan, evaluate whatever information he was bringing with him, and, if needed, take him to see the president. Cheney was briefed about the pending visit and decided to sit in on the meeting. He knew Dagan and figured that based on Olmert's special request, it must be urgent.

Dagan took a seat on the couch. Cheney settled into a large blue wing chair to his right. Not one for small talk, Dagan got straight to the point.

"Syria is building a nuclear reactor," the Mossad chief said in his thick Israeli accent.[2] "For Syria to have a nuclear weapons program, to have a nuclear weapon, is unacceptable."

Dagan then pulled the first folder out of his bag and spread a number of color photos on the coffee table. Cheney lifted one. Hadley and Abrams took another. They could clearly make out a concrete building under construction with some large pipes being installed inside. There was nothing yet that showed the building to be a nuclear reactor. It didn't have the typical dome or smokestacks, the trademarks of nuclear facilities.

"That is the nuclear reactor," Dagan told the group. It was

a gas-cooled graphite-moderated reactor, he explained, used to produce plutonium, and was being built as an almost exact replica of the Yongbyon nuclear reactor in North Korea. The concrete building on the exterior was a façade being built to hide what was really happening inside.

The Americans were speechless. There were dozens of photos. Cheney, Hadley and Abrams just watched and listened as Dagan pulled out one after another and explained in detail what they were. One of the photographs looked too good to be true. It showed two men posing in front of the concrete structure. One of the men, of Asian ethnicity, was wearing a blue tracksuit. The man he was standing next to, Dagan said, was Ibrahim Othman, head of Syria's Atomic Energy Commission.

Dagan then showed his hosts another photo. It was the same Asian man, although this time he wasn't wearing workout clothes but a tailored suit and black tie. From their intelligence experience, the Americans knew what they were looking at. It was a photo taken at a recent meeting of the Six Party Talks, the negotiations America and other Western superpowers were conducting with North Korea in an effort to stop its rogue nuclear program. The man in the photo, Dagan said, was Chon Chibu, one of the scientists in charge of the Yongbyon nuclear reactor.

The news was earth-shattering. Until then, there was no evidence in the US intelligence community to support what Dagan was claiming. None. Everyone knew about North Korea's nuclear ambitions—the hermit country had tested its first nuclear weapon just a few months earlier in October 2006—but there was nothing to even hint that Pyongyang was proliferating its technology and helping Syria build a nuclear weapon. It wasn't just shocking. It was a strategic nightmare of worldwide proportions.

Dagan continued to pull additional photos out of his bag. It was an intelligence treasure trove. There were photos of the vertical tube openings at the top of the reactor used to hold control rods and another of the reinforced concrete reactor vessel with its steel lining.

Israel, Dagan said, had already found the facility. It was buried deep in the desert in northeastern Syria in a region known as Deir ez-Zor, along the Euphrates River. The Syrians, he explained, had used the river to help conceal their rogue nuclear activity. They had built the reactor in a *wadi*, a valley, so it couldn't be seen by passing cars or hikers. The outer square structure that surrounded the reactor was built to look like an old Ottoman-era fort, no different from the countless other old guard posts scattered throughout the desert.

Cheney, who for years had tried to get US intelligence agencies to probe a possible link between North Korea and Syria, sat quietly. He had warned already in 2001 of the possibility that terrorist groups or rogue states would reproduce and sell nuclear technology on the black market and that North Korea would be at the top of the list of countries selling.

A few months before the meeting with Dagan at the White House, US intelligence agencies had detected that Chibu was making unusually frequent visits to Damascus. As head of the Yongbyon reactor, Chibu was on the US intelligence community's watch list. In his regular intelligence briefings, Cheney periodically asked the intelligence community what Chibu was doing there and if it meant that Syria and North Korea were co-operating on nuclear activity.

The answer he kept getting was "no." The US intelligence services said that while the countries were known to cooperate on missile technology, there was simply nothing to back up the possibility of nuclear collaboration. As Cheney later explained, what happened wasn't necessarily an intelligence "failure" but rather a complete "misinterpretation" of available intelligence.

Cheney's skepticism and high state of alert made these questions natural. He was selected by Bush to serve as his vice president largely due to his experience as a veteran member of Congress—he served six terms representing the State of Wyoming—as well as a stint as secretary of defense under Bush's father from 1989 to 1993. Cheney was in the Bush family's inner circle, and after taking office in 2001, the president sent him to visit all of the different US intelligence agencies and get up to speed on the national security challenges and threats the US faced at the time.

But then Dagan showed up and proved Cheney's intuition to have been right. North Korea wasn't just sharing nuclear know-how with Syria, it was building a nuclear reactor there.

When looking at the photos, the vice president saw clues that others had missed.[3] The reactor was almost completely built and seemed, from the photos, to be just a few months away from becoming operational. There were, for example, no power lines to the facility, or an electrical grid visible nearby that could provide enough power to run a nuclear facility.[4]

No military vehicles were visible in the area or anti-aircraft systems to intercept enemy aircraft. The Syrians, Cheney could tell, had gone to great lengths to hide what they were doing.

In Cheney's mind, this was a clear violation of a marker Bush had laid down half a year earlier after North Korea conducted its first nuclear test. Just hours after the detonation, Bush made a statement from the Diplomatic Reception Room in the White House, declaring that "the transfer of nuclear weapons or material by North Korea to states or non-state entities would be considered a grave threat to the United States, and we would hold North Korea fully accountable of the consequences of such action."[5]

What could be considered a greater "transfer" to another state than the construction of a nuclear reactor, Cheney wondered? No one knew at the time, but when North Korea tested its nuclear device and Bush made his statement, the ruthless regime in Pyongyang was already neck-deep in the midst of one of the gravest, greatest and most secretive acts of nuclear proliferation. Based on the photos, this was something that had been going on for years, possibly as early as 2000.

While Israel was convinced that the building was a gas-cooled nuclear reactor, the satellite images Dagan brought with him made it clear to the others in the meeting that whatever Syria was building, it wasn't some random warehouse. This was a unique structure built for some nefarious purpose that Syria had gone to great lengths to hide from the world.

Cheney knew Dagan from his first term as Bush's vice president, when the Israeli was appointed head of the Mossad. They were about the same age and shared a similar appreciation for military force as a viable way to solve diplomatic problems.

Nevertheless, they couldn't have come from more different backgrounds. Cheney was born in 1941 in Lincoln, Nebraska, and went to Yale University. Dagan was born in 1945 in a train car on the outskirts of Ukraine while his family was trying to escape to Poland.

Cheney had a particular respect for Israel's intelligence capabilities. He often recalled a meeting he had in July 1990 with then Israeli defense minister Moshe Arens and Ehud Barak, Israel's most decorated solider and, at the time, the IDF's deputy chief of staff. It was just a few weeks before Saddam Hussein invaded Kuwait, setting into motion Operation Desert Storm, which Cheney would oversee as secretary of defense.

It was a different time also for US-Syrian relations. Unlike 2007, in 1990 America was speaking directly with Syria and its leader, Hafez al-Assad. It was Cheney who was tasked with calling Assad a few hours before the beginning of the war to update him on what was about to happen. At the time, Syria sent a division to fight against Saddam as well as military representatives to sit in the joint command center set up by the Americans.

Arens and Barak shared with Cheney Israel's updated intelligence assessments on Saddam Hussein's nuclear program. Israel had destroyed the reactor nine years earlier but according to recent Israeli intelligence, Iraq was back to advancing its nuclear program. It was a starkly different assessment than the one reached by the US intelligence community, which at the time assumed that Saddam had forfeited his nuclear aspirations.

During Desert Storm, Cheney had a secure phone line installed in his office that he used to directly contact Arens's office in Tel Aviv. The two spoke almost daily as the US worked hard to keep Israel out of the war. With Saddam firing Scud missiles directly into Israel it wasn't easy. At one point, Cheney learned that Israel had ordered special forces onto helicopters to fly them to Iraq to hunt Scud launchers, jeopardizing the international coalition the US had worked hard to put together and which included Syria and other Arab countries. For the coalition to work, the administration thought, Israel needed to stay on the sidelines.

When the International Atomic Energy Agency (IAEA) gained access to Iraq after the war, Cheney was not surprised to learn that Saddam had in fact restarted his nuclear program. What Arens and Barak had told him months earlier turned out to be closer to reality than what his own intelligence agencies were saying.

"Israel was at least equal if not better than we were in terms of that subject," he would tell people.

Dagan's life story was a microcosm of Israel's never-ending fight for survival. Most of his family had been killed in the Holocaust, and instead of going to college, he spent his post–high school years participating in covert operations deep behind enemy lines in places like Lebanon and the Gaza Strip.

As a young IDF recruit, Dagan originally tried out for Sayeret Matkal, the IDF's most elite unit and a breeding ground for many of Israel's leaders, including two prime ministers— Ehud Barak and Benjamin Netanyahu. But he didn't get in, failing to pass the grueling selection process. Instead, Dagan was drafted into the Paratrooper's Brigade, where he slowly climbed the ranks, earning a reputation as a brave soldier and brilliant tactician along the way. His undercover experience and creative mind soon made him a key player in countering the Palestinian terror threat emanating from the Gaza Strip.

In January 1971, for example, Dagan—then a young captain—was leading a convoy of military jeeps through Jabalya, a Palestinian refugee camp north of Gaza City. On the way, a taxi passed Dagan's car. While it drove by quickly, Dagan—whose mind was always sharp and acutely vigilant to his surroundings—was able to identify one of the passengers as Abu Nimar, a known terrorist Israel had been hunting for some time. He caught up with the cab and ordered it to pull over. The soldiers took up positions around the vehicle as Dagan approached the passenger seat where Abu Nimar was sitting.

Abu Nimar got out of the car and pulled out a grenade, yanked the pin and yelled: "We are all going to die." Dagan shouted to his troops to take cover as he lunged directly at Abu Nimar and headbutted him with his helmet. As Abu Nimar fell to the ground, Dagan grabbed the Palestinian's hand and succeeded in securing the grenade before it could explode, an act for which he was later awarded the IDF Medal of Honor.

Abu Nimar was arrested and sentenced to a lengthy prison term. A few months after his capture, he expressed willingness to become an informant for Israel but had a condition—he wanted to meet the man who in a singular moment had both taken him prisoner and saved his life. Dagan agreed to the meeting and helped turn Abu Nimar into one of Israel's most strategic intelligence assets.

When asked about this period of his life, Dagan explained a simple equation: "We hit people who were involved in attacks on us. We hit them and deterred others."[6]

Ariel Sharon, then an IDF general in charge of the Southern Command, heard of Dagan and became fond of the young officer. Sharon was struggling to stop a wave of infiltrations by Palestinian terrorists from the Gaza Strip into Israel and gave Dagan the mandate to find a way to end this bloody reign of terror. Within a few months, Dagan had founded Sayeret Rimon, a crack commando unit of fearless soldiers who would disguise themselves as Palestinians and then raid Gaza to eliminate PLO fighters.

The Rimon commandos took on the most dangerous missions. They dressed up as Palestinian fishermen, farmers and women, doing whatever it took to get as close as they could to their targets. Israel was fighting a cruel and brutal battle for its life. Rules of engagement were left blurry.

When Sharon became prime minister in 2001, Dagan tagged along as his counterterrorism adviser. But Sharon had bigger plans for his former soldier.

When he took over the premiership, Sharon encountered a Mossad that he believed had become paralyzed. Its leadership at the time, Sharon felt, appeared to prefer talks with Arab diplomats at cocktail parties in Geneva over dangerous and risky operations in Tehran or Dubai.

It was a paralysis that had taken hold of the spy agency after the botched 1997 assassination attempt against Hamas leader Khaled Mashal in Amman. Two Mossad agents were caught trying to poison Mashal, and to get them back, Israel had to provide the antidote to save the Hamas leader's life and release Palestinian terrorists, including Sheikh Ahmed Yassin, the terror group's founder and spiritual leader.

"The motto at the time was 'don't get into trouble,'" one former security official explained.

On one occasion in the early 2000s, Mossad trainees were hearing a lecture about what to do if they were captured by police during a covert operation overseas. The trainees were told not to resist. "Talk your way out of it but don't fight," the instructor said. As an example, he told a story about a team of Mossad agents caught trying to tap a suspected Hezbollah operative's phone in Switzerland.

"Why shouldn't we resist?" one cadet asked the instructor. The answer was that violence was not the way the Mossad operated. It was the exact opposite of the ruthless and legendary spy agency that had once instilled fear in the hearts and minds of Israel's enemies across the globe.

In 2002, Sharon decided he needed to shake things up at the Mossad and asked Dagan, his old commando friend, to take over the reins of the dusty spy agency. Dagan, Sharon knew, was a no-nonsense soldier. He was brave, innovative and not afraid to get his hands dirty. On the contrary, that was his modus operandi.

It didn't take long for the change Dagan brought to the agency to be felt. Dagan came with a new sense of boldness and courage. When receiving his appointment, Dagan was given two main tasks by Sharon: combat the terrorist groups deployed along Israel's borders, and stop Iran's pursuit of nuclear weapons.

"Not to make a best effort, to stop it," Dagan later explained to one government minister.

The tone for Dagan's tenure was set by the way he decorated his office in Mossad headquarters, located in a nondescript building lined by a row of eucalyptus trees just north of Tel Aviv. There on the wall of his modest office hung a black-and-white picture of an old bearded Jewish man wearing a tallit—a Jewish prayer shawl—as he knelt down in front of two Nazi soldiers, one armed with a stick and the other with a rifle slung over his shoulder.

"Look at this picture," Dagan would tell guests. "This man, kneeling down before the Nazis, was my grandfather just before he was murdered. I look at this picture every day and promise that the Holocaust will never happen again."

Dagan took that mission statement seriously. After his appointment, reports began to surface of setbacks to Iran's nuclear program. Scientists began to disappear and equipment sent to Iran for its nuclear program arrived broken, believed to have been sabotaged. Warehouses in Europe where equipment for Iran's nuclear program was stored mysteriously went up in flames. In 2005, for example, Iran was plagued by a number of mysterious plane crashes, killing dozens of Iranian Revolutionary Guard Corps officers and several senior officers. All of the above was secretly attributed to the Mossad.

Over the next few years, with the reported success also came the money and respect. According to one former senior Israeli intelligence operative, by 2007, the Mossad's annual budget had jumped by half a billion dollars. The world also paid attention and noticed the difference in the Mossad. Relations with the CIA, for example, reached a new level of intimacy during Dagan's tenure.

Just months earlier, Ehud Olmert, who had succeeded Sharon as prime minister, decided to extend Dagan's term by a sixth year. In 2008, he would extend it by yet another, making Dagan one of the longest-serving heads of Mossad in Israel's history.

That same year, Olmert allowed a TV crew into his Jerusalem office to film the beginning of a meeting he was scheduled to have with Dagan. It was unprecedented access to what is the most intimate of settings—a prime minister sitting with his top spy. But Olmert approved the request after the news channel selected Dagan as its man of the year. The prime minister had a clear message he wanted to convey to the nation: Israelis, he said, owed Dagan more than they could even begin to imagine.

"Had you asked Dagan if he should be named man of the year he would have referred you to 25 or 30 other people in the Mossad who deserve the title more than him," Olmert said. "But since you didn't ask him I can say that you made the right decision . . . There is no salary that Israel can pay someone like Meir Dagan."[7]

That is why, that day in the White House, Cheney, Hadley and Abrams took what Dagan was showing them so seriously. They knew that the Israeli general wouldn't be in the White House if it wasn't of the utmost importance, and that Olmert would not have requested a private meeting for his intelligence chief without good reason.

Dagan wrapped up his presentation. "This has got to go away," he said. "Syria cannot be allowed to have nuclear weapons."

The Americans were left with a long list of questions. While Dagan made a strong case, Cheney, Hadley and Abrams knew that they would need to independently confirm everything they had just been shown within their own intelligence agencies. And if what Dagan had shown them was in fact true, they would need to answer the more difficult question: What do we do now?

The next morning, Dagan crossed the Potomac River and headed to Langley, Virginia, for a meeting with his CIA counterpart, General Michael Hayden. A decorated air force officer, Hayden had previously served as head of the National Security Agency (NSA) before taking up his post at the CIA. Hayden and Dagan had worked together on joint operations in the past. He referred to his Israeli counterpart as a "tough" and "tireless" friend. Under their joint leadership, coordination between their different agencies reached new heights.

Dagan went through the presentation again, showing Hayden the photos. He had brought multiple copies with him to the US, leaving the first batch with Hadley.

"Meir was very straightforward," Hayden later recalled. "He didn't say, 'And then you gotta go do this, and then you gotta go do this, and we gotta go do this.' It was, 'Michael, let me show you what we think.'"

It was a different conversation than the one he had a day earlier at the White House. There, Dagan had come to discuss policy and told Cheney, Hadley and Abrams that the reactor needed to go away. At Langley, he was there to share the intelligence, a requisite for any decision that would have to be made at a later date by Israel and the US, either together or independently.

What took Hayden by surprise was Dagan's decision to share the raw intelligence the Mossad had collected on the reactor with the CIA. While Israel and the US often shared intelligence assessments with one another—like many allies do—it is unusual for an agency to share raw intelligence. The reasoning is simple: when the intelligence is raw the chances are higher that the source of the material will be compromised.[8]

But this time, Dagan didn't have a choice. Israel needed American assistance in understanding what role North Korea was playing in Syria. While Israel had relatively good coverage of its neighboring countries, North Korea was a big black hole for the Jewish state.

Hayden assumed as much. He guessed that Dagan had brought the photos to the CIA to gain some insight into what North Korea's role was in all of this.

"The pictures were certainly very impressive [but] they [the Israelis] didn't know much about North Korea and didn't have the historic technical knowledge of the region that we had with satellite photography and so on," Hayden explained. "It was a case of looking to improve Mossad's view of this by stimulating us to show: here's what we knew going up to this."

Even though it was on everyone's mind, the biggest question wasn't asked by any of the Americans Dagan met on his two-day trip to Washington: How the hell did Israel get those photos to begin with?

The answer dated back to a few weeks earlier in the beginning of March, when Prime Minister Olmert approved a rare and unique operation. The Mossad had received intelligence that Ibrahim Othman, director of Syria's Atomic Energy Commission, was coming to Vienna for some meetings. Olmert gave Dagan permission to track Othman and, if an opportunity presented itself, to hack his computer.[9]

In some measure, the State of Israel's conceptual roots were grounded in the Austrian capital of Vienna. It was there, on the shores of the Danube River, that Theodor Herzl, the visionary behind modern Zionism, studied law and received his first real taste of the anti-Semitism that would forever shape his personal life and the ideas that would lead to the birth of a nation.

Vienna also has a distinctive place in Israeli intelligence mythology. In 1993, two elite undercover Mossad agents were killed when their motorcycle crashed into a car on a stormy night near the Austrian capital. They were there on a surveillance mission, tracking a known arms dealer who was making illegal sales to Iran.

In 1972, Sabena Flight 571 took off from Vienna on its way to Tel Aviv when it was hijacked by Black September terrorists.

The plane was allowed to land at Ben-Gurion Airport in Israel, where it was later raided in a legendary Sayeret Matkal rescue operation led by Ehud Barak and Benjamin Netanyahu, who were disguised as mechanics.

And in January 2010, Vienna again featured prominently in another operation attributed to the Mossad—the assassination in Dubai of top Hamas commander Mahmoud al-Mabhouh.

A hit team of about a dozen Mossad agents—traveling on forged Irish, Australian, British and German passports—overpowered the Hamas commander in his hotel room, killing him by injection. Dubai investigators later discovered that the hit team used intermediaries in Austria to communicate with one another. The agents called a number in Vienna, which then connected them to other phones they were carrying in Dubai.

In recent years, Western intelligence agencies have been focused on Vienna due to the presence there of the IAEA, the United Nations' nuclear watchdog established in 1957 to promote the peaceful use of nuclear energy and to ensure that countries don't illicitly pursue weapons of mass destruction. The IAEA's massive boardrooms have, over the years, hosted countless meetings with intelligence officials from Israel, the United States, the United Kingdom and other countries eager to share information they had discovered on countries like Iran whose nuclear programs are in violation of international agreements.

To conceal those meetings, IAEA reports often cite the source of their information as "member states," a reference to those countries' intelligence agencies. In 2013, for example, following the release of yet another incriminating report against his country, Iran's envoy to the IAEA accused the Mossad and the CIA of feeding the UN agency false information.

The Mossad reportedly tried to do more than just use information and intelligence to influence IAEA reports. One plot, albeit never carried out, was hatched to discredit Mohamed ElBaradei, the Egyptian diplomat who headed the IAEA from 1997 to 2009. Israel believed ElBaradei was being too soft on Iran, so some agents came up with an idea to deposit large amounts of money in one of his bank accounts and then leak that he was being paid off by the Iranians.[10]

As suspicions grew about Syria's nuclear program, the head of the Israeli Military Intelligence Directorate (known by its Hebrew acronym Aman) Major General Amos Yadlin met with Dagan and asked him to pool their resources and conduct a raid. While Aman is far larger in resources and budgets than the Mossad, it does not conduct covert operations in faraway places like Europe. That is the responsibility of the Mossad.

Yadlin's request was based on more than a hunch. About half a year earlier, in mid-2006, officers from Aman's research division came to Yadlin and voiced suspicions of what seemed at the time to be impossible. They claimed to have picked up a few crumbs of intelligence that—when put together—made it seem like Syria might be engaged in some kind of illicit nuclear activity. The assessment wasn't based on one single piece of intelligence but on a combination of a bunch of bits of information that together presented something of a puzzle. The problem was that more than half the pieces were still missing.

The suspicions didn't come out of nowhere. When Libya announced in 2003 that it was dismantling its nuclear program, Israel was completely shocked. It had no clue that Gaddafi was developing a nuclear program, let alone one that was so advanced. A state commission of inquiry was set up by the Knesset, Israel's parliament, and it came back with clear recommendations for the country's intelligence agencies, which were already worried about what else they might be missing.

When it became clear that Abdul Qadeer Khan, the rogue Pakistani scientist who peddled nuclear technology around the world, had helped Libya start its program, Israel decided to look back at where else he had visited over the years. One of the countries was Syria.

But when Israel started investigating, it initially didn't find much. It seemed that Khan had been turned away by Hafez al-Assad, Bashar al-Assad's father, when he was president. What made Aman suspicious now was Syria's growing and covert relationship with North Korea. The countries were known to have ties, but this seemed like something bigger.

"Intelligence work is about putting together a puzzle that consists of 1,000 pieces and all we had at the time was about 100," one senior intelligence officer involved in those efforts explained. "The picture was far from being complete."

What stood out was the discovery of a building under construction in northeast Syria, not far from the Euphrates River. Aman detected the building during random satellite sweeps of Syria, a country that is routinely a primary target for Israeli intelligence collection. But Aman could not identify the building. The surrounding area looked like a garbage dump. There were some tents, which the Mossad would later learn were used as living quarters for the North Korean workers. Was it a weapons factory, an arms depot or a nuclear reactor? It had no way of really knowing.

What made the possibility of a nuclear facility even more far-fetched was the fact that Syria had barely any nuclear infrastructure or know-how. Besides Othman, there were just a handful of Syrian nuclear scientists. Their only nuclear facility was a miniature research reactor supplied by China, which had been built in the 1990s but was far from being large or sophisticated enough to make the fissionable material needed for nuclear weapons. At the time, the facility had a staff of just 13 people and was only operational about two hours a day.[11]

In a subsequent meeting with Olmert, Yadlin presented his suspicions. But lacking any decisive proof, the suspicions remained just that. Some top-secret papers were written and shared throughout the Israeli intelligence community but they didn't amount to anything conclusive. Anyhow, the government's focus was on curbing rocket fire from the Gaza Strip as well as Iran and its nuclear program, which from year to year was turning into a graver and more immediate threat to Israel.

It also didn't make sense that Syria would be building a reactor. After the bombing of Osirak, the Iraqi reactor Israel destroyed in 1981, the assessment in Israel was that no country would again put all of its nuclear eggs in a single basket. Instead, they would spread them out like Iran was doing at the time by constructing multiple nuclear facilities and investing in two parallel tracks to the bomb—enrichment of uranium and the refinement of plutonium. It went against conventional thinking for Assad to be building a single standalone nuclear reactor. The risk of exposure, everyone thought, was too high.

In November 2006 Yadlin had met with John Negroponte, the US director of national intelligence, during a visit he made to Israel. Olmert was scheduled to travel soon to the US to talk about Iran with President Bush, and the American intelligence community wanted to get an update on Israeli assessments before the two leaders sat down.

Negroponte first visited Mossad headquarters for talks with Dagan and came the next day to Aman's offices for talks with Yadlin and his senior staff. Yadlin knew that Dagan would update Negroponte on Iran and Israel's updated intelligence, so he decided to use the opportunity to present the visiting American intelligence chief with Aman's hypothesis on Syria. He wanted to test the waters and see if Negroponte knew anything.

Yadlin got straight to business. He showed Negroponte a satellite image of the building Aman had discovered in the desert. "It is a hypothesis," Yadlin said, "but I have serious concerns that there might be a nuclear reactor there."

Negroponte looked and shrugged. He said he knew nothing about it. "I was at Mossad headquarters and they didn't say anything about this either," he said.[12]

The answer was a setback to Aman's suspicions. If the Americans didn't know about illicit nuclear activity in Syria then it was unlikely that something was actually happening there. But Yadlin refused to give up. Something wasn't right about the building. It was isolated in the middle of the desert without any real purpose. Why was the government building something there? It had to be important, Yadlin told his staff. He felt it in his gut.

Around the same time, a team of analysts in Aman's research department put out a top-secret report titled "The Effort to Uncover the Possible Existence of a Nuclear Military Program in Syria." On the cover was a picture of Assad above a flag of Syria. The Syrian flag was connected by an arrow to a North Korean flag and by another to a Pakistani flag, the two countries Aman suspected might be helping the Syrians. In the middle was a large black question mark.

Othman's upcoming trip was an opportunity to finally solve the mystery. At first, though, Dagan resisted. He told Yadlin that he needed his agents focused on Iran. Other assignments like this one, he said, were a waste of time.

It was an argument that dated back to 2005, shortly after Yadlin had taken up his post as head of Aman. Dagan had already made a name for himself as a supreme spymaster while Yadlin had come to Aman from the outside after serving for two years as Israel's military attaché to Washington, DC.

In one of their first work meetings, Dagan told Yadlin to stay away from Iran. "Aman should focus on Lebanon and Syria," he said. "The Mossad will take care of Iran."

The demarcation Dagan was trying to impose between Aman and Mossad was based largely on the vague borders that already existed between the two spy agencies, as well as Dagan's general assessment that Syria was not interesting. Yes, it had the largest conventional military along Israel's borders that still posed a threat to the country, but that did not interest Mossad, which was focused on bigger issues like stopping Iran's race toward a nuclear capability.

But Yadlin insisted. He shared with Dagan his concern that the strange building along the Euphrates might be of a nuclear nature.

"Do it as a favor for me," Yadlin finally asked of Dagan. "This way we will know once and for all what the building is. Mossad has the capabilities to put this whole affair to rest."

Dagan's hesitancy was understandable. This wasn't the first time the Mossad had tried to gather intelligence on Othman. He had been in Israel's sights for years and had been followed by the Mossad in the past. Each time, though, the Mossad came back empty-handed.

In the end, Yadlin prevailed and Dagan approved the operation. While Syria was not really of interest, he figured that Othman might be in possession of valuable information about Iran's nuclear facilities that could help the Mossad's campaign to undermine the ayatollahs' program.

The most senior nuclear scientist in Syria, Othman received his doctorate in physics from University of Surrey in the United Kingdom and served for some time as a member of the American Nuclear Society. An expert on radiation protection, Othman at the time had authored more than 50 articles on nuclear safety and was cited in dozens more.

In 2004, for example, Othman wrote an article for the United Nations Institute for Disarmament Research in which he called for the establishment of a nuclear-free zone in the Middle East. He issued the typical Arab condemnations of Israel, which he wrote was the primary source of instability in the Middle East due to its purported nuclear arsenal.

He listed nine requirements needed to move toward a WMD-free zone. The last was particularly interesting: "Until the WMD free zone is established, parties should refrain from manufacturing, producing, testing or acquiring in any way new nuclear weapons and from allowing the placing of any nuclear weapons, explosives or devices on their territory or on territories under their jurisdiction."[13]

That was in 2004. By 2007, the Mossad would soon learn, Othman had apparently changed his mind.

Like the rest of the Israeli defense establishment, the Mossad was also reeling from the aftermath of the Second Lebanon War, which had ended just a few months earlier. For years, Mossad agents had carried out dozens of secret missions across the world—some in enemy countries—and had risked their lives to collect information about Iran and its proxies scattered throughout the Middle East.

Particular attention was given to the smuggling routes used by Iran to supply its nuclear needs but also to the ways it was feeding Hezbollah with sophisticated weapons and technology. Some of this information was what enabled the Israeli Air Force to destroy Hezbollah's long-range missile arsenal on the first night of the Second Lebanon War in 2006.

The young men and women sent on the mission to Vienna were part of the Mossad's Keshet Branch, known for covert overseas operations that involved collecting data and breaking into apartments and hotel rooms.[14] Despite the months that had passed since the war, many of them were still frustrated by be-ing left out of it.

Many of the Mossad's operatives were former combat sol-diers who had served in some of the IDF's most elite units. But during the war, the Mossad did not let them leave to fight with their reserves units. "You are too valuable," the head of the de-partment, himself a graduate of an elite IDF unit, explained at the time, "and besides, think about if you were needed for an immediate operation here."

Like other operations of this kind, this one too would have needed approval first by Olmert. While the defense minister in Israel oversees the IDF, the prime minister is the so-called commander in chief of the Mossad and the Shin Bet, a differ-ent security agency that primarily combats Palestinian terror-ism in the West Bank and the Gaza Strip. During his term as prime minister, Olmert made a point of knowing every detail and approving every single Mossad operation that took place outside Israel's borders.

On the day of the actual operation Dagan and a few other senior Mossad commanders came to the Prime Minister's Of-fice for one last briefing with Olmert. Operations like these seem simple; it's exactly for that reason they are often the ones during which spies embarrassingly get caught. In 1998, for ex-ample, a Mossad agent was captured in Bern, Switzerland, after he was found trying to tap the phone of a suspected Hezbollah operative.

The last thing Israel needed was for Mossad agents to be caught breaking into the hotel room of a Syrian diplomat. It would spark an international crisis and make Israel appear like a provocateur and aggressor on the international stage. A few years earlier, two Mossad agents had been caught trying to obtain New Zealand passports in Auckland. The two had to appear in court, had their covers blown, and Israel later was forced to issue an official apology. It did not need a repeat now.

That is why operations such as these are usually carried out by two teams—the agents who break into the room and another team of agents who conduct the surveillance and ensure that the coast remains clear. After about two hours, Olmert gave the green light for the mission. It was to be carried out that night.

During the last briefing, a strong emphasis was put on Othman's laptop. The agents reportedly hacked his computer, downloaded files and installed a Trojan horse, providing the Mossad with permanent access to his computer. Othman had become careless. He had taken photos on a digital camera and simply downloaded them to his personal computer.

The agents were in and out of the hotel room in no time. Othman never knew they had been there. Within minutes, the computer was already transmitting back to Mossad headquarters in Tel Aviv. By 11:00 p.m., the operation was completed and Israel now had a front-row seat to one of Syria's most important computers.

Strangely, when the material sucked out of Othman's computer was brought back to Israel, the Mossad decided to send it to Aman to be developed. It's unclear why the Mossad didn't sift through the files on its own. This caused a delay. The material was brought to an Aman officer who wasn't aware of the urgency. Two weeks later, in mid-March, the processed material was finally returned to the Mossad, where the jaws of the intelligence officers there literally dropped.

Dagan immediately called the Prime Minister's Office and asked to speak with Olmert. It was an unusual request. While the two men met quite frequently, the meetings were usually set up in a phone call between Dagan's assistant and Olmert's chief of staff. This time, though, Dagan insisted on speaking directly with Olmert. He wanted to keep the meeting off the prime minister's regular schedule.

"I need to see you urgently," the Mossad chief told the prime minister. "Today."

Olmert already had a packed schedule that day with a planned visit to the Gaza border in southern Israel, but he knew that if Dagan was calling him directly, something was up. He told Dagan to meet him at his office in Jerusalem at 5:00 p.m. Dagan showed up at the meeting with Tamir Pardo, his deputy at the time and the man who would later succeed him as head of the Mossad. After sitting down across from Olmert, he pulled out a brown envelope and spread a collection of photos across the prime minister's mahogany desk.

"This is an atomic reactor and it is in Syria," Dagan told Olmert. "This is what we got in the operation."

In the meantime, since the operation, new satellite images had come back from Aman showing that the Syrians were in the early stages of digging a canal from the suspicious building to the Euphrates River, further proof that the building was a reactor and needed a constant flow of water to cool its core. Olmert was stunned into silence.

"What do we do about it?" he finally asked.

Just at that moment, there was a knock on his door. "Not now," the prime minister shouted. But that didn't stop the man entering. It was Olmert's spokesman. One of the news channels, he said, was going to be airing a story in a few hours about new criminal allegations against the prime minister. "We need a comment," the spokesman said. This was the last thing Olmert wanted to be bothered with right now. "Tell them to go to hell," Olmert replied.

He then took a deep breath. It was a rare moment, not just for him personally, but also for the State of Israel. Here he was, Israel's prime minister, being presented with a clear and present danger that threatened the very existence and future of the world's only Jewish state.

While he had known about the suspicions that had prompted the Mossad raid, he was shocked to see that the threat was real. The photos Dagan showed him were the kind of intelligence that leaves no doubt or room for questions. This wasn't digested intelligence—an analysis of a news report or a speech by some enemy commander. These were photos taken from a computer belonging to the head of Syria's Atomic Energy Commission showing that next door to Israel, in its backyard, a nuclear reactor was in the final stages of construction.

At this early stage, Israel faced three primary questions: Could it verify that the building was in fact a nuclear reactor? Could Israel live with a nuclear reactor in Syria? And last, if the answer to question 2 was "no," what were the options at Israel's disposal to stop it?

Olmert was not a novice when it came to military operations. He had overseen the Second Lebanon War as well as extensive operations in the Gaza Strip. But what he was now looking at was on a whole other level of threat. Syria, he understood, was building a capability that could potentially be used to try and destroy Israel. For Olmert, it was that simple. Nuclear weapons in the hands of Syria posed a direct and immediate threat that Israel could not live with. The reactor had to be eliminated.

"Okay," he finally said to Dagan. "We will destroy it."

If there was going to be a military operation, Dagan told Olmert, it would have to happen soon, before the reactor went "hot."

The clock, he warned, was ticking.

2

WHAT DO WE DO NOW?

No core, no war," George W. Bush instructed his top advisers. It was the day after Dagan had visited Langley and Hayden was at the White House to update the president on the bombshell his Israeli counterpart had just dropped on his desk.

Hayden had finished his meeting with Dagan convinced—based on the evidence the Mossad director showed him—that Syria was building a nuclear reactor, one Israel had learned was being called "al-Kibar."

He knew that the intelligence had to be 100 percent accurate. There was no room for any doubt. Mistakes could not be tolerated, especially when it came to the CIA and allegations of weapons of mass destruction being developed in an Arab state in the Middle East.

The CIA had been down that road just a few years earlier in 2003 when it helped validate the Bush administration's justification for launching a war against Iraq. In 2007, the war had very few supporters left in Washington, let alone in the general public.

One of the first steps Hayden took was to immediately assemble a team of analysts to pore over the photos Dagan had left behind. They were tasked with two assignments: verify that the photos were not doctored and scour all available intelligence to confirm the Mossad's assessment.

Hayden would later learn that a few years earlier, during random satellite sweeps of Syria, the CIA had detected work on a facility along the Euphrates River but was unable to identify what exactly it was being built for.

The National Geospatial-Intelligence Agency, responsible for providing satellite imagery to support US intelligence operations, had classified the building as "enigmatic," a category within the US intelligence community that meant the target was important but had an unknown and mysterious purpose. With Dagan's photos, the purpose was now becoming clear.

When it came to the photos, all seemed to be in order except for one, which showed some writing on the side of a pickup truck that appeared to have been pixelated out: Someone— either Israel or the Syrians—had not wanted anyone to see what was written on the side of the truck.[1]

"We went through everything very, very carefully," Hayden recalled a few years later. "It wasn't out of distrust, but you have to understand, we've gotten this very question wrong five years before that. We were very, very cautious that we had to get this right and be able to defend against any doubts or pushback from the White House."[2]

And pushback there would indeed be. It began at Hayden's White House meeting the next day with President Bush.

By then, Hayden had been able to digest his meeting with Dagan and prepare his presentation. Israel, he now assumed, had decided to share the intelligence with the CIA because as much as the Mossad thought it knew, there was a great deal it didn't. It was a normal facet of the CIA-Mossad relationship. Due to its size and almost unlimited resources and capabilities, the CIA will always be richer and have a wider and more global reach. Smaller partners, like Israel, will always be more focused on their region, more detail-oriented and more adaptable when it comes to the specific linguistics and cultures in the target country. The sharing of intelligence on the nuclear reactor is a perfect example of how that "marriage"—as Hayden called it—works in practice.

At the morning meeting with Bush in the Oval Office, Hayden laid out the photos and briefed the president on the CIA's own findings. He then leaned over to Dick Cheney, who had long suspected that Syria was building a nuclear program, and said: "You were right, Mr. Vice President."

The president quietly took in the news. Bush had two immediate requests: get more information to be sure this is a reactor, and maintain complete secrecy while doing so.

His stated policy—"no core, no war"—would later be engraved on a coin minted by the CIA in honor of the team that worked on the problem presented by the al-Kibar reactor. But in the meantime, Bush stressed, the US could not risk having this information leak out. As Hayden later half-joked with his staff, if word got out, Assad would turn the site into a day-care center, making a military operation virtually impossible.

A few days later, Olmert called Bush and made it clear that from Israel's perspective, the only acceptable option was for the reactor to be destroyed. "George," Olmert told the president, "I'm asking you to bomb the compound."[3]

Bush thanked Olmert for raising the issue but asked for patience. "Give me some time to look at the intelligence and I'll give you an answer."

Olmert agreed to give the US some time but urged Bush to take steps to ensure that the news did not leak out. The last thing we need, he told the president, was for Assad to find out that Israel knew about his secret pet project.

Understanding the urgency from Israel's standpoint, Bush instructed his staff to get to work on two different issues—the intelligence and the policy.

The work was essentially split into two teams: Hayden and the CIA worked to confirm the intelligence and ensure that what the Israelis had brought them was verifiable and rock solid. Another team, overseen by National Security Adviser Stephen Hadley, consisted of the principals' deputies. Called the "Drafting Group," this was the main team established to formulate different policy options for what to do with the reactor.

There were a handful of members—Abrams, a deputy national security adviser in charge of the Middle East; Stephen Kappes, deputy director of the CIA; Eric Edelman, the under secretary of defense for policy and a key aide to Secretary of Defense Robert Gates; Eliot Cohen, a renowned political scientist who earlier that year had been appointed counselor of the State Department; and James Jeffrey, another NSC official, who would later serve as deputy assistant secretary of state for Near Eastern Affairs. These men did the heavy lifting.

Their job was not just to draft the different courses of action in hypothetical terms, but to actually plan them out to the finest detail while considering all of the possible scenarios and obstacles.

Secrecy was a key concern, which Bush stressed in every meeting. He personally approved the list of officials who would be "read in" to the intelligence. Edelman, for example, was summoned one day in May to Gates's office. Usually other people were present. This time, when Edelman walked in, no one else was in the office.

"You're going to be read into an intelligence program," Gates told him. "You're going to be looking at intelligence that has been provided to us by one of our allies. This is going to be very, very restricted."

Edelman went over to the CIA, where he signed some papers and received a briefing on the reactor. He later joked that to get the security clearance he had to do everything short of signing away his firstborn child.

"Go over this with a fine-tooth comb," Gates told him.

Gates had actually been the first American official to learn about the existence of the nuclear reactor. A few weeks before, on April 18, Gates had arrived in Israel for the first visit of a US secretary of defense in eight years. Dagan's trip to Washington was already scheduled and Olmert feared that Gates would hold a grudge against Israel if he found out that Olmert and Defense Minister Amir Peretz, with whom he held talks during his two-day visit, had intentionally kept him in the dark. As a result, Olmert asked Peretz to briefly update Gates about the discovery of what might be a nuclear facility in Syria but not to make it the main focus of conversation. Peretz brought it up with Gates but spoke in vague terms. He told the secretary of defense that Dagan would soon be traveling to Washington to provide the White House and the CIA with more details about the shocking discovery.

Like Edelman, Eliot Cohen had a similar meeting with Secretary of State Condoleezza Rice. A few days after Dagan's visit, he was called in to meet Rice at the State Department. Like Edelman's meeting with Gates, no one else was in the office.

"There are only two people in the State Department who know what I'm about to tell you," Rice told Cohen. "I'm one and you're now the other."

She went on to explain that Israel had come to the administration with what appeared to be concrete intelligence showing that North Korea was building a nuclear reactor for Syria. She asked Cohen to be her representative in the Drafting Group.

"At that time, we thought we had about a month before it went hot. It was just a stunning kind of revelation," Cohen later recalled.

A sign of just how concerned Bush was with possible leaks played itself out during one of the Drafting Group's first meetings, held in the White House Situation Room. Located under the West Wing, this is the conference room the president uses to oversee military operations and hold confidential and secret meetings.

The Drafting Group had just sat down when Bush suddenly walked in. Almost all of the members of the group had participated before in Sit Room meetings with the president, but it was rare for him to attend a meeting of deputy principals without prior warning.

"If anything leaks out of here about this, I'm going to fire all of you," Bush said. Then he walked out.

The team took Bush's threat seriously and strict ground rules were put in place. Nothing, for example, could be written or stored on computers. Files had to remain in the offices of the National Security Council and could only be moved between offices with an escort. When the files were handed out, they were used, analyzed, updated and then almost immediately handed back. No copies were allowed to be made and nothing was allowed to leave the West Wing or CIA headquarters.

Only a handful of people were allowed to see the raw intelligence stored at Langley. Their names had to appear on what the US intelligence community calls the BIGOT List, an acronym that stands for "British Invasion of German Occupied Territory" and is a reference to the list of officials who had prior knowledge of the top-secret plans for the D-Day invasion during World War II.

Edelman, whose poor penmanship was notorious throughout the Pentagon, had to handwrite his list of about 150 questions for the CIA about the origin of the intelligence, the chances of it having been manipulated, what exactly it showed, timelines and anything else he could come up with.

"The scope of what our Israeli colleagues had was just too great," he later explained. "In a modern world, I thought I suppose anything can be fabricated, but that seemed like a pretty far reach. Nevertheless, we all felt that we had to do due diligence to make sure that we had gone through this."

As Hadley's deputy, Abrams played two roles throughout the process. He was a member of the Drafting Group but also sat in on all of the principal meetings as the official note taker. Many of these meetings took place in the president's living room in the residence, also known as the Yellow Oval Room for its shape and wall color.

After one meeting, Abrams left the residence and when he got back to his office at the National Security Council realized he had left his notes under his chair in the Yellow Oval Room. He ran back to the residence, sweaty and out of breath, where to his luck the notes were exactly where he had left them, right under the chair.[4]

If the butler stays quiet, Abrams thought to himself, I might not be shot after all.

Being a member of the Drafting Group and the note taker of all the principal meetings was exactly why Abrams was in government. A strong supporter of Israel, Abrams was married to the daughter of Norman Podhoretz, one of America's most prominent conservative thinkers and longtime editor of *Commentary* magazine. He was something of neoconservative royalty in the Bush White House.

He had worked in government since the mid-1980s, when he served as an assistant secretary of state in the Reagan administration. He was later one of the officials implicated in the Iran-Contra Affair but was pardoned in 1992 by President George H. W. Bush.

Abrams was about as pro-Israel as someone could get in the US government. He was the point man in the White House under George W. Bush for all things related to Israel and therefore was a logical choice to be the official note taker for the al-Kibar discussions.

When he wasn't participating in deliberations about what to do with Syria's nuclear reactor, his main portfolio was working to advance the Israeli-Palestinian peace process. In that capacity, he was often at odds with Condoleezza Rice, Bush's powerful secretary of state.

Abrams was of the opinion that to get Israel to make concessions to the Palestinians—the kind that would be needed to advance peace talks and Palestinian independence—America needed to give Israel a strong sense of security. The way to do that was for Israel to feel like America had its back. "Only when Israel feels strong will it be able to make the necessary compromises," Abrams would tell people.

Rice was of the opposite opinion. She believed that the way to get Israel to take steps toward peace was for it to be as dependent on the US as possible. Rice believed that the more leverage America had over Israel, the easier it would be to pressure the country to do its bidding, especially when it came to the peace process.

It was a disagreement that would surface in the final stages of the debate in Washington when deciding what to do about al-Kibar. While everyone recognized the threat the reactor posed to the world, they also were aware that this was a political game of high-stakes poker with global repercussions. Whatever America chose to do had the potential to lead to a regional war.

But first, the CIA had to sign off on the intelligence. Hayden instructed his team—which became known as the Al-Kibar Team—to keep its eyes on the site and to collect as much information about it as possible. The analysts went back into CIA archives to dig up clues, particularly on Syria's relationship with North Korea. There, they found a few reports of various mysterious shipments between the two countries dating back to 2001.[5] Back when the reports were filed, they didn't mean much. Now, they suddenly were looked at through a whole new prism.

Bush had said that the CIA needed to be 100 percent confident, so Hayden brought in a civilian nuclear expert to look over the intelligence. He had him sign a bunch of nondisclosure agreements and only then gave him all of the available data. He then created a Red Team within the agency to come up with all of the other possible explanations for what the facility could be if not a nuclear reactor. In the end, everyone agreed—the building had to be a nuclear reactor. The Red Team, for example, told Hayden that if it wasn't a real nuclear reactor then it was definitely a really good fake one.

With the possibility of war looming on the horizon, the president needed to update Congress. If something happened and Congress later discovered that the administration had known about it beforehand, the president could find himself again being accused of instigating conflict in the Middle East, or at the very least of hiding intelligence. That was a risk he couldn't take.

One morning in June, Director of National Intelligence Admiral Mike McConnell called for a meeting of the Gang of Eight, the eight congressional leaders who are briefed on classified intelligence matters by the executive branch. The list includes the Speaker of the House, the House minority leader, the majority and minority leaders in the Senate and the chairs and ranking members of the House and Senate intelligence committees.

Meetings of the Gang of Eight were a rare occurrence back then and usually happened once a year. They are, however, mandated by law, according to which the president is required to "ensure that the congressional intelligence committees are kept fully informed of US intelligence activities of the United States, including any significant anticipated intelligence activity."[6] There was no question that what was happening along the Euphrates fell into the category of "significant intelligence activity."

Before the briefing started, the members were sworn to secrecy. McConnell went on to explain how an "American ally in the Middle East" had discovered a nuclear reactor in northeastern Syria. He spoke a bit more about the intelligence and how the CIA had previously identified construction of the facility, but it had not been sure about its purpose and had classified it as enigmatic. McConnell showed the elected officials some of the photos that Dagan had brought to Washington. While Israel was not explicitly mentioned as the source of the intelligence, the eight officials were made to understand during the briefing that it had played a prominent role in the collection of the intelligence.

One of the officials present at the briefing was Michigan congressman Pete Hoekstra, who served as the ranking member on the House Intelligence Committee. Born in the Netherlands, Hoekstra moved to the US when he was a young child and served for almost 20 years in Congress until his retirement in 2011. In 2017, when Donald Trump became president, Hoekstra was appointed the US ambassador to his birthplace.

Hoekstra walked out of the meeting with McConnell with three conclusions: Israel was behind the intelligence; someone— either the US or Israel—was going to bomb the reactor; and Iran must have been involved.

"You can expect that sometime you will receive a call that this facility will be taken out," Hoekstra was told during the briefing. According to Hoekstra, the intelligence seemed to indicate that the reactor was not just a Syrian project.

"This seemed more of them acting as an agent to help the Iranians get to a nuke," he recalled years later. "It seemed like it was an Iranian facility that's in Syria, the Iranians are funding it, it's a North Korean design, and in Syria because that's the place maybe that people wouldn't look."

While interesting, the question of who funded construction of the reactor was less important at this stage than the more pressing dilemma—what was Bush going to do about it?

With the intelligence hurdle out of the way, the Drafting Group's discussions turned to focus on policy. While Israel never came out and explicitly said so, the general working assumption among the different US groups was that if America refused to take military action, Israel would strike the reactor on its own. That was the impression Hadley and Hayden got from Dagan as well as what Bush understood from Olmert.

The general thinking in Washington was that a military strike against the reactor would be fairly easy for Israel. Yes, it had been badly scarred by the outcome of the recent war with Hezbollah in Lebanon, but the reactor in Syria was a single target not too far from Israeli Air Force (IAF) bases. Destroying the reactor was the easy part. A subsequent war with Syria was a different story.

The group's main dilemma was to figure out what was in America's best interest.

Bush made two points clear to the Drafting Group early on: America would not act unilaterally and would coordinate whatever it decided to do with Israel, which, he felt, had earned that right after bringing the initial intelligence to the US. Without Israel, he reminded his national security staff, this whole debate would not even be taking place.

In addition, he stressed, the Drafting Group needed to come up with a plan that was not just about attacking. It had to be aggressive, enforceable, reasonable and strong enough to convince Olmert that it would work. Otherwise, he said, the Israelis would simply act on their own.

While everyone was concerned with the construction of the nuclear reactor by Syria, the debates within the Drafting Group and among the principals were overshadowed by a number of existing regional concerns.

First was the role Syria played at the time in Iraq. US intelligence was pretty confident that Syria was serving as an entry route for foreign fighters coming to Iraq to fight against American soldiers. Assad, US intelligence believed, knew about this but was turning a blind eye. Some of the more hawkish elements in Washington were already publicly calling for the use of force to teach Syria a lesson.

Attacking the reactor would have been in line with that thinking. On the other hand, other elements within the government thought Bush needed to open a sincere dialogue with Damascus and use diplomatic means to get Assad to stop the foreign fighters.

"While Assad seemed to be doing everything in his power to undercut what we were doing in Iraq, we didn't know if there were more active measures he could take in retaliation," one member of the group explained.

Then there was the question of timing. The CIA estimated that the nuclear rods could be installed in the reactor as early as August. That meant that a strike after that time would scatter nuclear waste into the Euphrates and contaminate large parts of Syria and Iraq, America's number one priority at the time.

The third concern was of an international legal nature. Was the intelligence rock solid, and would all of the US intelligence community stand behind a presidential decision to attack?

"If we didn't have full intelligence community concurrence with a very high degree of certainty, then obviously this would be a hard sell to Congress and to the American people after Iraq," the same member of the group explained.

The fourth concern was the precedent an American strike

would set. America simply didn't attack countries without first giving warning.

"We've never done that," explained James Jeffrey, one of the key members of the group. "We've always given a country warning first. We did that with the Taliban. We did that with Saddam. We did it in Korea. We did it with Saddam in Kuwait."

That meant that if past practices were to be followed, diplomacy would have to be given a chance first; at the very least, the US would have to first give Assad a warning and attack only if he didn't heed it.

The fifth concern was the impact this whole process would have on North Korea's nuclear program. North Korea had been caught red-handed proliferating nuclear technology and helping another rogue country obtain weapons of mass destruction. This was a direct violation of all international understandings, but also an act that put into question the purpose of the Six Party Talks the US led at the time with Pyongyang, which were aimed to pressure the regime to close its plutonium reactor at Yongbyon and dismantle its illicit nuclear weapons program.

Launched in 2003, the Six Party Talks included North Korea, China, the US, South Korea, Japan and Russia. The disjointed process had been undermined over the years by North Korea's repeated missile tests, but in February 2007 there seemed to suddenly be a breakthrough.

That month, during the sixth round of talks, the sides agreed on a phased denuclearization plan with a 60-day deadline for Pyongyang to freeze its nuclear program in exchange for aid and the release of much-needed cash. By June, Pyongyang began disabling its reactor, removing thousands of fuel rods under the guidance and supervision of US experts.

But now, with this new intelligence, the US had discovered that North Korea was actually participating in the talks while negotiating in bad faith. At the same time as it was supposedly working with the West to reduce its nuclear arsenal, it was in the midst of committing one of the most flagrant international crimes of all—nuclear proliferation.

How could the US trust that North Korea would abide by the denuclearization plan? How could it know that North Korea wasn't selling nuclear reactors elsewhere in the world? And if America took action against Syria would it also need to exact a price from North Korea? Would the bombing of the reactor encourage or discourage North Korea from moving forward with its own nuclear program? It was difficult to know.

And finally, there was the biggest elephant in the room— Iraq.

Here, the issue split into two problems. America didn't have a lot of credibility when it came to intelligence, WMDs and the Middle East. Another war based on intelligence that could end up being faulty was not an easy sale. The American people wouldn't agree to their government taking military action against another Arab state if the case was not airtight and rock solid.

Then, there was the actual war in Iraq. Bush was in the middle of implementing the Surge, his new plan to increase American troop numbers in Iraq to try to give the country a chance to stand on its own two feet. The president needed a win. Another war, in another Arab country, would be a distraction that the White House could not afford.

"The last thing the president needed was this: an action that couldn't stand, in a part of the world where any move could precipitate a war . . . with an ally [Israel] who could and would act on its own," Hayden later explained.

Over a period of about a month and a half, the Drafting Group met weekly in the White House Situation Room. Only the members were allowed inside the room. To conceal what they were doing from their own staffs, they left the blocks of time on their schedules blank. While some staffers had suspicions, they were left unconfirmed.

The group came up with three rough tracks. The first was the most straightforward: simply attack. The second was not to attack but to extend Israel any assistance it might need in carrying out the strike on its own. The third was to expose Syria's nuclear violation by revealing the existence of the reactor to the United Nations Security Council and the International Atomic Energy Agency (IAEA).

The group then dove into each option, providing detailed analysis of how each track would work, what steps would need to be taken as well as potential timelines. For most members of the group, it was a model example of interagency collaboration. They had to think through every step—how it would be carried out, when and who would be told what, as well as what parts would be kept secret.

One of the big questions was what Syria would be told. Would the US, if it carried out the strike, remain silent, something it rarely did when attacking a country? Or would it say something? If so, what would it say, how would it say it, and what could it expect in terms of a Syrian reaction?

The Israelis had told Hadley that in their assessment, Assad would contain the attack and not retaliate. But the Americans were skeptical. They knew that even if Assad didn't retaliate on his own, he had the option of increasing aid to the foreign fighters and insurgents who passed through Syria on their way to Iraq. With two wars already under way, the thought of a third, even if the chances were low, or of a further destabilization of Iraq, was quite daunting.

Despite the skepticism, the team carefully thought out and planned the military option. Two different plans were put on the table and considered by the Drafting Group. The first was an airstrike, plain and simple, something that would not be difficult for the powerful US Air Force. The site's location was known and there were no Syrian air defense systems in the vicinity. A pair of B-2 stealth bombers could easily get the job done.

The other option was to launch a covert operation. The CIA and the Joint Chiefs drew up some plans. The idea seemed good on paper—a small team would infiltrate Syria, make its way to the reactor and plant explosives inside. While this option was appealing—if successful, there could be deniability—it had a lower chance of success and a greater risk of exposure.

"It became very clear, very quickly, that given the size and strength of this reactor—it was a big building built of reinforced concrete—there was no covert option that would get enough explosives to the site," Abrams recalled. "You couldn't do that. You couldn't put it in a knapsack and simply walk there."

One interesting proposal was put forth by Jeffrey, the deputy assistant secretary of state. It was a multistage response. First, America would notify the international community and put the Syrians on alert that if they didn't immediately let the IAEA inside the reactor to inspect it, the US would attack within a preset number of days. Basically, it was a diplomatic track with a stopwatch counting down to an airstrike.

In the meantime, new intelligence constantly flowed in. The CIA had cranked up its satellite coverage of the facility and saw in early June that the Syrians were digging two trenches from the reactor to the Euphrates River. The images, shared and assessed with Aman, reinforced the confidence that this was a reactor. One of the trenches was going to be used for a pipe to carry water from the river to the reactor to cool its core. The other trench was for the pipe that needed to send the used and hot water back to the river.

Usually nuclear reactors have large cooling towers—the big, roundish concrete structures at nuclear reactors—that are used to disperse heat into the atmosphere. The fact that the Syrians were digging trenches added to the clandestine nature of the whole facility.

The CIA also started to more carefully monitor the movements of North Korean officials—like Chibu—known to be affiliated with Pyongyang's own nuclear program as well as the frequent and claimed-to-be-civilian cargo shipments between the countries. They were believed to be ferrying additional hardware needed for the reactor.

According to Jeffrey's plan, if Syria refused to allow inspec-

tors into the facility, the US would bomb parts of the reactor—
like the water pump house along the Euphrates—that would
render it unusable in the short term. Such a strike wouldn't
destroy the reactor but would make it impossible to operate.
The idea was to leave the reactor intact so it could be exposed
to the world and prove what Syria was doing. If Syria still refused to comply, America would hit Damascus with tough
and crippling sanctions, and then, if needed, a full-scale military strike.

The problem, the Israelis pointed out in their discussions
with Hayden and members of the Drafting Group, was that a
strike against the pumping station would tip off Assad that his
greatest secret, his most prized possession, had been discovered.
Within hours, buses filled with schoolchildren would be there
and then, even 100 UN Security Council resolutions would not
be able to stop him. Due to the potential loss of civilian lives,
military action would be off the table.

This is pretty much how the principals—Cheney, Gates,
Rice, Hadley and Hayden—ended up split between diplomatic
and military options. The five met regularly around a conference
table in Hadley's West Wing office, just feet from the Oval Office. There, while eating lunch or munching on chips and salsa,
they went over their options and each raised their concerns.

From the beginning, Cheney felt that America should attack.
He was a strong proponent of preemptive military action and
pushed hard for the president to approve a strike. He believed
that a military strike against Syria would also send a powerful
message to Iran, which had its own nuclear ambitions. By at-

tacking Syria, Cheney argued, the US might even be able to get Assad to cut off his alliance with Iran, to isolate Hezbollah and to dramatically change the region for the good.

Gates and Rice disagreed. They opposed American military action. First, they said, military action could spark a wider regional war if Syria decided to retaliate against US troops in Iraq. Second, they had doubts about entering another conflict based solely on intelligence, particularly the kind that, even if it was verified, was obtained by Israel.

Rice was also personally skeptical about Israel's military capabilities. The Second Lebanon War, which had ended about eight months earlier, left her unimpressed with the IDF. She feared that Israel would fail to execute its mission even though the target was a single building without any air defense systems around and was located within the operational range of Israel's combat aircraft fleet.

For Cheney, this was ridiculous. He had worked with the IDF numerous times throughout his political career and was always impressed by its capabilities. The end result was proof, he would later say. The crater from the Israeli bombing was inside the confines of the reactor.

Rice, it seemed, carried some personal baggage from the rocky relationship she had with Olmert. One particular incident was burned in her memory. It took place on July 30 at the height of the Second Lebanon War, when a bomb dropped the previous night by the IAF landed inside a building in the southern Lebanese village of Kana. The bomb had failed to detonate upon impact but exploded hours later.

Dozens of people, including children, were reportedly killed.

Rice happened to be in Israel that day as part of her shuttle-diplomacy efforts to get Israel and Lebanon to agree to a cease-fire. The explosion took place just before a scheduled meeting with Israel's defense minister at the time, Amir Peretz. But Peretz didn't say a word about it. Instead, one of Rice's assistants interrupted the meeting to show her an email he had received from the US ambassador in Beirut. When she asked Peretz about it, the Israeli defense minister admitted that he had known about the attack before the meeting began.

That made Rice even more furious. Now she would have to tell the press that she had sat through a meeting with Peretz despite the bombing. When she and Peretz finished their talks, she returned to her hotel room, turned on the TV and watched the live feed of the bodies being pulled out of the rubble.

Rice then called Lebanese prime minister Fouad Siniora, who told her not to bother flying to Beirut later that day as she had planned. The message this would send the world, she knew, was that the US was no longer a broker in the conflict. Upset, Rice asked for an urgent meeting with Olmert, who agreed to see her within the hour at his home in Jerusalem. There, she pressured the prime minister to suspend airstrikes over Lebanon for humanitarian purposes for the next 48 hours.

"Get it over with," Rice said to Olmert about the war. "After today, you have no ground to stand on and I'm not going to let the United States go down with you."[7]

To some members of the Drafting Group it seemed that Rice was using the reactor as an opportunity to get back at Israel. If America attacked and destroyed the reactor, it would be providing Israel with unique military and diplomatic support.

Going the diplomatic route and refraining from striking the reactor, while exposing it instead to the United Nations, would have the opposite effect—it would weaken Israel's position and force it to be dependent on whatever moves the US chose in the UN.

Eliot Cohen sensed his boss's antagonism toward Israel and particularly toward Olmert. A few weeks after the reactor was initially discovered, Cohen traveled to Israel to try and get the pulse of the country and, specifically, figure out what Olmert was really thinking. Usually when a high-level American diplomat comes to Israel for meetings, he or she is accompanied to their meetings by the US ambassador. The problem was that the US ambassador was not read into the intelligence on the Syrian reactor, and as long as he was in the room, Cohen couldn't ask whoever he was speaking to about it.

So, Cohen had to be crafty. After the formal meeting with Olmert, for example, he asked the ambassador if he would mind allowing him to spend 10 minutes alone with his old friend. He did the same when meeting with IDF chief of staff Lieutenant General Gabi Ashkenazi.

What Cohen was trying to evaluate was how serious a threat Israel considered the reactor to be and whether it was willing to attack even if it came at the risk of a full-fledged war. Rice had told him that she did not believe Israel would follow through with the attack. She was sure that following the failures of the war in Lebanon, there was no way Israel would carry out an attack that could easily spark a regional conflict, one that would make the war with Hezbollah pale in comparison.

In his meeting with Ashkenazi, Cohen asked him straight

out whether the IDF was prepared for another conflict. A fluent Hebrew speaker, Cohen spoke to Ashkenazi in his native tongue.

"Yes," Ashkenazi replied. "We are aware of the possibility and we are ready."

Cohen left Israel convinced that Olmert was going to take action if America didn't. When he returned to Washington, he met immediately with Rice.

"Boss," he said, "let me give you a kind of a condensed version of Israeli military history." The IDF's record, he went on to explain, is "one of unremitting failures followed by extremely fast recovery." There was the expansion of the pre-state Jewish paramilitary force Haganah after the Hebron riots in 1929, the establishment of the elite Unit 101 after the failure of the retaliatory raids against Palestinian terrorism in the 1950s, and more.

"What you should expect is that after 2006 there will be a really rapid recovery and focus on the basics," he said. "Besides, in 2006 the Israeli Air Force actually did very well, all things considered, taking down the long-range missiles. So actually, I would expect them to perform quite well and I think you're making a mistake if you think that Olmert won't have the guts to pull the trigger."

But Rice was insistent. At the same time as the al-Kibar deliberations were taking place, she was trying to renew peace talks between Israel and the Palestinians ahead of the Annapolis Conference that would be held in November. If the United Nations was informed, Israel would have to rely on the US to diplomatically get Syria to disarm. Taking out the reactor would achieve the opposite. Additionally, it was important for Rice that

Syria participate in the upcoming peace conference, and she feared that bombing the reactor would keep them away.

For Cheney this was ridiculous. Trying to solve the Israeli-Palestinian conflict, he said, was a "disease" that afflicted all secretaries of state. Each one, he would tell people, thinks they are going to solve the conflict. The problem is that no one ever does. The same would happen in this case, he predicted, and instead of exacting a price from Syria, it would get a free pass because of a cause—the Palestinians—that simply wasn't worth it.

Abrams also disagreed. He believed that to get Israel to make concessions necessary for a peace deal, it needed to feel secure. With two nuclear programs now threatening it—in Iran and Syria—Israeli security was dramatically undermined and its sense of vulnerability dramatically growing. This, he said, wasn't the way to advance a peace deal.

While Gates agreed with Rice in objecting to an attack, his approach was different and was based mostly on a desire to stay out of another war in the Middle East. "Every US presidential administration gets to have one preemptive war against a Muslim state, and we've already had ours in this administration," Gates told Edelman one day. "I don't think the US should do it."

On June 14, at his weekly private lunch with the president, Cheney brought up the Syrian reactor. Cheney told the president that nuclear proliferation was "the ultimate threat to the homeland."[8]

Cheney gave a detailed review of recent history. Saddam Hussein had been removed from power in Iraq, Muammar

Gaddafi had come clean and dismantled his nuclear program in Libya, and the black market nuclear network run by the rogue Pakistani scientist A. Q. Khan had also been taken down.

But, the vice president reminded his boss, there were still Iran and North Korea, two countries that were moving ahead with their own illicit nuclear programs. At the time, estimates were that Iran would have 3,000 operational centrifuges by the end of 2007.

Cheney tried his best to push for US military action against Syria. For him, it was necessary for the US to take action to restore its deterrence and to show North Korea that America meant business in its negotiations. Cheney thought back to America's failure in 1941 to predict the surprise Japanese attack against Pearl Harbor. A few months later, he recalled, Admiral Chester Nimitz, commander of the Pacific Fleet, received intelligence that the Japanese were headed for Midway Atoll to launch another attack against the US. At the time, all the Navy had left were three active aircraft carriers. But Nimitz, Cheney recalled, decided to send all of them into battle to intercept the Japanese fleet. The ships made it in time, sank four of the Japanese vessels and saved Midway, turning the tide of the war in the Pacific.

The lesson, Cheney explained, was simple. "Had Admiral Nimitz refused to act on intelligence warnings in the aftermath of the intelligence failure at Pearl Harbor, the outcome of the war in the Pacific may well have been different," the vice president said. "I was afraid we were doing just that in this case."[9]

Cheney knew that he was up against a strong opposition from within the administration but at the end of lunch he appealed to Bush's heart. The evidence against Syria was solid, he said. A US-led strike against Syria's reactor would be the first step in a "more effective and aggressive strategy to counter these threats," the vice president concluded.[10]

Bush listened but refrained from making a decision. He told Cheney that he needed more time and, before deciding, he wanted to hear from the rest of his national security team.

The first long debate with the principals and the Drafting Group was convened at 6:50 p.m. on June 17. It was once again in the Yellow Oval Room, up on the second floor of the Residence. Holding the meeting there kept it off the president's public schedule and would keep people from asking unnecessary questions. Olmert was coming to town later that week and Bush knew that the Israeli leader would want to discuss the reactor. He first wanted to get the latest update from his team.

Cheney, Rice, Gates, Hayden, Hadley, Abrams, Jeffrey and Edelman were all there, joined by the chairman of the Joint Chiefs, General Peter Pace. The president turned management of the meeting over to Hadley, who asked Hayden for a review of the most recent intelligence.

Hayden went over all of the intelligence—what Dagan had brought to the US a few months earlier and what the CIA had gleaned on its own. "We've got four key findings for you," he said. "One, that's a nuclear reactor. Two, it's clear that the North Koreans and the Syrians have been cooperating on nuclear questions for about a decade. Three, the North Koreans built this thing. And four, this is part of a nuclear weapons program."

He continued: "It's a nuclear reactor. High confidence. Can't be anything else. Take it to the bank."[11]

But, Hayden continued, there was one major problem. The CIA, he said, could not find the other parts of Syria's weapons program. They couldn't find the reprocessing facility or the so-called weapons team, the scientists and engineers tasked with assembling the final nuclear bomb or warhead.

"No weaponization effort that we can see," he concluded. "So, I can only give this to you with low confidence."

The moment Hayden said the words "low confidence," the final decision was pretty much predictable. The war in Iraq, and particularly the intelligence failure that got it started, hung over the people present in the room like a guillotine. No one wanted to be caught again approving a war based on intelligence that ultimately ended with a "low confidence" assessment.

For Bush this was particularly concerning. If the "low confidence" report leaked out—which it was safe to assume it ultimately would—the administration would be attacked again for carrying out a bombing raid despite having a hole in the intelligence.

The two options prepared by the Drafting Group were then presented before the entire forum. There was the military option, which Pace said was pretty straightforward and could be carried out easily by the US Air Force.

On the other side was the diplomatic option, which consisted of three primary steps. First, the US would take its intelligence to the IAEA and make the incriminating findings public in what would be designed to be a dramatic session. The US would then demand that access be granted immediately to UN inspectors and that work be halted on the reactor. The second stage would depend on what Syria did. If it opened the facility to international inspectors, the IAEA would come, make its assessments and proceed. But if it failed to comply, which everyone expected it would, then the US would go to the Security Council and demand action. The third step would depend on the Security Council. If action was not approved or not deemed aggressive enough, then the US would still have the military option, assuming the reactor had not yet gone hot and the proverbial kindergarten had not yet been built at the site.

Bush turned to Gates, who had brought some prepared remarks. Gates's opinion was strongly shaped by the two wars already raging in the Middle East. The military, he said, was overstretched, and the US was already considered by most countries as being too quick to use military force. "Without specific proof of a state taking hostile action against Americans, I am aware of no precedent for an American surprise attack against a sovereign state," Gates said. "We don't do Pearl Harbors."[12]

US and Israeli credibility, he added, were both equally suspect. US action, based on intelligence provided by a third party, would not go over well with the American people once it got out. Israel, he added, might be viewed by the world as instigating this whole conflict as a way to try and restore the deterrence it lost during the Second Lebanon War a year earlier.

Gates concluded his remarks by noting that although he agreed the reactor needed to be stopped he thought the US should not assume that it could solve all of its problems in Syria by bombing it. His preferred course of action, he said, was diplomacy. "I suspect no one in the world doubts this administration's willingness to use force," Gates told the president. "But better to use it as a last resort than as a first step."[13]

Hadley agreed. Syria, he said, was engaged in a lot of troublesome activity. The reactor gave the US an opportunity to put pressure on Bashar al-Assad to change his behavior on multiple fronts, similar to the way the US and France got Assad to pull his military forces out of Lebanon in the aftermath of the assassination of Lebanese prime minister Rafik Hariri in 2005.

The US, Hadley reminded Bush, was already working with the United Nations on a long list of grievances regarding Syria. He recalled his frequent meetings with Terje Rød-Larsen, the Norwegian diplomat and UN under secretary general charged with the Middle East. Hadley and Rød-Larsen would often strategize how to pressure Assad; Rød-Larsen would then talk to the Syrian leader, who would initially agree to whatever they were asking and then a few days later suddenly change his mind. This was just another issue for the list.

Hadley also believed that it would make more sense for the US to attack than for Israel. If Israel attacked, it would make it seem like Syria's nuclear reactor was strictly an Israeli problem and not a challenge for the entire international community. Israel, he argued, would want the entire world to face the challenge head on, similar to the way it was trying to enlist support for global action against Iran and its nuclear program.

The US plan—of diplomacy followed by a military strike if needed—should have been, according to Hadley, an Israeli interest. If America attacked, a Syrian response would not immediately be directed at Israel. "We would do it better, it would reduce the risk of retaliation and it would avoid the diplomatic isolation of Israel," he said.

Cheney saw this as his opening. Repeating what he had told Bush during their private lunch a few days earlier, he made the case for US military action. Cheney reminded the group of the marker Bush had laid down after North Korea's nuclear test six months earlier. "It is extraordinarily important for us to give substance and meaning to our diplomacy and this is a classic opportunity to do that," he said. "Not only would it make the region and the world safer but it would also demonstrate our seriousness with respect to non-proliferation," he added.

The vice president argued passionately, stressing that a US strike would enhance American credibility in the Middle East. "Within days of when we captured Saddam Hussein, Gaddafi announced he was going to surrender his nuclear materials to us and he did, and we got centrifuges and the uranium feed stock and the weapons designs which all reside in the United States today," Cheney said. "That is a direct result of our use of force against Saddam."

If done right, Cheney said, the use of force against Syria's nuclear reactor could have a similar effect not just on Syria's other rogue activities but also on North Korea, Iran and anyone else thinking of getting into the illegal nuclear business. The world needed to see, the vice president continued, that America meant business and "if you're gonna proliferate nuclear reactors, or nuclear technology you're gonna get hit."

Bush had heard enough. "I need more time," he told the group. It was premature for him to make a final decision on such an important issue, especially considering that Olmert was arriving in Washington, DC, in just a few days. The president first wanted to hear where things stood from Israel's perspective. He needed to meet his old friend Ehud Olmert, or as he frequently referred to the Israeli prime minister: "my buddy."

3

NUCLEAR DÉJÀ VU

A mos, come into my office."

It was January 1980 and a few days earlier, Major Amos Yadlin had returned to Israel from joint flight training at Hill Air Force Base in Utah. His squadron commander, Lieutenant Colonel Zev Raz, wanted to see him.

Yadlin, the deputy commander of the Israel Air Force's (IAF's) 117th Squadron, strode into Raz's office at the Ramat David Air Force Base, located in the picturesque Jezreel Valley. If it weren't for the occasional fighter jet taking off, a visitor would be forgiven for mistaking the base's rolling green pastures for those in Tuscany.

Tall, lean and blessed with a full head of brown hair, Yadlin was something of Israeli royalty. Born in 1951, he was raised in Hatzerim, a small kibbutz in the Negev. When he was 15, an air force base opened next door to the kibbutz. All day, he would watch planes take off and land. He was bitten by the flying bug.

His father was Aharon Yadlin, a former member of Knesset and education minister. His grandfather, David Hacohen, served in Israel's first Knesset, and one of his uncles was Uzi Narkiss, the famous IDF general who during the 1967 Six Day War commanded the Israeli forces that liberated Jerusalem's Old City and Temple Mount.

Yadlin stepped into Raz's office and closed the door behind him. Raz welcomed back his 29-year-old deputy and then dropped the bombshell. "We have been ordered to prepare for a long-range mission against a target far away," he said. "I need you to prepare the pilots."

As deputy commander of the squadron, Yadlin was responsible for overseeing the F-16 pilots' regular training regimens. Something about Raz's request, though, was different. Israel's enemies were not usually far away. Damascus, for example, is just 70 miles from Ramat David's runways.

For this mission, Raz told Yadlin, the pilots would need to fly 10 times that, about 700 miles. Later, when Yadlin looked at a map, he was puzzled what the target could possibly be. A year earlier, Israel had finalized a peace deal with Egypt so it didn't make sense that the target would be there. To the north, 700 miles put the target in Turkey, way beyond Syria. The only country that made sense was Iraq. But what exactly would the pilots be going after there? It was a mystery.

Israel wasn't supposed to even have F-16 fighter jets. In 1979, Iran was swept up in the Islamic revolution. The Shah fell and

Ayatollah Ruhollah Khomeini returned from exile and took over the country. Seventy-five F-16s, which Tehran had ordered from the US before the revolution, were ready and General Dynamics needed to find a new buyer. So, the Pentagon decided to offer the planes to Israel, which was in the middle of its own negotiations to buy the supersonic multirole fighter jet.

The air force jumped at the opportunity. Yes, it would mean that the planes would not come with the ingenious technology that the air force usually requires for its aircraft, but the F-16s would give the IAF a major boost in range and enable its pilots to fly distances they couldn't with their current combat fleet.

Yadlin got straight to work. While he still didn't know the exact target or its location, the additional instructions he eventually received gave some hint of what to expect. The F-16 was designed for dogfights—the dream of any fighter pilot—but IAF commander Major General David Ivry told Raz and his men that they needed to train for an air-to-ground bombing mission.

"An air-to-ground mission far from Israel," Yadlin and the other members of the squadron would often whisper to one another. "What could it be?"

While they were curious, there was a mission to prepare for and one that had never been done before, not in Israel, not in the US and not anywhere else in the world.

There were a number of challenges. First was technical—how to get a plane designed to fly 500 miles to fly 700. Israel, at the time, did not have midair refueling tankers, which meant that the planes would have to carry their own fuel.

The second was physical. Until then, IAF pilots were used to flying for an hour at a time; maybe 90 minutes. This kind of mission would require them to fly for nearly four hours straight. To do that, they needed to build up stamina, endurance and resistance to stress. Simpler needs also had to be dealt with. What, for example, would a pilot do when nature came calling in the middle of the flight? It's one thing to hold it in for an hour. It's another for four.

The third challenge was how to train for a long-range mission in a country that was only a couple hundred miles long and a few dozen miles wide. To train, the pilots would need to fly deep out over the Mediterranean.

And last—how do you fly from Israel to Iraq without being detected? It would require the pilots to fly over other enemy countries, each one of which could sound the alarm and try to down the aircraft. On a flight where every drop of fuel would count, having to burn thrusters to evade enemy aircraft could be the difference between a pilot making it home or falling into captivity.

The first step was making sure the planes could fly the necessary distance. Yadlin and the other pilots worked closely with the IAF's engineering division. The engineers smoothed the planes to minimize the drag and then installed fuel tanks that, once empty, could be dropped like a bomb—something that had not been done before by Israel. The pilots then trained for combat and learned new ways to evade surface-to-air missile systems.

Yadlin and the rest of his fellow pilots were still traumatized by the Yom Kippur War Israel had fought seven years earlier.

More than 2,000 Israeli soldiers were killed and over 100 air-craft were shot down; countless tanks and armored personnel vehicles were also destroyed. The nationwide sense of vulner-ability was particularly acute in the IAF, which had difficulty during the war flying in enemy airspace against Soviet-made surface-to-air missiles, or SAMs. It lost a third of its fleet as well as 53 pilots. Forty-four more were captured.

Yadlin awoke the morning of the Yom Kippur War to the sound of sirens at Hatzerim Air Force Base. By evening, he was getting his first taste of war as he flew his A-4 Skyhawk over the Suez Canal, dropping seven 500-pound bombs over Egyp-tian forces.

It was Yadlin's first live combat mission and it went against everything he had learned as a young pilot. He was sent to the front lines lacking quality intelligence and without aerial pho-tos to match to his target. He flew at a mere 100 feet above ground in an attempt to evade enemy radar and SAMs. It was deadly as hell.

He had one close call when his plane was damaged by a mis-sile on a flight over Ismailia, an Egyptian town along the west-ern bank of the Suez Canal. But Yadlin managed to retain control of the aircraft and land safely back in Israel. A few days later, he was back in the cockpit successfully evading another missile that chased him for what seemed like a lifetime until it blew up just 10 yards behind his Skyhawk.

Eighteen days and 25 combat sorties later, Yadlin finally un-derstood what it meant to fight in a war. He understood what it meant as a nation to fight for mere survival. His squadron lost 17 planes during the war. Seven pilots were killed and another five were POWs; Yadlin was now a changed man, a veteran of Israel's bloodiest debacle.

He grieved for his fallen comrades but, on a national level, he felt frustrated by the military's failure to prepare for the war. On a personal level, paradoxically, Yadlin gained confidence by surviving the war and living up to his commanders' expectations. Yes, planes were downed and pilots were lost, but the war ended with the IDF just 60 miles from Cairo and within artillery range of Damascus.

He learned about vulnerability but also about strength. About weakness, but also about resilience. A few weeks after the war ended, Yadlin told his commanders that he was signing up for additional years of military service. He was going to dedicate his life to rebuilding the IDF and restoring Israel's power, pride and deterrence.

By January 1981, the squadron was ready. Yadlin still didn't know the identity of the target, but he was prepared for whatever would come. He and his pilots had trained long enough.

A few weeks later, Raz gathered his men.

"I know you all have been wondering for a while what our target is going to be," Raz said.[1] "I can tell you now. On May 10 we will take off from Etzion Air Base and fly to a nuclear facility south of Baghdad in Iraq. There, we will bomb the Osirak nuclear reactor."

The pilots were silent. While they knew that the mission would be difficult, no one in their wildest dreams had assumed that it was going to be against a nuclear reactor, let alone one that was being built by Saddam Hussein, the ruthless Iraqi leader. Until then, some in the IAF had heard rumors that the target was going to be Iraq's Habbaniya Airfield, where a Soviet Tupolev Tu-22 supersonic bomber was scheduled to land.

Iraq had started its nuclear program back in the 1960s but it was not until the mid-1970s that it succeeded in convincing France to sell it a 40-megawatt light-water nuclear reactor called Osirak. While the Iraqis claimed their reactor was purely for research purposes, Israel believed otherwise. The Mossad was carefully following the Iraqi nuclear project and believed that Hussein intended to build a nuclear bomb.

Raz went through the mission plan and discussed the defenses around the reactor, which had been beefed up since Iran tried bombing the facility in January. It was going to be tough but Raz and Yadlin were confident that the pilots could do it.

In May, the pilots were flown from Ramat David to the Etzion Air Force Base in the Sinai Peninsula. While Israel had signed a peace deal with Egypt, it was still in control of the Sinai for almost another year. There, they were surprised to be met by Ivry, the air force commander, and an even more senior guest—IDF chief of staff Lieutenant General Raful Eitan.

Eitan's son Yoram, a fighter pilot, had died just a few days earlier in a training accident and he was still in shiva, the seven-day Jewish period of mourning. But that didn't stop him from seeing the pilots off. Armed with predictions that at least two pilots would not make it home, Eitan felt a need to shake each one's hand before they boarded their aircraft. His own personal mourning could wait.

But as the pilots started their final preparations for the flight, back in Jerusalem politics were getting out of hand and Israeli prime minister Menachem Begin decided to postpone the mission. News of the raid had leaked to Shimon Peres, then head of the opposition. Peres went to Begin and urged him to postpone the mission until after the French elections, scheduled for that same day. François Mitterrand, Peres argued, would be elected and would end technical and logistical support of the Iraqi reactor. If it only waited, Israel, he said, would not need to use force.

Begin was devastated but felt that because of the leak he had no choice but to postpone the strike. For him, Osirak was the modern manifestation of the Nazi death camps. It needed to be destroyed before Saddam could complete the job Hitler had started.

Begin had come to power in 1977 as head of the right-wing Likud Party, ending almost 30 years of left-wing rule. It was the beginning of a new era for the country and Begin's government adopted policies very different from those of the previous Labor-led governments. He was a strong believer in the settlement enterprise and began the process of moving the country away from its socialist roots to the free market economy it is known for today.

Born in Lithuania, Begin was drawn to Zionism and the dream of an independent Jewish state at a young age. The anti-Semitism he witnessed at home left a lasting impression on him. Despite his short height and pale complexion, Begin was a natural fighter. His life changed after meeting Vladimir Jabotinsky, a Russian author who had founded the Revisionist Movement, in 1930.

Jabotinsky advocated a revised version of Zionism, according to which the Jewish state needed to be established on all of the ancient land of Israel without compromise. It was a hard-line ideological approach, different than what David Ben-Gurion, Israel's first prime minister, was advocating—acceptance of the United Nations–proposed Partition Plan, under which the Jewish state was to be established on a sliver of the historic land.

When World War II broke out, Begin joined the Free Polish Army and was sent to fight in Palestine. A year later, the Nazis arrived in his hometown, rounded up his father and a group of 500 Jews and drowned them in a nearby river. Weeks later, his mother was pulled out of her hospital bed and murdered.

By 1943, the 30-year-old Begin had become head of the Irgun, an underground Zionist paramilitary group that had broken off from the Haganah. When he took over, the organization was falling apart. It had few members and even fewer guns. Begin put the organization back on track with a series of deadly attacks, including his most famous—the bombing in 1946 of the King David Hotel in Jerusalem, which killed 91 people.

It was a horrific attack but Begin viewed it as being part of a simple equation—the British had to withdraw from Palestine for Israel to be established. This meant that even devastating attacks like this were legitimate.

The Holocaust cast a large shadow over Begin's political career. It is what is believed to have ultimately motivated him to accept an invitation to Camp David in 1978 and to agree to withdraw from the Sinai Peninsula in exchange for a peace deal with Egypt.

Begin often invoked World War II during cabinet debates

about Osirak, declaring that he would not be "the man in whose time there will be a second Holocaust."[2]

But after Mitterrand took office, nothing changed. France was still helping the Iraqis complete the reactor. If Israel was going to act, Begin knew, it had to be soon.

A week later, Begin met with two of his most trusted ministers and reapproved the strike. He summoned Eitan and Ivry and informed them that the attack was back on. The new date: June 7, 14 years to the day from when the IDF liberated the Old City of Jerusalem and the iconic Western Wall. Israel, Begin thought, would once again be ridding itself of an incomprehensible existential threat.

The strike was planned for Sunday, when the facility was expected to be mostly empty, and at dusk, so that if needed, the IAF would have a long night to rescue downed pilots.

As deputy commander of the squadron, Yadlin was made the number two bomber in the formation of eight aircraft. The planes were instructed to fly low—very low—as they crossed into Iraqi territory, a tactic used to avoid radar detection. They were just a few hundred feet above ground and about 2,000 feet away from one another.

As he was approaching Osirak, Yadlin spotted the Euphrates River, one of the largest and most significant waterways of ancient Mesopotamia. What caught his eye was the sheer size of the river, going on and on as far as the eye could see from a perch in a fast-flying F-16 fighter jet. Israel, he thought, did not have rivers that size. Out of the corner of his eye, he spotted a group of Iraqi soldiers waving enthusiastically at the low-flying unmarked planes.

A few minutes later, Yadlin was diving down toward the reactor and dropping his pair of Mk-84 bombs. The other pilots followed suit and for the first time in history, one country—Israel—had destroyed another country's nuclear reactor from the air. Israel was once again changing modern warfare.

After the strike in Iraq, Yadlin became something of a national hero. It would take a few years before he could speak openly about his role in the attack, but the people who needed to know knew, and he quickly climbed IAF ranks. By 2000, he was appointed the deputy head of the air force after 30 years of combat service, during which he accumulated over 4,000 flight hours and 255 combat missions.

In 2004, as a major general, Yadlin was sent to Washington, DC, where he served as Israel's military attaché to its closest ally. In 2006, he was called back to Israel. His former commander at the air force, Dan Halutz, had been appointed the new IDF chief of staff and wanted Yadlin at his side as head of military intelligence, better known as Aman.

Commander of Aman is one of the most important positions in Israel but is, at the same time, also one of the most challenging. Numerous heads of Aman have finished their terms prematurely, marred by scandals and operational mishaps. The failure to predict the bloody Yom Kippur War in 1973 and the fallout from the Sabra and Shatila massacres in Lebanon in 1982 both led to the resignations of Aman chiefs. That is often the nature of intelligence work. It is anything but scientific and is easy to scapegoat in an operation-gone-wrong. Commanders

and politicians can easily blame faulty intelligence in an effort
to spare themselves.

Complicating matters is that the responsibilities of the head
of Aman are vast. In comparison, in the US, the responsibilities are split between five different generals: one is in charge of
signal intelligence, another of cyberwarfare, a third of special
forces, a fourth is the chief intelligence adviser to the Joint
Chiefs, and a fifth is an intelligence adviser to the government
and cabinet.

When Yadlin became head of Aman in 2006, the intelligence service was focused on strategic threats like Iran, Iraq
and Syria and less on providing ground forces with lists of potential targets—also known as target banks—one of the flaws
discovered during the Second Lebanon War when soldiers
crossed enemy lines with outdated maps of Lebanon and
Hezbollah-controlled villages. After the war, Yadlin initiated a
long set of reforms, aimed primarily at making Aman and its
intelligence products more accessible to the Operations Directorate and ground forces.

There was no way Yadlin could know that the Euphrates
River, which captured his imagination on the way to Osirak in
1981, would again be in his sights a quarter of a century later
as he plotted the bombing of another nuclear reactor, this time
in Syria. Fate, he would learn, worked in mysterious ways in a
place as complex and volatile as the Middle East.

Begin also didn't know back in 1981 that what he did—
authorizing the bombing of Osirak—would turn into what is
known in military and diplomatic circles as the Begin Doctrine,
a term that features prominently in Israeli strategic thinking

when it comes to emerging existential threats in Syria, Iran and beyond.

By 2019, for example, Israel had not launched a preemptive war against Hezbollah in Lebanon though the terror group has accumulated over 130,000 rockets and missiles they use to cover and threaten the entire country. Why? While those missiles and rockets are dangerous, they are conventional threats. They can hurt Israel, but they cannot be used to conquer territory or destroy the Jewish state.

Nuclear weapons are a different story. The detonation of a nuclear weapon over Tel Aviv, for example, would disperse radioactive material almost everywhere in the country. No one would be safe. Many of those not killed in the initial blast would die later from the radioactive fallout. A country like Israel, without strategic depth, cannot take such a chance. It might not have been immediately clear, but what Begin did was set a new standard for Israeli leaders, according to which Israel will act to prevent enemies from obtaining weapons that pose an existential threat to the Jewish state. If preemptive action is possible, Begin concluded in 1981, it should be used.

"If we stood by idly, two, three years, at the most four years, and Saddam Hussein would have produced his three, four, five bombs then, this country and this people would have been lost, after the Holocaust," Begin said two days after the Osirak bombing in a dramatic press conference in Tel Aviv. "Another Holocaust would have happened in the history of the Jewish people. Never again, never again! Tell so [to] your friends, tell anyone you meet, we shall defend our people with all the means at our disposal. We shall not allow any enemy to develop weapons of mass destruction turned against us."[3]

A few days later, in an interview with CBS, Begin hammered this point: "This attack will be a precedent for every future government in Israel. . . . Every future Israeli prime minister will act, in similar circumstances, in the same way."[4]

The Prime Minister's Office in Jerusalem is located inside an old Jerusalem stone building not far from the Knesset, the country's parliament. It is a gray, dull and unimpressive office building, a far cry from the elegance of the offices of heads of state around the world like the White House in Washington, DC, or the Élysée Palace in Paris.

Inside is a suite of offices used by the prime minister and his closest staff. It is on the second floor and is nicknamed "The Aquarium" after the massive and heavy bulletproof glass doors that one needs to go through to get inside.

Cell phones are deposited on a wooden shelf just outside and visitors sit on large brown leather couches as they wait to be summoned for their meetings. Just a few officials have offices within the cordoned-off suite. There is one for the prime minister's chief of staff, the head of the National Security Council, the prime minister's military adviser and a few other key staffers. At the end of the hall is the room where the Security Cabinet convenes and the prime minister's conference room, located adjacent to his wood-paneled office.

Prime Minister Ehud Olmert sat at his desk feeling the weight of the decision that rested on his shoulders. Twenty-six years after Begin courageously approved the operation to bomb Iraq's reactor, he now grappled with a similar dilemma. Was he going to risk a regional conflict and order a military strike against Syria's reactor to prevent Assad from obtaining a nuclear weapon, or would he wait for the Americans to decide what they were going to do? What would happen, he often sat up at night wondering, if Bush got back to him and decided to try his hand at diplomacy? It was an option, Olmert decided early on, that Israel could not tolerate.

From day one, in Israel, attention was divided into three different tracks: intelligence gathering, operational planning and diplomatic efforts.

While the Mossad initially led intelligence efforts, the burden now fell on Aman, which is the larger of the two agencies and operates the country's spy satellites as well as Unit 8200, the country's national SIGINT (signals intelligence) unit and Israel's version of the NSA.

Some of the photos obtained in the Mossad operation were a few years old, and while they were incriminating, Israel needed to get updated evidence on the reactor to know exactly what was happening there and what its status was. The intelligence teams focused on three primary questions: When will the reactor go hot? Who is operating it? And how soon after it is live will it be able to produce nuclear weapons?

Other pieces of the puzzle also needed to be put together. Where were the other components necessary for the production of a nuclear weapon, like the reprocessing plant where the spent fuel from the reactor would be turned into weapons-grade plutonium? Another mystery surrounded the "weapons team," the group of scientists that would then be tasked with assembling the nuclear warhead or bomb. Was there one and, if so, where?

Yadlin and his team of analysts begin to draw up a timeline for the reactor and possible Israeli military action. The general consensus within the defense establishment was that the moment the reactor became operational, it would be too late to attack.

"No one wanted to be responsible for radioactive material leaking into the Euphrates River and then adversely affecting the lives of generations of Syrians and Iraqis," Yadlin later explained.

Early on, Olmert warned of leaks. As long as Assad didn't know that Israel knew about the reactor, there was time to stop it before it went hot. The circle of those involved had to remain close-knit and small.

Nevertheless, it was constantly growing. Shortly after the discovery, Olmert convened a forum of ex-top defense officials to review the intelligence. He wanted to make sure that everything was airtight.

The forum was led by Major General Yaakov Amidror, the former head of Aman's research division. For six days the veteran officers sat and reviewed every piece of intelligence. They were sworn to secrecy but had been tasked personally by Olmert to find any mistakes in the Mossad and Aman's conclusions. The men told their families that they had been called up to reserves and wouldn't be available for about a week.

While this meant that the number of people who knew

about the reactor was growing, Olmert was confident that the discovery would stay secret as long as it was isolated to the intelligence community. Intelligence officers, even retired ones, are used to abiding by a creed of secrecy. This case was nothing different.

"Be devil's advocate," Olmert told them. "If you can, find what is wrong."

At the end of their deliberations, Amidror presented Olmert with a short document. The commission's conclusion was clear and unanimous—Syria was building a nuclear reactor and it needed to be destroyed.

To run the diplomatic efforts, Olmert tapped his most trusted adviser, Yoram Turbowicz. Nicknamed "Turbo," Turbowicz had been appointed Olmert's chief of staff shortly after the 2006 national elections. The two shared an affection for the good things in life—wine, cigars and high-end restaurants—as well as for American-style management. A trained lawyer, Turbowicz received a JD from Harvard Law School and later worked for Sullivan & Cromwell in New York. The two met when Olmert was mayor of Jerusalem and Turbowicz had come to his office with a group of parents complaining about the schools in their neighborhood. Olmert was impressed and the two men continued to cross paths over the years.

Olmert trusted Turbowicz. After Dagan's initial visit to Washington, DC, Olmert made him the point man in the discussions with the White House. It was Turbowicz, for example, who received assurances from the administration that they wouldn't go to the UN Security Council without first getting Israel's approval.

Then there were the military preparations. Those were handled by three generals: chief of staff Lieutenant General Gabi Ashkenazi, Yadlin and IAF commander Major General Eliezer Shkedi.

As the information flowed in, Ashkenazi—a no-nonsense general who had been appointed to his post a month earlier—reached the conclusion fairly early on that the strike, if there was going to be one, needed to happen before the winter. He also understood that it needed to be discreet and before the reactor went hot. He called the conditions the "Three Hets," since all three—hot, discreet and winter—started with the Hebrew letter "Het."

Like those of many politicians, Olmert's office wasn't without infighting. Shortly after the Second Lebanon War ended in 2006, Olmert's national security adviser, Ilan Mizrahi, announced that he was resigning. Mizrahi felt he had been sidelined by other members of Olmert's staff; while he had direct access to the prime minister, his ability to influence policy was limited.

Mizrahi had come to the Prime Minister's Office from the Mossad, where he had served as deputy director until 2003. While Efraim Halevy had recommended that Mizrahi replace him as Mossad director, then prime minister Ariel Sharon preferred Dagan.

Mizrahi had enlisted in the Mossad in 1972 and spent more than 40 years as an active agent. His specialty was HUMINT, human intelligence, specifically the recruitment and activation of agents around the world.

Syria was no exception. When Olmert first learned of the

reactor, Mizrahi was not in the loop. A few days later, though, he learned of the reactor from a conversation with one of his old Mossad colleagues. He immediately recalled a meeting he and other top Mossad officials had with the CIA in the late 1990s. At the meeting were Halevy and Mizrahi as well as George Tenet, at the time the CIA director. It was one of the regular gatherings where Israeli and US intelligence officials were meant to share assessments on the region and beyond.

But at this meeting, Tenet dropped a bombshell, telling the Israelis that they should "keep an eye" on Syria and possible nuclear activity. Tenet did not elaborate and the Mossad had no intelligence to back up what the CIA chief was talking about. After the meeting, Halevy ordered his staff to look into Tenet's warning. They came up empty-handed. Nothing in Israel's intelligence files could be found to substantiate Tenet's warning.

After learning of the existence of the reactor, Mizrahi met with Olmert and Turbowicz and was asked to stay on until the Syrian threat was taken care of, one way or another. Olmert asked him to prepare a paper outlining Israel's options but to keep it off the National Security Council's computer network. As a result, Mizrahi wrote it out by hand.

It dealt with three primary issues:

The first had to do with the readiness of the IDF and the home front for a new war. During the Second Lebanon War, Hezbollah fired over 4,300 rockets into Israel. If Israel attacked Syria and came under rocket fire from both Syria and Lebanon, would the home front be prepared to sustain such an onslaught? Would the IDF be prepared for an all-out war with Syria, which at that time had a formidable conventional military?

Mizrahi also analyzed the seeming contradiction between Assad's decision to build a nuclear reactor and signs that he was prepared to enter peace negotiations with Israel. In February, Olmert had traveled to Ankara for talks with Turkish prime minister Recep Tayyip Erdogan. During the meeting, the two agreed that Turkey would assist in mediating peace negotiations with Syria. A few weeks later, Nancy Pelosi, the US Speaker of the House, visited Damascus and reported back to Israel that Assad was prepared to talk.

Now that Israel knew about the existence of the reactor, Mizrahi wondered what all of this meant. Was Assad trying to deceive Israel by using peace talks to cover up the construction of the reactor and simply stall for time until he built a bomb? Or was he sincere and genuinely interested in achieving a lasting peace deal with Israel?

The third issue remains a mystery still today and revolved around the relationship between Syria and Iran. Was Iran, Mizrahi wondered in his memo, a partner to the construction of the reactor and, if so, would an Israeli action have the potential to open a multifront war with Syria, Hezbollah and Iran?

Mizrahi was one of the first members of Olmert's staff to push the prime minister to take the initial intelligence collected by Israel to the Americans. The argument was simple. America was getting hammered domestically and internationally for its continued war in Iraq. The criticism and growing casualty toll were eroding American deterrence and power. Mizrahi thought that a US-led strike against a proven nuclear reactor in another rogue state would serve American interests and restore its global deterrence.

For Israel, having America carry out the strike would be a win-win. The reactor would disappear without Israel's involvement, meaning that the chance of a large-scale war erupting was limited. In addition, if the reactor was dealt with and dismantled, the prospect for peace talks—supported at the time by the IDF General Staff—would still be viable.

"We should inform the Americans and then have them present the Syrians with an ultimatum to immediately dismantle the reactor," Mizrahi suggested during one of the first Security Cabinet meetings on the reactor.

The disadvantages, though, could not be ignored. If the US agreed to take upon itself the handling of the reactor, Mizrahi warned, it could potentially demand a quid pro quo from Israel in the form of concessions on the Palestinian front. This could force Israel to take severe security risks.

In addition, a deal with Syria—peace talks in exchange for the dismantling of its nuclear program—would embolden Assad and raise Damascus's international value and diplomatic clout at a time when he really needed to be punished, not rewarded, for actively working with North Korea, Iran and Hezbollah.

Mizrahi also wondered whether the US could reach a deal with Assad like it had with Muammar Gaddafi. Under that deal, Libya surrendered its nuclear program in exchange for the lifting of sanctions as well as the normalization of ties between Libya and the West.

While he was skeptical about such a deal, Mizrahi thought it was worth a try. Dagan, the Mossad head, disagreed. He advocated strongly for military action and did not believe that

Assad was sincere about reaching a peace deal with Israel. For him, peace with Assad was out of the question.

With the intelligence verified, Olmert began to more seriously consider his options. He let Ashkenazi bring in a team of three experienced former military officers to assist him in the operational planning: Amnon Lipkin-Shahak, a former IDF chief of staff; Uri Sagi, a former head of Aman; and David Ivry, the former air force chief who orchestrated and commanded the bombing of Osirak in 1981.

To keep the meeting off the books, the three men were briefed at Olmert's home on a Friday. Dagan and Yadlin presented the photos and the latest intelligence assessments on the reactor's status.

To the three officers, Olmert seemed to have already made up his mind. "We can't allow the reactor to go hot and we are already in the midst of planning how to take care of it," he told them. It was a race against the clock.

Syria, which at the time was in possession of advanced Russian SAMs, hadn't deployed a single missile battery or anti-aircraft gun near the reactor, likely part of the regime's attempt to keep the project a secret. A military presence in the area would have raised questions. That is why secrecy was so important. The moment the Syrians knew that Israel knew, this would no longer be the case.

Ivry was there for a particular reason. He was one of the few people alive in Israel who could give both Olmert and Ashkenazi the confidence they would need to make the fateful decision to act. A legendary fighter pilot, Ivry knew what it was like to send troops deep behind enemy lines with low chances of returning. He was the brains behind the bombing of the Osirak reactor. He also knew the toll war could have on a man and a family. One of his sons, Gil, a fighter pilot, accidentally crashed his F-16 in 1987. He did not survive.

Ivry knew what the air force was capable of doing but he also had a strategic view of the region. Since retiring from the military, he had served as director general of the Defense Ministry, the highest-ranking civilian position in the defense establishment; and as Israel's ambassador to Washington, which provided him with an intimate understanding of the Bush administration and particularly Vice President Dick Cheney.

After the Osirak strike in 1981, the US was furious with Israel for not informing it ahead of time of its plans and for undermining international efforts to stop Saddam Hussein's nuclear program. President Ronald Reagan decided to punish Israel by suspending the delivery of a new batch of F-16s and voted in support of a UN Security Council resolution condemning the raid. He also doubled down on a controversial arms package to Saudi Arabia, infuriating Jerusalem.

The suspension would ultimately be lifted by the end of 1981 when Israel and the United States signed the Strategic Cooperation Agreement, codifying the unique alliance between the countries and including an increase in military aid to Israel.

Nevertheless, it would take a decade for the US to thank Israel for destroying Osirak. In 1991, after the First Gulf War, Cheney, then the defense secretary, sent Ivry a satellite photo of the bombed-out reactor with the following inscription: "With thanks and appreciation for the outstanding job you did on the Iraqi nuclear program in 1981, which made our job much easier in Desert Storm!"

During his discussions with Olmert, Ivry shared two important insights. On the one hand, he said, while he felt that Menachem Begin had been partially motivated by political considerations when deciding to bomb Osirak—elections were just weeks away at the time—he still thought he made a smart move by not sharing his plans with the United States. The reason, he told Olmert, was simple. The moment the Americans know, they will make a decision one way or another. The best-case scenario, he said, is that they decide to attack. This way Israel does not have to risk the outbreak of another war. But, he added, if the Americans decide not to attack and to instead activate a diplomatic option, Israel will be forced to move up its timeline and attack sooner than it would have needed to.

"In every attack like this there is a red line," Ivry explained years later. "In 1981, we decided that inserting the uranium into the reactor was the red line. But in 2007, it didn't make a difference what we set as the red line since once the Americans said no, if Israel was going to attack, it needed to act sooner to prevent anyone from finding out that it knew about the reactor."

Israel, he continued, already had an earlier red line than the Americans simply because of its geographical location. "The risk will always be greater for Israel while the US interest will always be different," Ivry explained. "The downside is that if you share your information with the Americans, you increase the chances that you will not end up attacking."

Olmert, however, had already made up his mind. Telling the

Americans, he explained, was necessary in this case. The potential benefit from having the US carry out the strike greatly outweighed the risks Ivry had presented.

While the Syrian reactor presented a grave threat to Israel, it also was a unique opportunity, Olmert explained. His eye wasn't just on Syria but was also on Iran, whose nuclear program could only be stopped, he told the group, if the world superpowers—primarily the US and Russia—stepped up to the plate.

Syria would be the test. How it was handled, he said, would resonate throughout the region and particularly back in Iran. If Syria was allowed to get away with this, Iran would feel emboldened.

"But, if America were to say they will not allow anyone, in any place, to have atomic reactors and they do what they say and destroy the Syrian reactor, the Iranians will get the message," Olmert explained to the group. Additionally, the chance for retaliation from Syria was lower if America carried out the strike.

Olmert was thinking broadly and strategically, not about the current threat but about the next one. He was acting like a prime minister.

With a basic strategy outlined, Olmert decided it was time to start updating some of his cabinet members. While the president of the United States functions as the commander in chief of the military with the authority to independently authorize military operations of the kind needed to destroy Syria's nuclear reactor, in Israel, the prime minister's authority is limited. While Olmert was the head of government, the authority to go to war or launch such an operation rested in the hands of the Security Cabinet.

By law, the Security Cabinet needs to include the prime minister, the foreign minister, the defense minister, the internal security minister—responsible for the police—the justice minister and the finance minister. Usually, the prime minister also adds heads of the different parties that make up the coalition, assuming they do not already fill one of these positions.

Instead of convening the entire Security Cabinet at once, Olmert decided to update one minister at a time. In Israel, it is almost impossible to convene the Security Cabinet without the press immediately learning of the gathering. Questions would be asked, answers would need to be given, meaning that there was a possibility—even if small—that the true purpose of the gathering would leak out.

In addition, to some of the cabinet members, it seemed that the prime minister was trying to recruit each of them—from the get-go—to his position that an attack was necessary.

Some of the members he met privately at his residence in Jerusalem. Sometimes, Yadlin and Dagan were there to present the intelligence and what they could predict at that stage about Assad's potential thinking. The ministers were ordered to sign a written vow of confidentiality to emphasize the danger of leaks. By the time the reactor was bombed, some 2,500 people in Israel had signed the forms.

From the beginning, the Second Lebanon War, fought that previous summer, hung heavily in the air. The war had revealed two major flaws: the lack of preparedness in the home front, where bomb shelters were in ruin and in some cities nonexistent, as well as the IDF's difficulty in reducing Hezbollah's rocket attacks against the country.

An attack against Syria so soon after the war in Lebanon could again expose the country to another disastrous war. Olmert wanted to make sure everyone was on the same page in the event that a war—the likes of which Israel had not seen in decades—erupted.

The first two ministers brought into the loop were Defense Minister Amir Peretz and Foreign Minister Tzipi Livni. Peretz learned of the intelligence immediately after the Mossad raid. When Dagan drove to Jerusalem on March 13 to update Olmert about what had been discovered, he first stopped at IDF headquarters in Tel Aviv to brief the IDF chief of staff, who went immediately to update Peretz.

While Livni did not play a key role at this stage—that would come later—Olmert believed it was important to bring her up to speed due to the criticism he faced after the Second Lebanon War for leaving the Foreign Ministry out of the wartime decision-making process.

One Friday in late March, Livni was summoned to Olmert's Jerusalem residence, where he updated her on the intelligence uncovered in the Mossad raid. Already then, Olmert seemed determined to launch a military operation. When he met Livni, he told her that she could not discuss the reactor with anyone on her staff. Only later, as work on Israel's options picked up its pace, did Livni receive permission to bring two members of her senior team at the Foreign Ministry—Aaron Abramovich, the ministry's director general, and Tal Becker, the deputy legal adviser at the ministry—into the fold.

During that first meeting, Olmert, she later said, seemed to hint to her that the reactor could help turn around his political career. It was a rare intimate moment for the two politicians. Though both were from the same party—Kadima—Livni was already eyeing Olmert's seat. In a few weeks, the Winograd Commission—set up to investigate the failures of the Second Lebanon War—would publish its interim report, blasting Olmert. Livni would seize the opportunity and publicly call for the prime minister's resignation.

Another member of the Security Cabinet at the time was Rafi Eitan, a legendary Mossad operative famous for leading the team of agents that located and captured the notorious Nazi officer Adolf Eichmann in a daring operation in Argentina in 1960. Born in 1926 in a small kibbutz in northern Israel, Eitan played a key role in Israeli defense and intelligence circles throughout his career. He joined the Haganah, the underground Jewish fighting force, at age 12 and later became a member of its elite and secret commando unit, the Palmach.

After World War II, he helped smuggle Jews into the country, which at the time was still controlled by the British. One memorable escapade involved blowing up a radar station used by the British to detect ships illegally approaching the Haifa port. To reach the radar, Eitan had to crawl through an underground sewer pipe, earning the nickname "Stinky Rafi."

Throughout his career, Eitan's name has often been followed by controversy and mystery. In 1968, he paid a visit to a nuclear fuel plant in the United States, after which 200 kilograms of highly enriched uranium went missing; it was widely suspected that it had been diverted to Israel for its highly classified nuclear program.[5] He later tried to help the Shah in Iran establish a military force that would prevent Ayatollah Ruhollah Khomeini from returning to the country.

In 1981, while serving as an adviser to Menachem Begin, Eitan was appointed head of LAKAM, a secretive and shadowy organization that operated under the Defense Ministry and was responsible for collecting—some might say stealing—scientific intelligence and know-how. At LAKAM, Eitan was responsible for recruiting and overseeing Jonathan Pollard as an Israeli spy within US Naval Intelligence, an affair that would strain Israeli-US ties for decades.

In 1987, after taking responsibility for the Pollard affair, Eitan resigned and LAKAM was disbanded. He went into business with a particular focus on agriculture projects in Cuba. In 2006 he was asked to head the Pensioners Party, an almost defunct political group that ended the election with a surprise result—seven seats in the Knesset and two ministries, placing him within Olmert's government.

Eitan had first learned about the existence of the reactor directly from Dagan. The two were close from operations they used to run together against the PLO in Lebanon in the late 1970s. Eitan was working at the time for Prime Minister Begin, and Dagan was a top IDF commander.

That is why, when Sharon began deliberations ahead of the appointment of a new Mossad chief in 2002, Eitan went directly to his office and convinced him that Dagan, whose bravery and operational capabilities he had come to admire, was the best candidate. After a four-hour meeting, Eitan convinced Sharon and Dagan got the job. At one point, Dagan even asked Eitan to return to the Mossad to serve as his deputy.

When he was summoned to meet Olmert, Eitan told the prime minister: "We shouldn't waste any time. We should attack right away."

Other members of the Security Cabinet were Eli Yishai, leader of the ultra-Orthodox Shas Party; Avi Dichter, a former head of the Shin Bet, the intelligence agency responsible for combating Palestinian terrorism; Shimon Peres, the former prime minister who in July would become Israel's president; and Shaul Mofaz, a former IDF chief of staff and defense minister who was now serving as minister of transportation.

Haim Ramon, the justice minister, was supposed to get married that September. After learning of the existence of the reactor he convinced his fiancée to postpone the wedding until October. "There will be better weather then," he told her.

Olmert decided to update a select group of additional ministers who weren't members of the Security Cabinet, including Isaac Herzog from the Labor Party. Herzog had joined the Knesset in 2003. He was the son of Haim Herzog, a former head of Aman who later became Israel's sixth president. Herzog had also served as an officer in 8200, Aman's SIGINT unit.

While he wasn't a full-fledged member of the Security Cabinet, Herzog had "observer" status, which meant that he could attend the meetings and voice opinions but was not given a vote. He forged a close relationship with Olmert, built on mutual respect, even though they were in competing political parties.

One day in April, Herzog noticed something strange at the end of a cabinet meeting. After all the ministers had gotten up from their seats and were preparing to leave the room, Olmert announced that he had forgotten to discuss one last item.

"Due to the situation in the north, I want to establish a special ministerial committee for the north," Olmert said. "Its members will be the Security Cabinet members."

Herzog, who had served as cabinet secretary during Ehud Barak's short-lived premiership, knew that this was not the way cabinet decisions were taken. The establishment of a ministerial committee wasn't a decision thrown out at the last second to be voted on as ministers were halfway out the door. Also, what situation in the north exactly was Olmert referring to?

"Who's in favor?" Olmert asked the room. Everyone raised their hands and the meeting was adjourned.

While Herzog had his suspicions about the last-second vote, it was only a month later, in May, when he discovered what was really going on. One day, Olmert summoned Herzog to his office. It was just the two of them. On the desk was a folder. Olmert proceeded to open it and lay out the different photos—some from the Mossad raid and others from satellites—of the Syrian reactor.

"I'm setting up a small cabinet of ministers and want you to be part of it," Olmert told the astonished Herzog. Recognizing the significance of the information, Herzog readily agreed. The "ministerial committee," Herzog now understood, was a façade Olmert had created to convene the Security Cabinet without people asking questions.

Olmert pulled out a confidentiality form and asked Herzog

to sign. More and more people were being updated about the reactor, and while some—like Olmert himself—were determined to see it destroyed, Israel still had to wait. First, Bush needed to make a decision.

4

TICKING CLOCK

In 1998, George W. Bush made his first trip to Israel. He had just been reelected governor of Texas—the first governor to win a back-to-back second term in the Lone Star State—and was already plotting his presidential bid.

During the visit—together with a few other Republican governors—Bush made the standard gubernatorial stops: a meeting with then prime minister Benjamin Netanyahu; a tour of the Knesset, the Yad Vashem Holocaust Museum and the Western Wall. He then took a helicopter ride up to the Golan Heights. His guide for the flight was none other than Ariel Sharon, the fabled IDF general who was serving at the time as Israel's foreign minister. Little did the two know that in just three years they would meet again, although this time as president and prime minister.

The helicopter ride sparked a mini crisis between Israel, the US and the Palestinians. Sharon wanted to land the helicopter in the West Bank to show Bush the reality on the ground, but the Palestinians objected. They feared that Israel would use the visit to try and legitimize the settlement enterprise, which Sharon had long championed.

In the end, Israel compromised. The helicopter didn't land but it flew low enough for Bush to see Jerusalem's ancient rooftops, the ridges overlooking the Jordan Valley, the red-roofed stucco homes in the Israeli settlements and the densely populated Palestinian cities.

Sharon and Bush wore headphones so they could communicate over the noise made by the Blackhawk helicopter's rotors. The former IDF general shared with the Texas governor his own personal story, pointing along the way at hills and valleys where he had waged battle in past Israeli-Arab wars. When Sharon told Bush that at its narrowest point Israel was just 10 miles wide, the future president joked that some driveways in Texas are longer.[1]

Bush also met with Olmert, who was then serving as the mayor of Jerusalem. During their meeting, Bush asked Olmert what the biggest challenge was being mayor of one of the most contentious cities in the world.

"Collecting garbage," Olmert said without missing a beat. Bush couldn't believe it. A city as complicated and as tense as Jerusalem, and the mayor was concerned about picking up the trash!

The visit had a tremendous impact on Bush and his meeting with Olmert was a story he relished retelling. In 2004, for example, when he took the stage at the American Israel Public Affairs Committee Policy Conference in Washington, DC, he opened by saying that he had heard his old friend Ehud Olmert was in the crowd. To general laughter, he retold the garbage story.

While Bush's father had a tenuous relationship with Israel as president, the younger Bush fell in love with the Jewish state. His visit showed him not just how small and vulnerable Israel was, but also how committed its people were to the land and the Jewish nation. He was impressed by the country's vibrant democratic character as the only real democracy in the Middle East.

While in the Golan Heights, for example, he met a woman who had moved to Israel from Texas; her husband was one of the largest avocado growers in Israel. "It was really interesting to hear the human side of what it's like to love a country as much as she does and yet have the concerns about living so close to a border of a nation [Syria] that often posed a real threat to their way of life," Bush later recounted.[2]

The feelings he took away stuck with him. When he eventually became president, he told his national security team in January 2001 that the US would be "correcting the imbalances" of the previous administration.

"We're going to tilt back toward Israel and we're going to be consistent," he said, referring specifically to what he had seen during his helicopter ride with Sharon. "Looked real bad down there. I don't see much we can do over there at this point. I think it's time to pull out of that situation."[3]

While Bush and Sharon had a unique relationship, when Olmert became prime minister he worked to deepen those ties. Shortly after the elections in March 2006, he flew to the US for his first meeting as prime minister with the president. The two had a lot in common. They were around the same age—Olmert was born 10 months before Bush—and they both came from political homes. Bush's father was America's forty-first president. Olmert's father was a former member of the Knesset.

While the two had met several times in the past, Olmert's visit to Washington, DC, on June 19 was of strategic importance. To reporters, the Prime Minister's Office said he was going to the US to talk about the Palestinians. A few days earlier, Hamas had overrun the Palestinian Authority in the Gaza Strip. It was two years since Israel had unilaterally withdrawn from Gaza; it was now under the control of a terrorist organization. There was plenty for the two leaders to discuss.

Olmert spent hours with his staff preparing for the meeting. He knew that this would be his opportunity to convince the president about the need for US action against Syria's reactor. A people person, Olmert can turn on his charm when needed. What he couldn't do by phone, he hoped to be able to do in person.

At their meeting later that day in the Oval Office, the two leaders sat in blue-and-yellow-striped armchairs in front of the fireplace, under the portrait of George Washington. With the cameras in the room, the two spoke primarily about Gaza and the Palestinians. Bush reaffirmed American support for a two-state solution, while expressing hope that the Palestinian Authority would be able to regain control of the Gaza Strip. After the leaders' opening remarks, Bush turned to the assembled reporters and offered to take some questions.

Most of the reporters focused their questions on Gaza, except for one, who asked about Iran's nuclear program and the viability of renewing Israeli-Syrian peace negotiations. Assad had recently told a US congressional delegation in Damascus that he was prepared to open peace negotiations with Israel.

Bush dismissed the question. "They [the Israelis] can handle their own negotiations with Syria. If the Prime Minister wants to negotiate with Syria, he doesn't need me to mediate," he said.[4]

Syria, though, took up much more than just one question. Later, once the press left the room, Olmert and Bush got down to business. Cheney sat in on the meeting but remained mostly silent. Time, Olmert told the president, was running out. "If we are going to act, it needs to be soon," he said.

At a certain point, Bush kicked out the staff and took a walk with Olmert upstairs to the Residence. There, the two men could sit in a more intimate setting. It was a gesture Bush reserved for world leaders he wanted to make feel special and at home. There was also a practical benefit to meeting in the Residence: conversations were not recorded.

Bush shared with Olmert some of his concerns. In a meeting a few days earlier, for example, Hayden, the CIA chief, had confirmed that Syria was building a reactor but said that he could not find the weapons team, the group that typically takes the enriched material and assembles a nuclear warhead for a ballistic missile. This situation, he explained, would make it difficult for him to approve a military strike.

The Israeli prime minister was decisive in his response. First, he said, it was possible that within Syria's secretive Scientific Studies and Research Center there was a section that was working on the country's nuclear program. And, he argued, even if that could not be guaranteed, Syria's nuclear program still posed an existential threat to Israel and the entire region.

"In the history of mankind, to the best of my memory, there were only two times that atomic bombs were used against two cities," Olmert told the president. "Your country did it. Did they have missiles? They had a bomb and dropped it from a plane, so what's the difference?"

Imagine, Olmert continued, what would happen if thirty-five Syrian planes, two of which have nuclear devices on board, take off at the same time and start flying toward Israel. Even if the Israeli Air Force is fast and succeeds in intercepting most of the planes, some will get through, and one of those might be one of the two planes carrying a nuke. "When their planes take off, they are above Israel within one minute," Olmert said. "They don't need to have a missile."

Time was running out. America needed to act. A US-led strike would "kill two birds with one stone." "I think this is a great opportunity for America and for you to send a signal to the Iranians that will not be missed," Olmert said.

Bush was noncommittal and mostly listened. He told Olmert that he needed some more time and would give his answer in the coming weeks.

Nevertheless, Olmert had a sense of the direction this was going. He got the impression that the president's hands were tied. The war in Iraq, and the faulty intelligence that had led to it, left the president with very little room to maneuver. The fact that US intelligence agencies were not giving Bush a written recommendation due to the missing weapons team tied the president's hands even more.

Later that evening, Olmert met Cheney for dinner. The Israeli prime minister was staying at Blair House on Pennsylvania Avenue, directly opposite the White House. The two had known each other for years. Cheney was the former chief of staff of President Gerald Ford and participated each year in the World Forum, a gathering of leaders that took place annually in Beaver Creek, Colorado, and was hosted by Ford and the American Enterprise Institute, a conservative-leaning think tank. Olmert had been a regular attendee since the 1990s, when Cheney was secretary of defense. They weren't the closest of friends but they knew each other well.

Cheney spoke bluntly and told Olmert what he genuinely believed—America, and not Israel, needed to use military force to destroy the reactor. Olmert agreed but knew that Cheney was up against fierce opposition from Rice, Gates and Hadley. He told the vice president that if nuclear proliferation was allowed to continue, it would send a dangerous message to Iran and North Korea. If America didn't act, Israel would.

Cheney agreed. Like the Israeli prime minister, he viewed the Syrian reactor as an opportunity for the US to "demonstrate we're serious and those of you who are thinking about proliferating, to think twice." Cheney had been a longtime supporter of preemptive military action to destroy nuclear capabilities. To Cheney's credit, he was consistent in his worldview. In 1981, when Israel bombed Osirak, he was in Congress but publicly came out and supported Israel even as it took flak from the Reagan administration.

Olmert told Cheney that if America decided in the end to

go ahead with the bombing, the administration would need to consider whether it publicly took responsibility. He said that if Israel ended up acting, it would remain quiet in order not to provoke Assad and push him to retaliate. Cheney completely disagreed.

"On the contrary," the vice president said. "We don't only need to do it but need to make sure that everyone knows the policy that we will not tolerate this and the Iranians will know."

While it was reassuring for Olmert to hear the vice president of the United States side with him, he knew it wasn't yet the success he was looking for. The ultimate decision was up to the president, but the opposition to American military action was greater than he assumed.

A few days later, the president gathered his national security team—again in the Yellow Oval Room—for a final meeting on the issue. Olmert was back in Israel and it was decision time. Israel was pressing to get an answer and Bush felt it was only right, considering that Israel had discovered the reactor and come to the US with the intelligence, that he get back to them as quickly as possible.

The principals again laid out their positions and impressions from Olmert's trip. Gates and Rice urged a sequenced approach—go to the UN and try to stop Assad with diplomacy. If that didn't work then use a military option, but only as a last resort. General Pace, chairman of the Joint Chiefs, agreed. "It gives you two chances to win," he told the president.[5]

Rice mentioned the Israeli-Palestinian peace conference she was in the midst of trying to put together for the end of the year. An American attack on Syria, she said, would blow up the conference before it even took place.

Gates went a step further. While he was a self-declared supporter of Israel, he didn't like the amount of influence Olmert had over the president. He told Bush that Olmert was trying to push his hand and get him to do something that was not necessarily in America's own national interest. The US needed to decide for itself. If it chose diplomacy and Israel refused to fall in line, then, Gates said, Bush needed to make it clear to Olmert that US-Israel ties would be on the line.

While Israel had pushed the theory that if it remained quiet after an attack Assad would not feel compelled to retaliate, many in the group did not buy into the idea. Gates, for example, believed that an Israeli attack would trigger a war with Syria that would have fallout and consequences for the US and the entire Middle East.[6]

It was similar to what Edelman had asked earlier. If, for example, something went wrong with the operation—even one carried out by the US—and search-and-rescue teams needed to be flown in, could they even enter Iraq and land there? How would the Iraqi government react?

Cheney sensed defeat but again pushed for US military action. That was the only way, he insisted, to send a real message to Iran, North Korea and anyone else who would ever contemplate building a nuclear weapon in the future. For America, he said, it would be an easy military operation.

When Cheney finished, Bush asked: "Is there anyone in the

room who agrees with the vice president that we should bomb this site?"[7]

No one said a word. Abrams actually supported attacking the reactor but believed the strike needed to be carried out by the Israelis, not the US. Israel, he believed, needed to do it on its own to restore the deterrence it had lost during the Second Lebanon War a year earlier. If the bombing was carried out by the US it would seem as if Israel was too weak to do it on its own. Striking a secret nuclear reactor no one knew about, Abrams thought, would send a powerful message that Israeli power was back on the rise.

Edelman, Gates's representative in the Drafting Group and the under secretary of defense for policy, also sympathized with Cheney. But he took a different approach. Gates's comment to him in the beginning of the process—that each administration gets one war with a Muslim nation—remained stuck in his mind. So, he kept his hand down due to concern about the fallout an American strike would have on US efforts to stabilize Iraq.

"There was potential for blowback in Iraq where we were at that point in the midst of the Surge, which was extremely sensitive in the US, politically. And we already were taking the highest casualties that we had in that period," Edelman explained a few years later.[8]

None of this really mattered, though. In the end, Cheney was on his own. The result reminded the vice president of an old term he picked up as a kid in Wyoming—snakebit. The people in the room had been traumatized or "bitten by a snake" and were too scared to take the necessary action. The snakebite in this case was the intelligence flop on Iraq. The fear of launching another military operation based on similar intelligence was apparently too intimidating.

So, Bush said, if no one else agrees with Cheney, America will go to Vienna, update the IAEA and take Syria to the UN under a threat of military force. If diplomacy failed, only then would military action be considered.

In principle, Bush seemed to agree with Cheney's view that the reactor was an opportunity to rein in Assad. He just didn't think military action was the route to go at this stage. He preferred to first go public with the reactor and shame Assad on the global stage. That, the president seemed to believe, would give the US leverage over Assad on the other pressing issues as well.

Bush asked the team how Olmert would respond. Rice said she believed Israel would accept the diplomatic option and go along with a UN-led initiative. Cheney completely disagreed. Olmert, the vice president said, "meant what he said about taking action."

To some extent, the writing had been on the wall. Three years earlier, during the Sudanese massacre in Darfur, human rights groups had pressured the White House to take military action to prevent a genocide. Bush had asked his team to find a viable solution. The military command suggested attacking the Sudanese Air Force to relay a clear message: genocide will not be tolerated. Bush was convinced and was prepared to give a green light for the operation. For him this was a classic case of good versus evil, with the goal of preventing the murder of the weak and oppressed. It was a simple operation. The US Air Force could have completed it in a single sortie.

But then his closest advisers convinced him to back down, arguing that he was already up to his neck in trouble in Afghanistan and Iraq. Another attack against a Muslim country would only increase hatred toward America throughout the Arab and Muslim world. "Any complication there will increase public sentiment against you. It is more important to focus on solving the problems where we already are," they told him.

"Had the Israeli prime minister understood this dilemma," Abrams later explained, "he would never have expected Bush to order an airstrike against the Syrian reactor."

The question now was how to tell Olmert. Bush wanted a little more time to think. In the meantime, the different sides on the national security team tried to make some last-minute changes to what Bush would end up telling his Israeli counterpart.

A few days later, Gates met privately with Bush and again tried to push the president to insist that Israel not do anything without American consent. Yes, Israel had brought the intelligence to the US, but even if Israel acted on its own, America would appear complicit, he told the president. "Tell Prime Minister Olmert that we will not allow the reactor to become operational but Israel must allow us to handle this in our own way," Gates said. "If they do not, they are on their own. We will not help them."

In the meantime, Abrams met with Hadley and presented him with a new memo he had drafted on the reactor. Abrams was concerned about political and diplomatic fallout if Bush went through with the diplomatic approach.

Look at the region, Abrams said. Hamas had just taken over

the Gaza Strip; Hezbollah had rearmed itself, despite the beefed-up presence of UN forces in southern Lebanon and Security Council Resolution 1701 that had ended last summer's war; Iran was moving forward with its own nuclear program; and now, we've learned that Syria is also building a nuclear reactor. And what is America's response to all of this, Abrams asked? To go to the UN.

The administration's friends on the Right, Abrams warned Hadley, will think we've lost our senses. Instead of being forceful, he said, we are going to the UN and, at the same time, pushing Israel into final-status peace talks with the Palestinians. It appeared ridiculous.

But it was too late. Bush had made up his mind. On the morning of July 13, Bush called Olmert from the secure line in the Oval Office. It was 8:00 a.m. in Washington and 3:00 p.m. in Jerusalem. Hadley and Abrams were in the room with Bush while Olmert was joined by Turbowicz and his diplomatic adviser Shalom Turgeman.

"I cannot justify an attack on a sovereign nation unless my intelligence agencies stand up and say it's a weapons program," the president told the Israeli premier. He explained his decision to take the issue to the IAEA. It will "protect your interests and your state and makes it more likely we can achieve our interests as well."[9]

Olmert mostly listened as Bush continued. If I attack, the president said, I would need to update Congress and would then be asked where I got the intelligence from. "I would have to say it came from Israel and in no time it would spread throughout the world that America attacked another country because of Israel." This, Bush stressed, would undermine the Israeli-US relationship and erode Washington's ability to run Mideast affairs.

Already, some parts of Washington were pushing a theory that Israel had pressured Bush to attack Iraq.

"Is that what you want?" Bush asked Olmert. "Let us take care of it."

Bush said Rice would arrive in Israel on Monday and hold a joint press conference with Olmert during which the two would reveal the existence of the reactor and set into motion the diplomatic process needed to take it down.

Abrams thought Olmert would listen and ask for a day to consult with his staff before responding. He was wrong. Olmert responded immediately and forcefully.

"Mr. President," he started. "I understand your reasoning and your arguments but don't forget that the ultimate responsibility for the security of the State of Israel rests on my shoulders and I'll do what needs to be done and trust me—I will destroy the atomic reactor.

"This is something that hits at the very serious nerves of this country," he continued. "I must be honest and sincere with you. Your strategy is very disturbing to me."

Bush was taken aback by Olmert's fierce reaction. Abrams was nervous that the president was going to snap back, but he decided to let Olmert vent. "Have at it," he said when wrapping up the conversation. "We will not get in your way."

Olmert had one last request. "Whoever knows, knows," Olmert said. "But from now on, I urge you to make sure that it will not spread since the only advantage we have is that they do not know that we know. So please, Mr. President, make sure that no one speaks."

Bush completely agreed: "I'll be buttoned up, my friend."

When the call ended, Bush surprised Abrams and Hadley with his reaction. "That guy has guts," the president said. "None of this is going to leak. Everybody just shut up."

The US, Bush concluded, couldn't actively assist Israel in carrying out the strike, but he told Hadley and Abrams to ensure that no one in the US got in Israel's way. What this practically meant was that America could only continue working with Israeli intelligence.

Basically, intelligence cooperation, yes; military assistance, no.

For Hadley, the reaction was typical Bush. "That is the kind of leader he admired and that is the kind of leader Olmert showed to be," Hadley explained years later. "Olmert said that this is an existential threat to the State of Israel and the Jewish people and I am not willing to leave the elimination of that threat in anyone else's hands, even in the hands of the US, Israel's best friend in the world. Bush's decision was that he respected that."

The next day, Bush again met with his national security team. Gates was furious. Olmert, he told Bush, had asked America for help, but was unwilling to accept anything as an answer if it wasn't a US attack on Syria. America, he said, was being held hostage by Israel.

Gates felt that by not giving Olmert a red light, Bush was in reality giving him a green light to attack. A secret strike by Israel, he said, would put the focus on the bombing as opposed to what was really important—North Korea's nuclear proliferation, which would have been exposed had the diplomatic approach been implemented.

In addition, Gates warned, the end result would make America look weak. "Our [diplomatic] proposal will emerge, making it look like the US government subordinated its strategic interest to that of a weak Israeli government that already had screwed up one conflict in the region."[10]

Bush listened but refused to put any pressure on Olmert. He said that he was impressed with Olmert's "steadfastness" and that he would not do anything that would preempt Israel.

But while the assumption in Washington was that Israel would strike, no one knew the exact date. The rough timeline was clear—the strike had to take place before the reactor went hot. The reactor's exterior was complete and the cooling system was in its final stages of preparation. If there was going to be a strike, it had to be soon.

A few days after the phone call, Olmert convened the Security Cabinet. He needed to update the ministers about the American decision. Like previous meetings, this gathering was also disguised so the public would not know the true reason behind the unscheduled gathering of the ministers.

Olmert opened with updates from his conversation with Bush, and then Yadlin and Dagan presented the latest intelligence. The ministers were then each given an opportunity to ask questions and speak.

"The Americans gave us their answer," Olmert said. "They will not be taking action."

One minister around the table had a "told-you-so" smirk on his face. It was Ehud Barak, the former prime minister who, after six years out of government, had returned to the defense ministry the month before.

In June, Barak managed to win the Labor Party primaries and unseat its chairman, Amir Peretz. The same day that he won the party's top spot, he faxed Peretz a dismissal letter, firing him from his post as defense minister. Barak didn't just want to be the party chairman. He wanted to return to the cabinet.

Peretz received the letter in the middle of a meeting with Olmert about the Syrian reactor. It was almost surreal. Here he was discussing the fate of the State of Israel, and his new party boss was firing him by fax.

At the time, some political analysts believed that Peretz's dismissal was a cheap shot and disrespectful. Barak explained that he did so because of the reactor. As a former prime minister, he had been briefed on it by Olmert shortly after the Mossad raid and felt a sense of urgency to immediately join the Security Cabinet so he could help plan for the eventual attack.

Olmert had invited Barak to the Prime Minister's Residence in Jerusalem one day back in April. Yadlin and Dagan were also there and they gave him the full brief on the discovery of the reactor. "We can't allow this to go hot and we are planning how to deal with it," Olmert had told Barak at the time. A similar briefing was held for Netanyahu.

Barak mostly listened. He agreed that a reactor in Assad's hands posed an existential threat to the State of Israel and he told Olmert that it seemed like he knew what he was doing.

A former IDF chief of staff and one of the country's most

decorated soldiers, Barak's military and political career is part and parcel of Israel's history as a nation. Born in a kibbutz in 1942, Barak never gave thought to public office or even a military career growing up.

All that changed when he was drafted into the IDF and joined Sayeret Matkal, eventually becoming its commander and making a name for himself as a crafty tactician and brilliant strategist. He was one of the key architects of the raid on Entebbe in 1976 to free a group of Air France hostages, and was a member of the force that boarded a hijacked Sabena flight in 1972 disguised as a mechanic to free it from Black September terrorists. A year later, Barak dressed up as a woman and led his Sayeret Matkal troops deep into Beirut to eliminate three of the PLO's top terror chiefs.

His career didn't stop there. Barak continued to climb the IDF ranks, serving as head of Aman and the Planning Directorate before being appointed chief of staff in 1991. A mere six months after his retirement in 1995, he joined the Labor Party and was appointed Israel's interior minister.

When Shimon Peres lost the 1996 election to Benjamin Netanyahu, Barak had his opportunity to take over the Labor Party. Three years later, he defeated his former soldier Netanyahu and became Israel's prime minister. But Barak's premiership was short lived. By 2000 elections were held again and he was ousted by Ariel Sharon, the famed general. Barak left politics and went into business.

After the 2006 Lebanon war, though, Barak saw an opportunity. All of the government ministers involved in the war were now in the public's crosshairs. He, the former IDF chief of staff and prime minister, could sweep in and retake the country's mantle. So, he ran for the head of the Labor Party and ousted Peretz.

Apparently, returning to the Defense Ministry was not enough. From the moment he returned to the government, he clashed with Olmert, at almost every single meeting.

A few days after he moved into the fourteenth floor of the Defense Ministry, Barak came to the Prime Minister's Residence in Jerusalem for a routine work meeting with Olmert. Known for being chronically unpunctual, Barak was late to this meeting as well. But when he finally walked in, he immediately attacked Olmert for meeting privately with the IDF chief of staff. Olmert tried to calm him down but failed. As he would learn over the coming months, working with Barak was not going to be easy.

For some of the ministers who sat with Olmert and Barak, it was uncomfortable to even be there. "It was like that feeling you get when you go out with friends and the other couple fights the whole time," one of the ministers recalled. "All you want to do is get the hell out of there."

Often accused of being condescending and aloof by political colleagues, Barak believed Olmert lacked strategic depth. While he agreed with Olmert on the end result—that the reactor needed to go away—he felt that the prime minister was moving too quickly and wasn't considering all of the available options.

When he took up the defense portfolio in June, Barak dived straight into the reactor file and immediately held a couple of briefings with the Mossad and IDF to get up to speed on where things stood. Olmert updated him separately on his talks with Bush and his hope that the Americans would carry out the strike.

Barak disagreed. He told Olmert that from his experience working with the Americans, there was no way Bush would authorize a strike against Syria. "They are already engaged in too many wars in the Middle East," he said.

At the time, Barak claimed he was presented with a handful of military options that were being discussed seriously. One was an extensive airstrike involving layers of aircraft in case something went wrong along the way.

While this option would most definitely accomplish the mission and destroy the reactor, it would also make it impossible for Israel to deny its involvement. It would be so loud that Assad would likely feel compelled to respond, something Israel wanted to avoid. Another option discussed was a ground operation by Israeli special forces.[11]

Barak wasn't happy with any of the options and made his opinion clear in a series of meetings Olmert convened at the Prime Minister's Residence with top IDF and Mossad officers. At each meeting, Barak would open by saying that he was in favor of destroying the reactor and "I am going to say this again in the middle and at the end." But, he said, "we need to be smart how we are going to go about doing this."

"We need to do it in a way that there is confidence we will destroy it and, at the same time, allow Assad to pretend nothing happened," Barak told the forum.

To some, including Olmert, it seemed that Barak was operating out of political considerations. These people viewed

Barak's arguments as an attempt to stall for time and delay the attack so more time could pass between his return to the Defense Ministry and the eventual strike. This way, if successful, the attack would be connected to him and not just to Olmert.

Olmert suspected that Barak was banking on the final Winograd Commission report on the Second Lebanon War— scheduled to be released later that year—to be so critical that it would force Olmert to resign. Barak would then oversee the strike on Syria and use its success to propel himself back into the prime minister's office.

"He wants to postpone everything so after you are thrown out of here, he will be elected prime minister and the glory from the strike will all be his," Finance Minister Roni Bar-On told Olmert one day.[12] Olmert's political instincts were telling him the same thing.

To others, it seemed that Barak was acting responsibly. Mizrahi, for example, agreed with Barak that Israel had time and did not need to rush to attack the reactor. To him, Barak seemed genuinely concerned with the prospects of a war with Syria and whether Israel was sufficiently prepared.

For Barak, all this political talk was nonsense. Barak told Olmert that the work done was impressive but that there was no reason why the army needed to stop planning even if the strike date was getting close. While he wanted to use the air force for the strike, he wanted something quiet that wouldn't embarrass Assad in a way that would force him to retaliate.

According to Barak, Olmert was dead set on attacking and showed little interest in the details. It was a pattern he felt Olmert had developed already during the Second Lebanon War. On the first night of the war, for example, Olmert launched a top-secret operation against Hezbollah's long-range missile arsenal. These were the rockets and missiles, secretly obtained over a period of several years from Iran, that had the ability to reach Tel Aviv.

The intelligence on the location of the missiles had been obtained by the Mossad back in the early 2000s when Barak was prime minister. In May 2000 he had pulled the IDF out of Southern Lebanon, where it had maintained a security zone since 1982. Five months after the withdrawal, though, Hezbollah abducted three Israeli soldiers, and some members of the defense establishment pushed Barak to strike the long-range rockets. He refused to attack the missiles, wanting to avoid a larger-scale war.

The same happened five years later when Ariel Sharon was prime minister. Then too Hezbollah launched a cross-border attack with the aim of kidnapping IDF soldiers. This time, however, thanks to a single IDF marksman, the mission failed. The Israeli sniper hit an RPG the Hezbollah guerrillas were carrying, setting off an explosion and killing three members of the raid squad. He then shot and killed a fourth. But again, Sharon refrained from attacking the missiles, knowing, like Barak, that if he did so it had the potential to escalate into a larger confrontation.

Olmert, on the other hand, adopted the plan to attack the missiles immediately, just hours after the two reservists had been kidnapped in 2006. "It sometimes seemed that there was uncontrolled and unrestrained excitement by Olmert. When he saw an available option on the shelf he just went for it," Barak would tell his confidants.

While Barak had been out of government during the 34-day war in Lebanon, he closely followed developments and remained plugged into the defense establishment and his old party, which kept him up to date. His feeling was that Olmert should have waited before responding to the initial Hezbollah attack. Barak believed Olmert could've taken a week to prepare the IDF, draft the reserves and seriously consider what was in Israel's best interest. Barak had a special appreciation for time. During drawn-out and long security meetings, he would get up from his seat, walk around the room, pull a clock off the wall, sit back down, take it apart and then put it back together again.

The meetings about the reactor often went on for hours and were an opportunity for everyone to brainstorm. At one meeting, a minister suggested leaking a few hints about the existence of a nuclear reactor in Syria to an international news network like BBC. The idea, the minister said, would be to gauge Assad's reaction and see what effect the knowledge that his reactor might have been discovered would have on its continued construction. Maybe, the minister said, Assad would suspend all of the plans until he felt safe enough to continue.

The idea was nixed out of intelligence concerns that such a leak would have the opposite result and motivate Assad to get the reactor up and running faster than he had originally planned.

Many of the ministers would later describe the experience of sitting in the Security Cabinet meetings as the highlight of their political careers. They had participated in an operation that removed an existential threat hovering over Israel. For the most part, politics were set aside and the goal was pure—how to keep the State of Israel safe.

One day, at the Knesset, Herzog bumped into Livni and asked whether she was planning on taking a vacation over the summer. He had spoken to his wife about going on holiday but was nervous about traveling too far in case the Syrian situation heated up. Livni said that she and her husband were flying to Cyprus, a mere 45-minute flight from Israel. Herzog decided to do the same. The two agreed that if needed, they could always charter a private plane to fly back to Israel at a moment's notice.

Meanwhile, at Aman headquarters in Tel Aviv, Yadlin's top analysts came up with a new concept—"the Deniability Zone." It was the brainchild of Brigadier General Yossi Baidatz, head of Aman's research department, a brilliant intelligence analyst and one of the country's top experts on Syria.

Baidatz's idea was simple. If Israel attacked but remained silent and did not "stick the reactor in his face," there was a good chance that Assad would restrain himself and refrain from retaliating.

Basically, Israel could create a "deniability zone" for Assad, in which the Syrian leader would never have to admit that he had been building a nuclear reactor to begin with. If Israel was quiet, Assad could carry on after a strike as if nothing had even happened.

The strategy was based on two lines of thinking: The number of people aware of the existence of the reactor was extremely limited. According to Aman, top generals in the Syrian military didn't have a clue that the reactor was even being built and Assad, the thinking went, would most likely prefer to pretend that nothing had happened than have to explain to his cabinet members and military officers what he had been doing along the Euphrates River. The Iranians didn't know, nor did the Russians. In addition, Aman believed that Assad would be so shocked that Israel had discovered the reactor and destroyed it, that he would actually prefer to sweep the whole thing under the rug rather than go to war. It would be painful, but for Assad, it might be the preferred option.

On the other hand, Assad had repeatedly been humiliated by Israel. Twice, in recent years, the IAF had buzzed the Syrian leader's summer residence after terrorist attacks in Israel that were carried out by groups supported by Assad. On both occasions, he bit his tongue and refrained from responding. There was no assurance that this time he would do the same.

Livni, the foreign minister, considered and ruled out a diplomatic option early on. It was not an easy decision to take. As the country's top diplomat, Livni had pushed from the beginning of the Second Lebanon War for the government to think and plan out its "exit strategy." At the time, no one wanted to listen to her. But in the end, diplomacy was what ended the war when the UN Security Council passed Resolution 1701, reached after intense negotiations with Condoleezza Rice.

But with the reactor in Syria, Livni knew that diplomacy wouldn't work. If Israel called out Assad and tried to get the world and the UN to clamp down on Syria, it would likely have the opposite effect. The world, she assessed, would be more inclined to try and reach a deal with Damascus, along the lines of the Joint Comprehensive Plan of Action, the infamous nuclear deal reached with Iran in 2015.

Livni's concern was that the moment the world started negotiating with Syria about al-Kibar, Assad would want to include other outstanding issues in the talks—like the future of the Golan Heights, the territory Israel had conquered from Syria during the Six Day War, as well as the regime's interests in Lebanon. Israel wanted those issues kept off the table.

Together with the Mossad, Livni oversaw the compilation of "incrimination dossiers" filled with the photos captured in the original Mossad raid as well as other key pieces of intelligence. The dossiers were placed in safes in Israeli embassies in France, Germany, Russia and Turkey. All were governments that Israel knew it would need to update after the reactor was destroyed.

At the same time, Livni drafted a statement to use if and when foreign counterparts of hers called to ask about the strike and if Israel had been involved. It was simple: "We appreciate the concern, and there was something, but we are keeping a low profile," Livni's text read. She then planned to cut off the call by saying: "I have to keep this conversation short since I have other phone calls to make. Someone will come to you soon and give you a detailed briefing."

Livni also began to prepare for the possibility that war would erupt. She had her top aide, legal expert Tal Becker, draft a Security Council resolution that would explain what had happened, how Israel had acted in self-defense, and would end by calling on the world to condemn Syria for violating the

Non-Proliferation Treaty and trying to illegally build a nuclear weapon.

Throughout this period, Aman and the Mossad consulted with expert psychologists and psychoanalysts to try and predict what Assad would do after the bombing. During one meeting with the prime minister, the analysts were surprised to discover that Olmert had actually studied psychology in university.

While Olmert's academic background helped, it was still a difficult prediction to make. Predictions are easy when they are based on facts, not on what a single person will do.

"If you ask me technical questions like how many planes does Assad have or how many missiles does he have and what can they all potentially do, I can answer with 100 percent," Yadlin, the Aman chief, explained to Olmert.

But trying to predict what is going on in the mind of a foreign leader is always going to be harder since it depends on so many different factors that are almost impossible to take into account. The dry facts could strongly suggest that Assad would not retaliate, Yadlin later explained. But what happens if he has a fight with his wife the night before? This might motivate him to decide to retaliate without us even knowing why.

"To know what a leader, who doesn't even know that you have discovered his secret, will do is very complicated," Yadlin said. "We have to be modest."

Ashkenazi explained that the real test would be if Israel's politicians could remain quiet. At one of the cabinet meetings, he explained that in his opinion there was a 50 percent chance that Assad might retaliate. But, he said, the 50 percent chance that he won't will depend largely on what we do and whether we remain quiet.

"If you don't stay quiet you will be responsible for the war that comes," the IDF chief warned the ministers. "We have to give Assad the opportunity to lie."

5

OLMERT'S WAR

On July 12, 2006, almost a year before the Syrian reactor was discovered, Ehud Olmert arrived at his office in Jerusalem early in the morning for another day of political and military battles. It was a short ride from the prime minister's official government residence in the upscale neighborhood of Talbiya in West Jerusalem where he lived with his wife, Aliza. What waited for him, he never could have imagined.

He had a busy morning. The IDF was operating on the ground in the Gaza Strip for the first time since Israel unilaterally pulled its settlements and military positions out in the summer of 2005 in a plan known as the Disengagement.

Two and a half weeks earlier, Gilad Shalit, an IDF soldier, had been abducted by Hamas, the Palestinian terrorist organization that was the true ruler of the Gaza Strip. Hamas terrorists, shortly after dawn, had crossed into Israel through a tunnel, attacked a nearby IDF Merkava tank, killed two soldiers and dragged Shalit, who had been lightly wounded, back into Gaza. Most of the tank crew was asleep and never saw the Hamas terrorists coming.

The night before, Olmert had given the IDF his approval to escalate the operation and send ground forces into Gaza. Until then, all operations had been carried out by the air force. Troops from the Givati Infantry Brigade crossed the border under the cover of Apache and Cobra attack helicopters. Their stated mission was to conquer land near the border that was being used by Hamas to fire rockets into Israel.

As the troops were moving into the Palestinian territory, Israeli intelligence managed to locate the most wanted and elusive man in Gaza: Mohammed Deif, the notorious leader of Hamas's Izz ad-Din al-Qassam military wing. This was the group behind some of the most vicious terrorist attacks against Israel. Deif had been an Israeli target for years but always managed to slip away. Locating him was one of those rare moments in the lives of intelligence officers. They had to move fast.

The lights went on and the screens flickered to life inside the special command center at IDF headquarters in the south, not far from the Gaza border. Officials took up their positions around the oval-shaped desk where they watched the intelligence flow in from different informants, drones and satellites.

At air force headquarters, the dimensions of the building where Deif was hiding were being analyzed, and experts there were carefully selecting the bomb that would be dropped. It had to be small enough to limit collateral damage but large enough to get the job done and kill the man who for years had managed to elude Israel.

The intelligence was checked and rechecked. Deif appeared, beyond a reasonable doubt, to be in the building and the commanders were confident enough to go ahead with the strike. The green light was finally given and the F-16 fighter jets took off toward their target, a three-story concrete apartment building in the Gaza City neighborhood of Sheikh Radwan.

At 3:00 a.m. the bomb was dropped. It scored a direct hit, demolishing the building. Deif was inside but somehow, despite sustaining serious injuries, emerged alive. Nine others were killed.

When he arrived at his office, Olmert received updates on the ongoing operation as well as a more detailed briefing on the strike against Deif.

At 10:00 a.m., Shalit's parents, Aviva and Noam, were led into the "Aquarium." Olmert wanted to update them on where things stood with their son. Everyone knew that the chance Hamas would simply free Shalit because of the ongoing military operation was slim, but Olmert and the IDF were hoping to extract a heavy price from the terrorist organization, so at the very least, Hamas demands for his future release would not be disproportionate. It was also important to show Hamas that the abduction of a soldier would not be tolerated. Israel needed to think about the next soldier as well.

In the middle of their meeting, Olmert's military aide walked in and handed the prime minister a note. Olmert looked up, took the small paper, unfolded it and read it. He then read it again and then a third time. He couldn't believe it. Without saying a word, he handed the note to Noam Shalit and told him to show it to his wife.

Olmert's military aide had scribbled that an attack had taken place in the north, along Israel's border with Lebanon. Two soldiers, he wrote, were missing. "It smells like a kidnapping," the officer said.

Olmert's heart sank. His mind started to race. Here, in front of him, were the parents of an abducted soldier held in the Gaza Strip. IDF troops were operating in Gaza for the first time since Israel's withdrawal a year earlier. And now, the winds of war were blowing in the north.

"The military better be careful," Olmert shouted to his military aide as he left the office. "Hezbollah will be waiting for them."

The prime minister didn't know yet how right he was. An IDF tank, stationed near the border, crossed into Lebanon to try and cut off the kidnappers as they were making their getaway. Hezbollah was prepared and had planted a massive landmine in the tank's path, which blew it to smithereens and killed all of its crew. If the abduction hadn't been bad enough, now the death toll was starting to climb.

Olmert wrapped up the meeting with the Shalits and promised to keep them updated on the progress in Gaza. He then gathered his closest advisers and asked to hear their opinions how they thought the IDF should respond to the cross-border attack in the north. Everyone seemed to be of the opinion that an aggressive response was needed. The problem was that Olmert had a visiting dignitary he needed to host that day. Japanese prime minister Junichiro Koizumi was in town on a trip that had been repeatedly postponed and Olmert was supposed to meet him at his official residence for lunch, to be followed by a short statement to the press.

"I want to make it clear," Olmert said a couple hours later at the press conference. "This morning's events were not a terrorist attack, but the action of a sovereign state that attacked Israel for no reason and without provocation. The Lebanese government, of which Hezbollah is a member, is trying to undermine regional stability. Lebanon is responsible and Lebanon will bear the consequences of its actions."

Olmert continued: "The State of Israel and its citizens now stand in an hour of trial. We have withstood difficult tests in the past, even more difficult and complex than these. We, the State of Israel, the entire nation, will know how to now overcome those who are trying to hurt us."

Olmert spoke a bit prematurely. The war that would ensue would be marred by mishaps, failures and political trials and tribulations. The Winograd Commission of inquiry would later call it a "severe failure" and place a large chunk of the blame squarely on Olmert's shoulders.

A few minutes before Olmert got word of the attack, his defense minister, Amir Peretz, heard about it in Tel Aviv. Peretz was sitting in his office on the fourteenth floor of the brand-new Defense Ministry tower, a large techy-looking office building located at the entrance to Tel Aviv. He was in a meeting with a group of generals discussing the ongoing operation in Gaza.

The head of the IDF's Operations Directorate gave an ini-

tial update on the incident—two Humvees, he said, had been
hit in a Hezbollah ambush—and the Northern Command, the
IDF branch responsible for Lebanon, had activated "Hanni-
bal," a code name for the military procedure initiated when there
is a fear that a soldier has been abducted.

Peretz wrapped up the meeting and instructed everyone to
divert their attention to the north. "This is the most important
event right now," Peretz said. "Otherwise, we will go into a tail-
spin." Before adjourning the meeting, Peretz gave the air force
approval to strike Hezbollah positions along the border and to
carry out additional bombings deeper inside Lebanon, against
roads the terrorists could potentially use to escape with the abducted soldiers.

The irony was that Olmert and Peretz weren't even supposed
to have been in their respective positions. Olmert landed in the
job half a year earlier after Ariel Sharon, the legendary general
and cunning politician, suffered a devastating stroke that per-
manently incapacitated him.

In 2003, Olmert only managed to come thirty-second in the
Likud primaries that set the ranking for entrance to the Knesset. Due to his loyalty, though, and as compensation for his low
ranking, Sharon made him minister of industry and trade, and
then—after Benjamin Netanyahu resigned ahead of the Disengagement from Gaza—finance minister. When Sharon eventually broke away from the Likud and established the new party
Kadima, he appointed Olmert deputy prime minister, a position that usually only comes with a title but in this case, due to
Sharon's fatal stroke, would end up meaning much more.

Olmert was born in 1945 in northern Israel in an old Turkish fortress used by Etzel, one of the pre-state Jewish militias, as a base of operations for fighters heading out on missions against the British. His father, Mordechai, was born in Russia but moved to Harbin, China, where he founded a local branch of Betar, the Revisionist youth movement associated with Vladimir Jabotinsky. He moved to Israel in the 1930s, became a politician and served in the Knesset as a member of Herut, a party that advocated territorial expansionism and later morphed into the Likud, the party that has mostly ruled Israel since the late 1970s.

In 1963, Olmert was drafted into the IDF's Golani Infantry Brigade, but after an old high-school injury acted up, he left his combat unit and was transferred to *Bamahane*, the IDF's weekly magazine. He completed his service as a journalist, a past his critics later mocked him for following the Second Lebanon War.

Olmert joined the Knesset in 1973, at the age of 28. For most of his career, he was considered an outsider but also one of the more hawkish members of the Likud Party. It was just four years before Menachem Begin would oust the Labor Party from power and establish the first right-wing government in Israel's history.

At the time, Olmert was known as one of the bad boys of the Knesset. A former journalist with a sharp and cynical tongue, Olmert went after the establishment, every establishment. Together with some other rookie Knesset members, Olmert led a campaign against government corruption. One of his first targets was organized crime and its control over Israeli soccer clubs. He then went after drug rings in Jerusalem and teamed up with reporters to take down arms dealers.

Olmert's political career took off. In 1988, he earned a seat at the cabinet table as a minister-without-portfolio, and two years later was appointed Israel's health minister. In 1993, Olmert decided to capitalize on his newfound fame and threw his hat in the Jerusalem mayoral race. Early polls showed him losing to Teddy Kollek, the city's longtime legendary mayor, but Olmert ended up prevailing, moving across Jerusalem from the Knesset to city hall.

As mayor of Jerusalem, Israel's contentious capital, Olmert had a platform that he could use to speak to the world but also to consolidate his right-wing credentials. He became a regular speaker at demonstrations against the Labor Party government and the peace process Yitzhak Rabin was advancing with Yasser Arafat. He also made a name as a massive builder. During Olmert's term as mayor, Jerusalem's infrastructure boomed—new roads were built, tunnels were dug and the planning began for the city's innovative light rail system.

After a decade as mayor, Olmert returned to the national stage in 2003. He was a changed man. Gone was the bad boy of the 1970s as well as the flaming right-wing rhetoric from his days at city hall. Olmert had undergone a metamorphosis and became known as one of the more moderate members of the Likud and the new government. On December 1, 2003, Olmert filled in for Sharon as the cabinet member to speak at the annual memorial for David Ben-Gurion, Israel's first prime minister and founding father.

He quoted extensively from Ben-Gurion: "We could, militarily . . . have occupied all of the western land of Israel. And then what would happen? We would become one state. But that state would want to be democratic, there would be general elections—and we would be in the minority. Thus, when the question arose of the wholeness of the land without a Jewish state, or a Jewish state without the wholeness of the land, we chose a Jewish state without the wholeness of the land."

Olmert went on. "In the near future leaders of this nation will need to gather all of their spiritual strength and Zionist beliefs to determine our future . . . and justify a painful compromise for peace."

Shimon Peres, Israel's former prime minister and future president, was sitting in the audience. He turned to Ehud Barak, another former prime minister, and said: "Nu, what you do think? Look who's become a Ben-Gurionist."[1]

Olmert never fully explained what led to this transformation, but it seemed to be a sober realization that the revisionist ideologies he had been raised on could not ensure Israel's long-term Jewish character. In addition, there seemed to be a political calculation that if he ever wanted a chance at being prime minister, he needed to move to the center to appeal to the general public. He was following in the footsteps of Sharon, the godfather of Israel's settlements in the Palestinian territories, who then went on to raze Israel's presence in the Gaza Strip. He was becoming a leader.

Olmert had huge plans for Israel after he was elected prime minister in March. Already before Israelis went to polls, Olmert revealed his flagship diplomatic plan—the "Convergence." The idea was similar to what Israel had done in the Gaza Strip in the summer of 2005 when it unilaterally removed its settlements and military bases. Olmert believed the same needed to happen in the West Bank, a large swath of territory Israel had conquered from Jordan during the 1967 Six Day War. While prime ministers before him had tried to negotiate a deal with the Palestinians, with the goal of establishing an independent Palestinian state, Olmert was disenchanted with bilateral negotiations and had lost faith in the Palestinian leadership's readiness and ability to make the compromises needed to reach a deal. As a result, he pushed for the Convergence Plan, under which Israel would remove its settlements and simply leave the land for the Palestinians to control.

In interviews he gave on the eve of the elections, Olmert spoke about his vision for "a different Israel." "We will have different borders and will separate from most of the Palestinians. It will be a country that is less violent and has more security. It will be a country that will better deal with the social problems and will be fun to live in. People won't just love it, they will love saying how much they love it."[2]

Olmert was so sure of his plan that he gave it a timeline—four years, after which Israel would have settled on defined borders even in the absence of a final status agreement with the Palestinians.

He swept the elections. Kadima, the party he led, won 29 seats, trouncing Benjamin Netanyahu's Likud Party, which garnered just 12 seats, a third the size of what it was in the previous government. A few weeks later, Olmert embarked on a world tour aimed at selling his new plan to different leaders. In May, he flew to Washington, DC, where he held meetings with President Bush and addressed Congress, becoming the third Israeli prime minister to do so.

A week later he flew to Sharm el-Sheikh in the Sinai Peninsula and met with Egyptian president Hosni Mubarak. Four days later, he flew to Amman to meet Jordan's King Abdullah and then four days after that, he went to London to sell his plan to British prime minister Tony Blair. A week after that, he was in Paris meeting with President Jacques Chirac.

This was a carefully crafted tour aimed at giving Olmert some quick diplomatic wins. The responses were mixed. In London, Blair said, "I do not want to go down any other path than a negotiated settlement."[3]

In the US, Olmert received a more positive response, with Bush calling his ideas "bold" and "an important step toward the peace we both support." Nevertheless, the US president pushed for a sincere effort to renew bilateral negotiations with the Palestinians and not to give up on a negotiated deal.

The meeting with Bush was the most important of them all. It was his first sit-down with the president as prime minister and Olmert recognized the significance of first impressions. The two leaders had similar backgrounds. Both were sons of politicians and were considered political princes from birth. While Sharon and Bush had a close relationship, it was more of a younger man—the president—looking up to someone 20 years his senior. Olmert, who was just 10 months older than Bush, was more of a peer.

The president and prime minister met in the Oval Office. Olmert pressed his plan but Bush tried to keep him focused on negotiations. Assume that Palestinian president Mahmoud Abbas can deliver, Bush urged Olmert, and try to work with him. Olmert promised to give talks a chance but cautioned that they were unlikely to succeed and when they didn't, his unilateral plan would have to be adopted.

Later that day, Bush invited Olmert and his wife, Aliza, for a talk on the Truman Balcony overlooking the South Lawn. In this intimate setting, the two leaders could really get to know one another. Bush came away feeling that Olmert was committed to peace and would be a worthy successor to Sharon's legacy.

The war in Lebanon cut all of this short. What Olmert might have lacked in experience, he made up for in guts. Twelve hours after the abduction of the IDF reservists by Hezbollah, Olmert convened his cabinet. The IDF had used the day to try to repel Hezbollah from the border but it wasn't working.

"Enough is enough," Olmert told his staff. Israel, he said, needed to use the attack to try and change the situation that had prevailed along the northern border since the IDF withdrew from Lebanon six years earlier. He didn't know it just yet but Israel was on its way into its first war in over 20 years.

That evening, after the losses of the first day, Olmert gathered his ministers to discuss how Israel should retaliate. The IDF chief of staff, Lieutenant General Dan Halutz, pushed for a massive bombardment of Lebanese national infrastructure. His logic was simple: Israel needed to show that it had gone a little crazy to get the international community to wake up and come rushing to the region.

Olmert disagreed. His instincts told him that destroying Lebanese infrastructure—water plants, electrical grids and roads—would turn the average Lebanese against Israel and straight into the open arms of Hezbollah and Iran. "I will not turn 2.5 million Christians in Lebanon into enemies of Israel, or the international community against us," he said.

The position didn't come out of nowhere. In the afternoon, Olmert had called Condoleezza Rice as the fighting was just getting started. Rice was sympathetic. She conveyed the Bush administration's understanding that Israel would need to retaliate. But she asked him not to attack the Lebanese government. The prime minister, Fouad Siniora, was, in Washington's view, a promising leader and shouldn't be harmed. Olmert agreed to the request.

At 5:00 p.m., though, Sheikh Hassan Nasrallah, the popular and charismatic Hezbollah leader, held a press conference in Beirut before dozens of journalists. Those were the days when the Hezbollah chief still traveled freely throughout Lebanon. That would change with the war, after which Nasrallah rarely showed his face in public.

The abducted IDF reservists, Nasrallah announced, were already tucked safely away in Lebanon and would only be released in a prisoner exchange with Israel. He then tried to take responsibility for the abduction of Shalit, saying that he was willing to negotiate a deal that would include him as well.

He finished with a jab at Olmert, Peretz and Halutz. "Olmert is a new prime minister and the defense minister and chief of staff are also new to their roles," the arrogant Hezbollah chief declared. "I want to urge you before you convene the cabinet this evening to seek advice from former prime ministers and ministers about their experiences in Lebanon . . . If you want confrontation, get ready for some surprises."[4]

Nasrallah tried to goad Israel and had reason to believe that it would work. He assumed that Olmert would restrain himself like Barak and Sharon had done after Hezbollah abducted and tried abducting soldiers in 2000 and 2005, respectively. He was wrong. At 8:00 p.m. that night, Olmert and his ministers approved a plan to attack all of Hezbollah's long-range missiles.

Operation Specific Weight had been in the planning for years. The Mossad had led the charge, gaining access to Hezbollah's most carefully guarded secret—the location of its long-range rockets. These were not the Katyusha rockets, 4,300 of which would pound Israel during the 34 days of the war, but were Iranian-made Fajr artillery rockets, which had a range of nearly 100 kilometers and the ability to strike deep inside Israel like never before.

The Mossad and the air force told the cabinet that the rockets were being stored inside people's private homes; each home had a special room containing a hydraulic launcher that could be pulled out when it was launch time. When the IDF presented the plan, the generals were initially hesitant. Since the rockets were stored in homes, the IDF feared that there could be anywhere between 500 to 1,000 casualties. They also said that a strike would show that Israel knew the rockets' location and potentially endanger the source of the intelligence.

Peretz, the defense minister and former labor union leader, pushed back. "Someone who goes to sleep with a missile shouldn't be surprised if they wake up one day without a house," he said.

Olmert agreed and the cabinet voted to strike. The operation took place that night. Sixty-eight targets were attacked by dozens of aircraft in an operation that lasted less than 40 minutes. Almost 100 percent of Hezbollah's Fajr arsenal was destroyed.

While the success gave Olmert and the IDF confidence, it also pushed Hezbollah to escalate its rocket onslaught against Israel. And while the IDF managed to locate and destroy the long-range rockets, that success could not easily be duplicated with the shorter-range Katyushas. They were smaller targets and more difficult to locate, identify and destroy. As the war ground on, northern Israel became eerily empty. Those who could leave fled south. Others remained holed up in their bomb shelters for days at a time. Israel was hostage to Hezbollah missiles.

By the time the war ended, Olmert had been badly burned and his Convergence Plan was pretty much history. At the height of the fighting, Olmert had tried to keep the plan alive. In interviews with the foreign press, he continued pushing the unilateral withdrawal plan from the West Bank, saying that a successful outcome to the war would boost the chances to achieve a sustainable and lasting peace with the Palestinians.

But the war didn't end in success and the settler camp in Israel attacked Olmert, accusing him of sending soldiers to die in battle so he could then evict the settlers from their homes. Two weeks after the war ended, in mid-August, a poll showed that 63 percent of Israelis felt that Olmert had failed in managing the war and needed to resign. Seventy-four percent said the same about the defense minister, Amir Peretz.

It was a stark contrast to the polls that had been taken a few weeks before, in the early stages of the anti-Hezbollah campaign. In the war's initial days, one poll in an Israeli daily showed 80 percent of Israelis supporting the military offensive in Lebanon. Seventy-four percent claimed that Olmert was doing a great job. The public sentiment had completely changed.[5]

The failures throughout the war were hard to miss. In what could only be a coincidence, the day before the war broke out, Olmert had met with the IDF General Staff. He sat at the front of a long table, next to Peretz and Halutz, the chief of staff. The wall behind him was engraved in gold letters with a quote from Israel's founding father, David Ben-Gurion: "Let every Hebrew mother know that she has entrusted the fate of her son to commanders worthy of the charge." It was a statement whose truth, over the next month, would be tested like never before.

In elections earlier that year, social issues had dominated and politicians took turns slamming the IDF and declaring that if they were elected, they would cut the defense budget. Halutz and his generals planned to use their first meeting with Olmert to warn of the repercussions.

One general told Olmert about a reservist brigade that hadn't trained since 2002. If it was called up to fight in a war, he said, there was no way it would be able to achieve its goals. Yadlin urged Olmert not to cut the budget, but to actually increase it. "It will be cheaper than the price we will pay of going to war," he said.

Olmert dismissed the criticism. "I have enough trouble finding the money to fund care for the elderly in Tel Aviv," he said.[6]

The war showed that the generals were right. When, for

example, Egoz—one of the IDF's most elite anti-guerrilla units—entered Lebanon, it encountered fierce and unexpected resistance from Hezbollah forces. It was the first deployment of ground forces in the war and the Egoz soldiers were sent to the Lebanese village of Maroun al-Ras, just over the border opposite the Israeli village of Avivim, marked by its stucco homes and red rooftops. The Lebanese village, Aman said, was home to Hezbollah's top regional command center.

The operation was supposed to be simple: gain control of the eastern side of the village, take up positions inside some of the homes and then, using heavy firepower, conquer the rest of the village. After six years of fighting in the West Bank and Gaza Strip, IDF soldiers were supposed to be experts at this tactic.

Egoz soldiers were also specially trained for these kinds of missions. Despite the years of quiet along the northern border, Egoz was one of the only units that still trained on rocky and mountainous terrains similar to southern Lebanon, where Hezbollah had established its bases, deployed its rocket launchers and dug its trenches.

Though the soldiers complained about what they believed was "useless" training, Egoz's experience in this terrain was supposed to have made its soldiers experts in fighting against Hezbollah.

As in Gaza, the soldiers were expecting some resistance. They thought there would be sniper fire and some mortar shells. Possibly an occasional roadside bomb. But when they crossed the border, they were immediately spotted by Hezbollah reconnaissance teams. In the ensuing battle, which included the unexpected use of anti-tank missiles by Hezbollah, five Israeli soldiers were killed. That was the way the IDF began its ground offensive in Lebanon.

At the same time as the battle raged in Maroun al-Ras, reservists were being called up. The IDF relies heavily on reservists during times of war as well as for routine operations, and the battle beginning in Lebanon was no exception. When the war broke out, the reservists enlisted in high numbers. Two soldiers had been abducted and rockets were pounding the home front. There was a feeling that this was a war for survival. But when the reservists arrived at the draft centers and started going through their gear, they were shocked to receive outdated equipment in all the wrong sizes. The magazines were rusty and did not fit their M-16 automatic rifles. The combat vests were the old brown ones they had seen in photos from the Six Day War and the helmets were full of cobwebs.

Outdated and rusty equipment was not the reservists' only problem. What really frustrated them was the lack of clarity from above and a feeling that their orders were constantly changing. Some units were sent into villages in southern Lebanon and ordered to simply sit for days at a time, turning them into sitting ducks for Hezbollah anti-tank missile squads. Others were sent to conquer targets without adequate intelligence or the right firepower.

As the war progressed and more mishaps took place, the press began to turn on the prime minister. One prominent columnist from the left-leaning *Haaretz* daily who had supported Olmert in the past wrote an op-ed published on the paper's front page titled "Olmert Must Go." Nahum Barnea, an Israel

Prize laureate and the country's most influential columnist, published a piece titled "Run, Ehud, Run." He recommended that Olmert cut his losses and get out of Lebanon. The IDF was not winning the war, Barnea wrote, and wasn't going to.

It was no surprise, therefore, when a few days after the war ended, hundreds of young men and women gathered in the Rose Garden opposite the Prime Minister's Office in Jerusalem and launched a sit-in protest calling on Olmert to resign. While some politicians slammed the reservists for undermining the government, the soldiers felt that they were actually continuing their service to their country. Though the lack of preparedness had been years in the making, for Israel's future security, the reservists said, Olmert, Peretz and Halutz had to go.

The protests had the quiet backing of Benjamin Netanyahu, a former Israeli prime minister who had returned to politics and had lost to Olmert in the last election. Netanyahu saw a political opportunity and helped the reservists secure funding for their demonstrations.

The press covered the protest extensively. The patriotic sentiment that had characterized coverage of the war in its early days had been replaced by descriptions of the war's failures and mistakes. Some focused on the mismanagement of the IDF. Others concentrated on Olmert and Peretz and their political paralysis. Either way, almost everyone agreed that something needed to change. This protest was too strong to ignore.

Olmert ultimately caved under pressure and on September 17, just weeks after the war had ended, appointed Eliyahu Winograd, a retired judge, to lead a state commission of inquiry into the war. The commission released its preliminary report in April 2007, sending shockwaves throughout the political establishment.

No one escaped criticism. The commission placed the burden of responsibility on the shoulders of Olmert, Peretz and Halutz, the last of whom had by then already announced his resignation.

According to the commission, Olmert went to war too fast and without proper planning or consideration. The cabinet, the commission claimed, was presented with ambiguous plans by the IDF, and the ministers voted on vague resolutions that were neither understood by them nor the top military command, let alone the battalions deployed on the battlefield. The war's goals, the commission concluded, were unclear and the IDF lacked creativity in proposing plans that could succeed. The military had failed to warn the political echelon of the discrepancy between what the ministers were asking for and what was realistically possible.

"The primary responsibility for these serious failings rests with the prime minister, the minister of defense and the (outgoing) chief of staff," Winograd wrote in his report. "We single out these three because it is likely that had any of them acted better, the decisions in the relevant period and the ways they were made, as well as the outcome of the war, would have been significantly better."

While not immediately obvious, the results of the Second Lebanon War had a direct impact on how some Americans viewed Israel and the IDF's ability to confront new threats and challenges. When war broke out, Bush and Cheney, thinking they were going to witness a reenactment of the Six Day War, expected a swift defeat of Hezbollah that would take, at the most, just a couple of weeks. Israel had a conventional military with US warplanes, smart bombs and sophisticated tanks and intelligence systems. Hezbollah was a small-time guerrilla organization. Yes, it had some Russian anti-tank missiles, but this was not supposed to be something the IDF couldn't easily take care of.

Condoleezza Rice was particularly disenchanted. Rice had been burned by the Kana incident in late July, but the end of the war and its poor results left a profound impact on her view of Israel and especially on her relationship with Olmert. She admired and respected Sharon, but Olmert she simply did not trust.[7]

Rice's growing and close relationship with Foreign Minister Tzipi Livni, Olmert's number two, made the prime minister suspicious that the US secretary of state thought he was on his way out. Rice, it seemed to Olmert, was already investing in his potential successor.

By 2019, the world's opinion of the war had changed. Almost 13 years of quiet along Israel's border with Lebanon—the longest period since 1967—showed that even with all of its presumed failures, the Second Lebanon War had been successful. It deterred Hezbollah and taught it a lesson. In the years that passed, and despite thousands of Israeli strikes in Syria, Hezbollah had yet to retaliate even once. With time, Olmert's war proved to have been right and effective.

Only a handful of people knew that as all of this was hap-

pening in 2007, a new and unprecedented threat was brewing
in the north. While Olmert was fighting for political survival,
he was also facing one of the greatest tests of his premiership—
what to do about the nuclear reactor discovered in Syria.

For Ehud Olmert, a strike against Syria's nuclear reactor had
the potential to be more than just the elimination of an existential threat to Israel; it was an opportunity to rehabilitate his
legacy and political career. If done right, the destruction of the
reactor would show Olmert as a decisive leader who stood up
to the US and took action to save the Jewish people.

What Olmert didn't know at this initial stage was that he
would never be able to publicly take credit for the bombing of
the Syrian reactor. It would remain an operation that, for more
than a decade, Israel would neither confirm nor deny. It was a
vow of silence he would personally take and an order he would
enforce with others.

For a politician like Olmert, this silence was possibly one of
the most difficult parts of the whole operation.

It was also a stark contrast to what happened when Israel
bombed Iraq's Osirak reactor in 1981, just three weeks before
national elections. While then prime minister Menachem Begin had made the decision to destroy the reactor before elections were announced, to many—especially the opposition—the
timing seemed to have been influenced by the looming vote.
Many suspected a political motivation behind Begin's announce-
ment that Israel was responsible for the strike, a revelation that
went against the initial IDF and government agreement to remain silent.

Olmert was facing genuine political trouble, and Israel is a place where, when politicians smell blood, they pounce and rarely leave survivors. In addition, Israeli politicians are known to not be above using security situations for political gain. Olmert was bloody from the war and extremely vulnerable. Taking credit for a successful operation would have given him a much-needed boost.

For any politician staying quiet would not have been easy. But Olmert understood what was at stake: the security of the country, as well as trying to avoid a war. All that outweighed any political benefit he stood to potentially gain.

6

TIME TO ATTACK

Under the cover of darkness, the pair of Sikorsky CH-53 Sea Stallion helicopters flew low to evade radar detection. Inside, the commandos—disguised as Syrian soldiers and armed with AK-47s instead of their usual M-16s—were doing one last review of their equipment. The heavy-lift Sikorsky choppers carried old, camouflaged Syrian-model military jeeps, which the troops planned to use for transportation once they were on the ground.[1]

It was August 2007, and Military Intelligence chief Yadlin had crafted a plan to send elite commandos from the IDF's General Staff Reconnaissance Unit—better known by its Hebrew name Sayeret Matkal—deep into Syria. It would be one of the top five covert ops he ran as head of Aman.

The mission was complicated: get as close to the reactor as possible and return home with pictures and soil samples. No one could know that the Israeli soldiers had been there.

Covert operations like these need to first be approved by the prime minister. Yadlin had explained that while the photos obtained in the Mossad raid were impressive, many of them were a few years old. It was true that the IDF had daily satellite imagery of the site, but that was not enough to know what exactly was happening there. Israel wanted to know if the fuel rods had been installed, an important indicator for determining how close the reactor was to becoming operational.

Beyond the intelligence collection, the raid served another purpose—to prove that the IDF could reach the site on the ground. The cabinet needed to know what its options were, and whether a ground operation was one of them, before approving an attack.

The helicopter pilots could see the small hills rising above the Syrian desert and the tranquil water of the Euphrates off in the distance. Behind the transport helicopters carrying the commandos were attack helicopters, as well as a rescue chopper with a team from the IDF's elite airborne search-and-rescue unit on standby in case something went wrong. A command plane, tasked with intercepting Syrian military communications, circled high above, far out of reach of any radar or surface-to-air missile system.

For missions of this kind, Sayeret Matkal usually has months to prepare. Sometimes, operators get assigned a mission a year in advance. Depending on the complexity, the operation becomes their lives. They train for it and build mock targets to practice. They live and breathe the operation. But sometimes, the missions get nixed. Military statistics show that a Sayeret

Matkal operator usually trains for three or four special operations during his military service. Fifty percent get canceled.

Sometimes it is the political echelon that changes its mind, or new intelligence comes in and changes the original operational requirements. For a Matkalist—the nickname for operators in the unit—there is nothing more frustrating.

Sayeret Matkal, which operates under Aman, is known for some of Israel's most breathtaking operations. During the 2006 Second Lebanon War, the commandos ran a number of special operations. One brought them deep into Lebanon's Bekaa Valley, a known Hezbollah stronghold, where the IDF wrongly thought the two abducted reservists were being held. Other operations included sabotaging Iranian arms convoys en route to Hezbollah.

For this mission, the battle procedure was shorter, a result of the narrow window that existed between learning of the reactor and the deadline for attacking it. The training began in early June and lasted a month and a half.

IDF Information Security made the operators sign special confidentiality forms, as they did before every special mission. Matkalists were used to telling their families they would be away for a couple of weeks and, after returning, not being able to say a word about where they had been or what they had done. Every few days, senior officers showed up to take part in the training or to see with their own eyes as the operators ran through the model one more time.

Before the mission, as always happens, a conversation broke out about the weight each commando should carry in his kit and whether it was more important to load up on firepower or scouting and camouflage materials. The commandos boarded the helicopters knowing that as soon as they hit the ground, they would be on their own. If something went wrong, the chances of getting rescued were not particularly high.

The helicopters dropped them a few dozen kilometers from the reactor. The rest of the way they made in jeeps and on foot. Matkalists are expert navigators and spend a good portion of their training learning how to get to places with nothing more than a compass, and sometimes even without. A lot of the preparation for this mission involved studying the terrain in Syria so they would be able to find their target.

On missions like this, the commandos usually split into groups. A small squad of scouts goes ahead and clears the way. Every half hour, the commander orders a planned stop. In between, the commandos suck water out of a long straw extending from between the straps of their bags and munch on energy bars, the wraps of which they'd stick in their pockets so as not to leave anything behind.

The scouts remain about 100 meters ahead of the main force. Before entering a new area, the commander of the scout force presses twice on his two-way radio, an agreed upon sign that it is safe for the rest of the force to proceed.

As Israel's top commandos, Matkalists get whatever equipment they need. Night vision goggles, anti-tank missiles, explosives and satellite communications are the basics. The unit also has a technical team that builds specially tailored weapons and hardware.

The operators had been briefed by geologists and scientists

before the mission. They were told what to look for and what samples they would need to bring back. When they were close enough to the reactor, the team leader gave the order and a few of the soldiers started filling plastic boxes with dirt, soil and plants. They had to dig deep to get the right samples. Radioactive exposure was not a concern. Israel was looking for tiny traces of uranium that would have naturally scattered during the reactor's construction.

The core part of the mission took just a few minutes. When they were done digging, another soldier walked around with a device that looked like a small broom to make sure that they hadn't left any tracks. The last thing they needed was a Syrian army patrol discovering the holes a few days later. Nothing could be left behind.

The force commander gave the signal and the soldiers headed back to the pickup point. When they crossed back into Israel, Olmert received an update. He let out a massive sigh of relief.

A few days later, the lab results came back. The soil samples were positive. Now there were no doubts about the site. This was definitely a nuclear reactor. The reactor was on its way to becoming hot. If there was going to be an attack it had to be soon.

Olmert and Yadlin had a close relationship. A few days earlier, during one of the cabinet meetings, Yadlin had taken Olmert aside and assured him that a narrow strike, one using just a few planes, would be enough to take out the reactor.

The attack on Syria, Yadlin explained, was nothing like the 1981 bombing of the Iraqi reactor he had participated in 26 years earlier. Then, he said, there was a real fear that some of the planes wouldn't return home or even make it to the reactor. "We needed a large fleet to make sure that the mission would get done," he said. In Syria, though, the target was close, fairly isolated and completely unprotected.

"A few planes are all we need to get it done," he concluded. While some of his advisers were advocating for a larger strike package, Olmert did not argue with Yadlin. It was hard to argue with your intelligence chief when he also happened to be one of the eight pilots who had risked their lives to fly the F-16s used to destroy Iraq's reactor.

A few days later, Olmert sent Dagan and Yadlin on a diplomatic mission overseas. Bush had already said that America would not be attacking the reactor but Olmert wanted to give a heads up to one more ally—Great Britain.[2]

Olmert called British prime minister Gordon Brown and asked that he authorize Sir John Scarlett, head of the powerful British espionage agency MI6, to meet with his two intelligence chiefs. His motivation for sharing the intelligence with the British was twofold. MI6 is one of the most powerful spy agencies in the world and has a strong presence throughout the Middle East. Olmert wanted a buy-in from London in case a war erupted, but he also wanted to ascertain that MI6 was unaware of the reactor and was not in the midst of its own operation that could potentially interfere with what Israel was planning.

Scarlett came to the meeting with two of his deputies. Opposite him were Dagan and Yadlin alongside two other Israeli

intelligence officers. What the Israelis pulled out of their brief-
cases took the British completely by surprise. Scarlett immediately classified it as an "intolerable situation."

They were shown the same photos that Dagan had brought
with him to the White House three months earlier as well as
some additional details the Israelis had gathered on the reactor
in the months since. The facility, Yadlin told Scarlett, was being built under a tight shroud of secrecy and outside of the
"normal Syrian government structure."

Scarlett was shocked. MI6 is known for penetrating deep
into Arab countries. He had also personally spent time with
Assad and thought he knew the Syrian leader quite well. But
MI6 knew nothing about this. Nothing about Assad pursuing
nuclear weapons.

While many states have tried to obtain weapons of mass destruction in the past, Scarlett was taken aback by Assad's boldness. The Syrian leader, it seemed, thought that if he built the
reactor far away in the desert and only allowed a limited number of people to know about it, he could get away with it. That
took guts.

For Scarlett and his agents, the three big takeaways from the
Israeli briefing were the following: Syria was building what definitely seemed like a nuclear reactor in a very desolate part of
the country, very few people knew about it, and it was being
done outside the normal structure of the Syrian government.
While the North Korean involvement was also disturbing, for
now the British were primarily concerned with what all of this
meant for stability in the Middle East and the wider world.

But the meeting wasn't just about getting London up to

speed on the brewing crisis. Israel was also interested in any insight into the background of the reactor: whose idea had it been, where did the money come from, were the Iranians involved and what exactly was North Korea out to achieve?

On this last point, the Israelis thought the British might be particularly helpful. The al-Kibar reactor under construction in Syria was a replica of the Yongbyon reactor in North Korea, which, in turn, was modeled after Calder Hall, a British reactor opened in 1956. Israel wanted to see what light the British could shed on the reactor, its design, output and capabilities.

After the meeting, Scarlett immediately updated Gordon Brown, who had taken up the premiership just two months before. Depending on what happened, this was news that had the potential to change the world.

As the end of August grew closer, questions still remained. One was about timing—how much time did Israel have to carry out the attack? All along, Olmert had set the beginning of September as the deadline for a strike, but the cabinet still needed to decide. The other question was about the attack method—by ground or by air, and if by air, how exactly?

In the air force, the man responsible for preparing the airstrike was Major General Eliezer Shkedi, a quiet, mild-mannered pilot. The son of a Holocaust survivor, Shkedi felt an obligation to do whatever it took to prevent Israel's enemies from having a capability that could threaten the very existence of the Jewish people.

His father, Moshe, was a Hungarian Jew who managed to jump off a cattle car traveling from Budapest to Auschwitz. Moshe eventually made his way to the "Glass House," a building used by a Swiss diplomat who issued "letters of protection" that saved thousands of Jews from the Nazis. His parents and four sisters weren't as lucky. They were never seen again.

Shkedi enlisted in the air force in 1975 and became one of Israel's first F-16 pilots, making a name for himself as a professional and daring combat operator. As head of the IAF, Shkedi helped hone Israel's targeted killing policy—a method based on a unique combination of quality intelligence and precise airstrikes—later replicated by the US and other Western countries in their own battles against terrorists across the globe.

One missile developed at the time came with a tiny warhead that was so accurate, it was capable of blowing up—without harming any bystanders—a single room in a high-rise apartment building or a lone car or motorcycle driving down a busy road.

Under his watch, intelligence-gathering methods also underwent modifications, with stricter procedures put in place to tighten control over the decision-making process that leads to a targeted killing.

It was a unique combination of innovative thinking, accurate missiles, high-quality intelligence and advanced command-and-control systems. With targeted killings, Israel saw a drop in collateral damage and civilian casualties. In 2002, for example, the combatant-civilian death ratio was 1:1, meaning that for every combatant Israel killed, it also killed a civilian. By 2008, when Shkedi stepped down as IAF chief, the ratio had dropped to 30:1, meaning only 1 civilian for every 30 terrorists.

The Holocaust cast a large shadow over Shkedi, as a pilot and as a senior military officer. He was deputy commander of the air force when he received an invitation to send a group of fighter jets to attend the air show in Poland in 2003. Shkedi helped secure approval but together with the flight commander added a condition—the IAF would only send its jets to Poland if it had permission to fly over the train tracks leading to the Auschwitz death camp.

The Poles agreed but added their own condition—the Israeli F-15s could fly over Auschwitz but they would need to fly high above, at an altitude that would put them way out of sight and make the whole gesture almost meaningless. The day of the flight, though, Shkedi decided that the flight would be below the clouds so the planes could be seen by a group of IDF officers who, at the same time, would be holding a memorial ceremony along the train tracks, which decades earlier had been used to transport over a million Jews to their deaths.

The picture of the three F-15s over Auschwitz—a demonstration of Israel's might and independence—can be found today in hundreds of IDF offices. Most of the pictures were given out personally by Shkedi, who wrote on all of them: "To remember. Not to forget. To rely only on ourselves."

It was a saying he lived by. As commander of the air force, he once asked the head of his branch's history department to prepare a research paper comparing public remarks made by Adolf Hitler in the 1920s and 1930s to those made by Iranian president Mahmoud Ahmadinejad since his rise to power in 2005. Coming from Shkedi, such a request was not surprising but the results of the research were. Both leaders voiced similar declarations regarding the Jewish nation, Zionism and race.

In 1922, for example, Hitler said: "If I am ever really in power, the destruction of the Jews will be my first and most important job." In 2005, at a conference called "A World without Zionism," Ahmadinejad said, "Israel must be wiped off the map." Shortly thereafter, he said: "The Zionist regime is a decaying and crumbling tree that will fall with a storm."

Shkedi kept the paper in the top drawer of his desk at IAF headquarters and often shared it with visiting dignitaries. For him, the conclusion was clear. Ahmadinejad, as well as Israel's other enemies—like Assad—could not be allowed to obtain nuclear weapons. The IAF's fleet of fighter jets, he would tell people, always needed to be ready to prevent a potential repeat of what his father's family had gone through some 70 years earlier.

Aman's "deniability zone" theory played a critical role in the debate over the right way to attack the reactor. On the one hand, everyone knew that a kinetic strike—an aerial bombing— would be the most effective method. But it would also leave the largest signature and be automatically connected to Israel. The planes might be spotted and traced back to their point of origin or landing.

Hypothetically, a covert operation could be made to look like an accidental explosion and—if successful—would not necessarily be traced back to Israel. On the other hand, it would be more complicated, especially if something went wrong: there would be no assurance that the commandos would be able to plant enough explosives to completely destroy the facility, a concern that led the Americans, months earlier, to nix that proposal.

Israel needed to reach this decision on its own. As Bush had ordered after his July phone call with Olmert, America could assist with intelligence but could play no role in planning a military strike.

In addition, if soldiers were captured, Israel would be looking at another debacle like the one Olmert was already facing with Gilad Shalit being held by Hamas in Gaza and two reservists being held by Hezbollah in Lebanon. The last thing Israel needed was another standoff, this time with an enemy country.

An airstrike, on the other hand, was almost risk free and ensured complete destruction. While Syria did have a sophisticated and advanced array of surface-to-air missile systems—purchased over the years from Russia—the IAF had experience flying over the country and it was unlikely that the missiles would suddenly now become a problem.

In 2003, four F-16s buzzed Assad's summer residence in the seaside resort town of Latakia in retaliation for the killing of a young Israeli boy by Hezbollah rocket fire from Lebanon. Israel wanted to humiliate Assad—who was vacationing there at the time—and send him a message to restrain his Lebanese terror proxy.

The planes flew so low, they reportedly shattered some of the palace windows.

Some months later, the air force bombed an Islamic Jihad training base in Syria in response to a suicide bombing that killed 19 people. And in 2006, after the abduction of Shalit, Israeli fighter jets again buzzed the Latakia residence to remind Assad of the price he would pay personally for giving refuge to Hamas's leadership in Damascus.

In the 1981 raid on Iraq, the IAF predicted that it would lose at least two aircraft. This time around, an airstrike had little downside. Yes, there were always risks when crossing borders and entering enemy airspace, but the reactor was just about 300 miles from Israel. All of the planes and pilots were expected to make it home safely.

The operation Shkedi put together involved three squadrons: the 69th Squadron, which operated the F-15I, Israel's longest-range aircraft known by its Hebrew name Raam (Thunder) and capable of carrying over 10 tons of ammunition; and Squadrons 253 and 119, which operated F-16Is known by their Hebrew name, Sufa (Storm).

During briefings, Shkedi constantly emphasized three points: the need to avoid detection, to destroy the target and to get home safely. The pilots trained for months but were given very few details. They were told the range, the fact that the target would be a building, and that they would need to fly in radio silence and low to avoid radar detection. The exact nature of the target was kept a secret. Only those who needed to know knew.

At least once a week the pilots would get together and conduct a practice flight somewhere over Israel or the Mediterranean.

The lead pilot, a major named Dror, drew an imaginary line in his head of the range and tried to calculate where and what the target could potentially be. Based on the range, it could have been anywhere—in Jordan, Saudi Arabia, Lebanon, Syria and beyond. Based on the secrecy, he knew one thing for sure—it was extremely important.

The pilots had been handpicked by the top IAF brass and included Dror, who had just completed a term as a deputy squadron commander, and his direct commander in the squadron. The oldest pilot was a 46-year-old reservist. The youngest was a talented 26-year-old fresh graduate from flight school.

As the military preparations continued, the question of timing came into sharp focus. One day, in mid-August, Dagan showed up at the Prime Minister's Office and urged Olmert and Barak to attack. The longer Israel waited, he warned, the greater the chance that Assad would discover that his secret was out.

The relationship between the two Ehuds was going from bad to worse. At one point, Olmert toyed with the idea of firing Barak. In the end, he decided not to. Firing a defense minister in Israel would raise too many questions. It would be extremely difficult to continue keeping the existence of the reactor a secret. Additionally, there was a chance that war would break out and Olmert needed the country to believe that it had leadership that was stable.

Dagan told the ministers that he had just gotten off the phone with Hayden, the CIA director, and new US intelligence seemed to indicate that Syria was close to activating the reactor. The Americans knew, Dagan said; the British knew; and now close to 2,000 people in Israel knew. It was becoming harder and harder to keep the information contained. All it would take, he said, was one news article or blog post. If Assad discovered that Israel knew, everything would change.

"We need to move faster," Dagan said.

Yadlin agreed and said that according to Aman's calculations, Israel had until early September. The reactor was nearing completion. The water canal was almost completed and the fuel rods were believed to be in place. The moment they went hot, Israel would not be able to attack.

"An attack would cause radioactive material to leak into the Euphrates," he told the ministers. "We do not want to be responsible for what will happen afterwards to generations of Iraqi and Syrian children."

Surprisingly, Barak seemed to disagree. But here, accounts of the disagreement differ. Some members of the Security Cabinet remember Barak claiming that Yadlin was wrong. First, he apparently said, the reactor could be attacked at a later date, even after it went hot. The dispersion of the radioactive material, he claimed, would not be as bad as Yadlin had made it out to be. Israel, he argued, could even wait until April.

Barak clarified his point: "If we learned of the existence of the reactor after it was already active, you want to tell me that we wouldn't have attacked?" he asked his fellow ministers. "We would have even then."

Barak then suggested the possibility of striking just part of the reactor. "We can hit the first floor but not the second floor," he told the cabinet, according to some of the participants. No one really understood what he was talking about but that often seemed to be the case with Barak, whose tactical brilliance was legendary in the IDF.

Olmert rejected this. "If there is a fire on the first floor of a building do you wait for it to spread before calling the fire department?" he asked. "People will say we could have avoided radioactive contamination but didn't."

Yadlin was in shock. He knew he would be risking his position in the IDF and that under the chain of command he was subordinate to the defense minister. But he couldn't contain himself. "Despite what the defense minister said, I think that he is wrong and if we are quiet, I think that Assad won't attack," Yadlin said.

Barak again felt compelled to clarify his argument: "What I meant was that if we had discovered the reactor after it was already hot, would we not attack because of the dispersion of radioactive material?" he asked the forum.

Israel, Barak said, did not need to chain itself to deadlines. There were other considerations, like preparations for war, he said, that needed to be accounted for ahead of a final decision.

At another tense Security Cabinet meeting on August 1, Barak cut off Major General Ido Nehushtan, the head of the IDF Planning Directorate, who was in the middle of a Power-Point presentation outlining the military's different possible options. "I didn't authorize you to speak," he told the general. "I am in charge of the army and I forbid you to speak."

The ministers sat in awe at the power struggle playing out before them. While Olmert knew that he could have the cabinet vote to bypass Barak and authorize Nehushtan to finish his presentation, he also knew that it would be the end of the general's career. Instead, he silenced Barak. "Sit down and listen," he told the defense minister. "Now the prime minister is speaking." Then, he took the presentation—he had gone over it the night before—and finished reviewing it for the ministers.

Yadlin, who was also present, became visibly upset. His face turned red and he banged on the table. "No one will shut me up," he said to Barak. "We, IDF officers, have an obligation to brief the cabinet."

Yadlin proceeded to give a detailed analysis of the Syrian nuclear program as well as the dangers it posed. Israel, he concluded, had no choice but to act.

Olmert adjourned the meeting but not before he looked each minister in the eye. Some of them were still in shock from the spectacle they had just witnessed.

A week later, there was another cabinet meeting and, to this one, Olmert came prepared. Together with Turbowicz, his chief of staff, he had drafted a long speech. It took 40 minutes to deliver and contained all of the details of the discovery of the reactor, the planning, the engagement with the Americans and the final issues that remained unresolved. Israel, Olmert said, had no choice but to attack and destroy the reactor.

"This is a threat that we cannot live with," he said. He went on to dissect every claim made by Barak and to reject it. "The defense minister says this," he repeated, "but the truth is . . ."

The tension between the two politicians continued. The day after Barak had cut off the general's presentation, he sent a courier from the Defense Ministry in Tel Aviv to the Prime Minister's Office in Jerusalem with a letter for Olmert. In it, Barak said that the presentation the general was giving at the cabinet meeting did not "represent the viewpoint of the defense establishment."

Olmert sent a letter back with the courier. "You don't speak for the *defense* establishment. You speak for the *military*," the prime minister wrote.

The exchange of letters dragged on for two days and included seven letters until finally Barak wrote: "Maybe we should stop this exchange." Olmert replied with his own letter: "Maybe we shouldn't have started it to begin with."

A few days later, Barak paid a visit to IAF headquarters. There, Shkedi took the defense minister aside and pulled a napkin from a nearby table. "Our plan today is heavy but I've given thought to how we can do it differently," Shkedi said, drawing the operation, which would require only a handful of aircraft, on the napkin.

"This is excellent," Barak said. "Take a few days and present it to the cabinet."

While to some of the other cabinet members it seemed like Barak was stalling for time, he was convinced that he was simply doing what he had been elected to do—challenge conventional thinking and come up with the best plan possible. As the final cabinet meeting approached, the large-scale airstrike was still on the table as well as other options, including the newly crafted "quiet" airstrike.

The problem was that even within the IDF, there were differences of opinion about the right option to use in the attack. Ashkenazi, for example, preferred an airstrike while Barak and Yadlin preferred one of the other more covert options. Nevertheless, Barak gave instructions to continue to hone all the different plans. Satellite footage did not detect any armed guards near the reactor. Barak, himself a former commander of Sayeret Matkal, had faith that all of the options could work. The decision would be made at the final cabinet meeting.

But Barak also knew what it was like being an IDF chief of staff. If Ashkenazi was opposed to one of the options, no matter the reason, Barak wasn't going to fight him. It was important, Barak believed, that they come to the final cabinet meeting with a unified recommendation.

As the debates continued, Yadlin arrived late one night at his house in a tranquil and picturesque farm community in the center of the country. Perched on a small cliff overlooking the Shfela—Israel's flatlands and a region known for its soft-sloping hills in south-central Israel—his house has a direct view of the runways at the Tel Nof Air Force Base.

Yadlin stood there in the dark, thinking about what would happen if the attack went ahead. On the one hand, he was confident that Israel could pull it off. He believed in Aman's assessment about the "deniability zone" as well as in the air force's ability to destroy the facility. On the other hand, he was concerned about another war and whether the country would be able to withstand the missile onslaught it would potentially face from Assad's well-stocked arsenal of Scud missiles.

According to updated intelligence in Israel, Assad was under the impression that Israel and the US were planning a joint simultaneous attack against Iran, Syria and Lebanon in the coming weeks, around the same time as the planned bombing of the reactor. As a result, he had put his Scud missile batteries on high alert. Some of them were even in their launchers, already pointed at their designated targets inside Israel.

Yadlin couldn't escape a sense of déjà vu. Here he was, one of the pilots who destroyed the Osirak reactor in 1981, involved in planning the destruction of another reactor. He was bothered by a nagging question—how long could this go on for? Is Israel destined to live by the sword forever? Will it need to continue bombing nuclear reactors throughout the Middle East for eternity or will Israel, at some point, find it has managed to establish enough deterrence to protect itself?

It was an impossible dilemma. If Israel attacked the reactor, it ran the risk of instigating a devastating war with Syria. If it didn't, one of its enemies would have nuclear weapons. As head of Aman, Yadlin had a front-row seat to the deliberations and debates that others sat in on in 1981. He used to think that being a pilot was difficult. Now, he understood the gravity of being a decision maker who, by making what might seem like a simple tactical decision, could be sending his or her country into a full-fledged war. The sense of uncertainty was overwhelming.

On September 5, Olmert convened his Security Cabinet for a final meeting. New satellite footage showed that construction of the reactor was nearly complete, as was the digging of the water canal from the Euphrates to the reactor. Aman believed the facility was close to being activated.

In addition, out of the blue, some journalists were asking questions about rumors they had heard of an impending Israeli military strike against Syria. One of the journalists worked for an American newspaper, one that was not bound by Israeli military censor rules. Ashkenazi started to genuinely fear that word was going to leak out. There was no time left.

It was going to be a long meeting. The ministers gathered at 10:00 a.m. and, to prevent anyone from asking questions, the Prime Minister's Office released a statement that the Security Cabinet was meeting to discuss ways to stop Hamas's rocket attacks from the Gaza Strip. It was a standard press release, like hundreds before it.

Yadlin and Dagan opened the meeting, going through the intelligence that everyone was intimately familiar with by now. Aman projected a graph it had prepared onto a screen to show the risks of each stage of the operation, with different arrows and different colors from red for high to yellow for low.

Once the intelligence chiefs finished, Shkedi and Ashkenazi presented the operational plans. There was still a debate over exactly how to carry out the attack. Ashkenazi asked the cabinet to approve the strike but to leave the decision on the way it should be carried out up to him and the trio who would ultimately determine the timing of the attack—Olmert, Barak and Livni. Ashkenazi had continued to work on all of the different options. As the cabinet was meeting, the air force was still in the process of making its final preparations.

Recognizing the significance of the moment, Olmert decided to let all of the ministers speak. It was dramatic. Each minister laid out his or her opinion, hopes and beliefs. Some expressed hesitation. Others, like Herzog, had little to say.

"May God be with us," he declared as he raised his hand in favor of the attack.

Livni gave an important insight. Unlike the Second Lebanon War, which Israel got dragged into following Hezbollah's abduction of two IDF reservists in July 2006, Israel this time didn't need to immediately retaliate to everything Assad would do next. In wars, she pointed out, countries often sought victorious images to be able to claim that they had won and their opponent had lost. Those images are usually obtained, if at all, at the end of the fighting—conquered territory, bombed-out enemy bases or a flag raised above an enemy capital city. In this case, she said, Israel will have the image—of the destroyed reactor—right at the beginning.

"We will have victory before the war even erupts," Livni told her fellow ministers. This meant that depending on the response from Assad, Israel could potentially restrain itself and not respond, thereby preventing a greater escalation.

As she said this, Livni knew there were circumstances beyond the government's control. If a Syrian missile landed on a kindergarten or shopping mall and caused mass casualties, the public would demand a fierce response. The path to war would then be quick.

All of the ministers except one—Dichter, the former head of the Shin Bet—voted in favor of attacking the reactor and authorized the ministerial trio to decide on the timing and method. While the ministers all leaned toward the option that would destroy the reactor and minimize the chance of war, the final decision was left up to Olmert, Barak and Livni.

At 3:00 p.m., after five hours, the Security Cabinet dispersed with a feeling of great anxiety. Herzog, who lived in Tel Aviv, looked out the window of his car as he made his way home. He couldn't shake the feeling that the people out enjoying a warm summer day might not be there by tomorrow if Assad decided to unleash his Scud missile arsenal on Israel.

"It was a feeling of tremendous trepidation," he later recalled.

In the meantime, after a ten-minute break, Olmert, Barak and Livni reconvened in the cabinet room. It was just the three of them and a stenographer, sworn to secrecy. One by one, Ashkenazi, Yadlin and Dagan came inside and presented their recommendations.

Yadlin urged the trio to approve a limited strike. He feared that a large-scale attack by Israel would be too much for Assad to ignore. "We can do it with just a few planes," the Aman chief said.

Dagan didn't have much to add. He agreed that the aerial strike was preferable since it would get the job done.

Olmert then asked the two intelligence chiefs to leave the room and for Ashkenazi to remain.

"What is your recommendation?" he asked the chief of staff.

It was a moment Ashkenazi would not forget and one he had prepared for long and hard. He didn't waste any time. "We need to attack tonight," he said. "We are ready for the operation and the army is prepared for whatever comes next."

Ashkenazi said that in his opinion the attack needed to happen by air. A narrow airstrike would definitely destroy the reactor and have a relatively small chance of sparking a war.

Livni was initially taken a bit aback. She supported attacking but didn't know that Olmert, Barak and Ashkenazi were of the opinion that the strike needed to take place immediately.

Now that the Security Cabinet had voted, the chance of a leak dramatically increased. Too many people knew about the IDF plans, which were just waiting for a green light. The whole system was on edge and wound up.

Livni suggested waiting a bit longer to see how things developed. Yes, the cabinet had voted to attack but there was still time, she thought.

Olmert wasn't willing to wait. "We need to do it now," he told her. "You don't want a situation that we vote, the three of us, and it goes down in history as two against one. Join us."

Livni raised her hand.

As the trio was voting, Shkedi was already making his way to Hatzerim Air Force Base, just outside the southern city of Beersheba. He wanted to personally meet with the pilots before they took off for Syria.

The night before, on September 4, the air force had carried out its last training flight, this time dropping live bombs over an imaginary target in the Negev Desert. After months of training, they were as ready as they would ever be. Ashkenazi and Shkedi had been there to watch.

Shkedi, who had flown with them on one of the earlier training sessions, now gathered the pilots in the squadron's briefing room. "Your mission is to bomb a nuclear reactor in Syria," he told the airmen, who looked at one another in disbelief. "It is of utmost importance for the safety and security of the Jewish people and the State of Israel."

Many of the pilots had flown top-secret missions before,

some deep behind enemy lines. But none had ever imagined that a nuclear reactor would be their target. They were literally embarking on an operation of existential importance.

"It was a shock but we didn't really have time to think about it," one of the pilots recalled years later. "It was definitely something that made me stop and say 'wow.'"

Shkedi told the pilots that the operation had three objectives: destroy the reactor, return to Israel without losing any aircraft, and complete the mission as quietly as possible and without detection. The name the IAF gave the operation said it all: Soft Melody.

As they picked up their helmets and headed out to their aircraft for a last checklist of inspections, Shkedi stood at the door and shook each airman's hand. "I trust you and I believe in you," he said. For the pilots it was a moment they would never forget.

The day before, Major General Gadi Eisenkot, head of the Northern Command (in 2015 he would be appointed the IDF chief of staff), convened his senior staff to prepare them for the possibility that war would break out. Eisenkot briefed them on the general intelligence picture without giving too many details about the target.

"There is going to be an attack in the next 24 to 48 hours," the general said, adding that while chances were low, there was a real possibility that war would erupt. Due to the need to maintain the element of surprise, Eisenkot told the commanders that they would not be allowed to make any preparations except in their own heads. If need be, he said, they would have to transition quickly into a state of conflict.

In the meantime, Olmert, Barak and Livni headed to Tel Aviv. They planned to watch the operation from the Bor, Hebrew for "pit" and the name given to the IDF's underground command center. On the way, Olmert went home to shower and rest. "I have a long night ahead of me," he told his wife, Aliza.

Olmert slept for just about two hours. He woke up at 10:30 p.m., got dressed and into his armed convoy for the drive to the Bor. On the way, he made some phone calls. One was to the editor of a local newspaper who had looked for him earlier that day about an unrelated issue. Olmert played it cool. He didn't give off even the slightest hint that something historic was about to happen.

Buried hundreds of feet beneath the Defense Ministry, the Bor is the IDF's main command nerve center, the place where all major operations are planned and overseen. It is accessed through massive steel doors that are sealed shut in the event of a chemical, biological or nuclear attack. A big sign warns visitors to leave their cell phones outside. With Iran and Hezbollah actively eavesdropping on Israel, no chances are taken.

The Bor has its own air-purification system and power source. Even if the buildings above ground are destroyed, the Bor will keep functioning.

The stairs seem to go down for miles. The halls are lined with rooms for each of Israel's different areas of interest. There is Gaza, Lebanon, Syria, the West Bank and what the IDF calls "Depth," places where troops might need to operate far from Israel's immediate borders. These are the rooms where operations are planned and units are allocated based on their expertise and capabilities.

The War Room, the IDF's main command center, is where the chief of staff oversees military operations. He has a seat in the middle of a long table lined with computers and phones of different colors, depending on their level of encryption. Each screen shows a feed from a different sensor: naval vessels, satellites or drones.

On special occasions, like this night, the prime minister and other government officials often gather to watch an operation unfold in real time. While the dignitaries sat in one room, Shkedi took his seat in a nearby communications center where he was able to track the planes on a large radar screen. Each plane had its own screen, showing fuel and weapons levels.

Before joining Olmert and Barak, Livni stopped off at the Foreign Ministry's Tel Aviv branch and met with all of the relevant spokespeople who were likely to be quizzed the following morning by the media. In a nearby room, an officer from the IDF's Spokesperson's Office was scouring the Internet to see if something had leaked. If word got out prematurely, the team agreed, Israel would treat it like gossip and try to play it down so as not to alert Assad.

By the time Livni arrived at the Bor, the IDF preparations had been finalized. At around 10:30 p.m., four F-15Is took off from the Hatzerim base in southern Israel and four F-16Is from

Ramon base in the Negev Desert. All together, the planes were carrying around 20 tons of bombs, more than enough to destroy a building less than 2,000 square meters. Some of the bombs were equipped with satellite guidance systems. Each had a different level of penetration. This way, if one didn't work, the others could compensate.

While the pilots had spent the day studying the route to the reactor and satellite imagery, there was still concern that something would go wrong. What if, the pilots wondered, Syria had hidden one of its surface-to-air missile systems somewhere near the reactor? Or what if one sortie wouldn't be enough to destroy the reactor and another mission would be needed? These were all risks they had no choice but to take.

They flew west till they were a safe distance over the Mediterranean Sea, all the time operating electronic warfare systems to hide their location. Then, they turned right, northward toward Syria. For most of the flight they straddled the Turkish-Syrian border, dipping into Syria for the last leg to the reactor.

To infiltrate Syrian airspace without detection, the planes flew extremely low—below 200 feet—and the pilots and navigators maintained strict silence. No one said a word. Any problems—there were some bumpy parts due to unexpected weather conditions—were dealt with by each individual pilot.

Barak lived on the thirty-first floor of an apartment building in Tel Aviv. It amazed him that the aircraft flew lower than his own apartment, almost the entire way to the reactor.

As expected, there was no resistance. The Syrians didn't even see the planes coming. The fighter jets were over their target a little after midnight and broke formation, climbing to a higher altitude and then diving toward the reactor, one after the other.

Within seconds each plane had dropped two bombs, nearly 20 tons of explosives altogether, over the nuclear reactor. The planes' wings reverberated with the discharge of each bomb. One after another, the bombs struck the roof as well as the exterior walls. Everything was captured on camera. The explosions were consecutive and massive. First the roof caved in. Then, the side walls. The building had been destroyed beyond repair.

The planes hovered above, watching as their bombs were dropped and hit the target. Thermal cameras gave the pilots a front-row seat to the explosion. They were on top of the target for less than two minutes. Each plane checked in and then the lead pilot broke radio silence. "Arizona," he reported back to Tel Aviv, the code word for a mission accomplished.

The Bor broke out in a round of applause and hugs but it was all still a bit premature. Shkedi could not yet relax; the pilots still had to get back home safely. By now, the Syrians knew they were there and they needed to get out quickly.

In the last briefing before the mission, Shkedi had told the pilots that they needed to do everything possible to avoid a direct confrontation with Syrian fighter jets. If, for example, a Syrian MiG tried to engage the IAF F-15s and got shot down, Assad might feel compelled to respond. He wouldn't be able to enter the "deniability zone." The same was true if an Israeli jet got shot down or a pilot got captured. It wasn't just about Israel keeping quiet. The whole operation needed to appear as if it never happened.

At this point, flying low would no longer help. The pilots kicked their boosters and shot northward back to the Turkish-Syrian border for the flight westward to the safe confines of the Mediterranean. Syria fired off some missiles but they were way off mark. By 2:00 a.m., less than four hours after the operation had begun, all the planes were back at their bases.

Relief swept through the Bor. The mission was a resounding success and the airplanes had returned safely. But this was just the beginning. In all of the other rooms, the IDF operations desks were fully manned. With war a real possibility, no one was allowed to leave. All eyes were on Aman, which was busy tracking the Syrian military.

Ashkenazi left the Bor and went back to his office on the fourteenth floor of the nearby IDF headquarters. He took out one of his Europa cigarettes, lit it and opened a window. As he took a drag, the chief of staff looked out at the Tel Aviv skyline. Would Assad mobilize his troops? Would he put his Scud missile teams on high alert? Every minute counted and any Syrian movement that seemed out of the ordinary could mean that war was coming.

Within a few hours, he thought to himself, the whole city could be in flames.

7

WHAT WAS ASSAD THINKING?

Bashar al-Assad was sound asleep in the Damascus Presidential Palace when the IAF jets bombed his most-prized possession in northeast Syria.

Designed in the late 1970s and known for its grandeur and massive—but mostly empty—marble rooms, the palace was completed in 1990. Assad turned it into his home after he succeeded his father as president a decade later. The palace's iron gates and doors, even the one to Assad's private office, were designed and built by a Syrian-Jewish artist who later fled the country.

This was the place from which Assad ruled over his people with an iron and violent fist.

At about 1 a.m. Assad's staff woke him up and gave an initial report about the bombing. He didn't have to ask too many questions to know what the target was. There was nothing else there. If Israel had infiltrated Syrian airspace near Deir ez-Zor it was for the reactor. His greatest secret, the asset that was supposed to make him invincible, untouchable and undefeatable, was now gone.

The question now was, what was he going to do about it? Was the attack an act of aggression worth going to war over? How important was the reactor and could he let the Israeli bombing pass without response? While Aman had come up with the "deniability zone" theory, in intelligence there is always a limit to what can really be predicted, especially when it comes to trying to envisage what is going on in the mind of a single person.

The IDF was preparing for a wide range of options. Assad could activate Hezbollah and ask the group to light up Israel's north with a barrage of Katyusha rockets from Lebanon. Or he could order his own commando units to invade the Golan Heights and try to capture an Israeli community. He could keep his response minimal and simply fire off a few long-range missiles into central Israel. Or he could do nothing. Anything was possible.

It was a daunting position to be in for a man who was never supposed to have become president. Bashar al-Assad was the second son of Anisa and Hafez, who had ruled Syria ruthlessly since 1971. The leader of the Baath Party, Hafez came to power after a series of coups that he led. To safeguard his regime, no act of violence was off limits. There was a reason he was nicknamed the "Lion of Damascus."

For Israel, Hafez was the bitterest of enemies. In 1973,

Hafez—together with Egyptian president Anwar Sadat—launched a surprise attack against Israel on the holy fast day of Yom Kippur. It was Israel's bloodiest war and its greatest intelligence debacle. In the initial days of the war, Syria made impressive gains on the Golan Heights, the territory Israel had conquered just six years earlier. The IDF sustained heavy losses but fought back hard and held on to its land.

At home, Hafez was no different. In 1982, his troops laid siege to the city of Hama, where the Muslim Brotherhood had launched an uprising against his regime. Large parts of the city were destroyed and while estimates varied, the death toll soared to almost 40,000.

Bashar was the quiet son, who avoided military service and politics. His older brother, Bassel, was the charismatic military figure in the family. The heir apparent. But in 1994, Bassel, who served as commander of the Presidential Guard, was killed in a car accident on a foggy highway as he sped to catch a flight from Damascus to Germany.

In the West, a story circulated that when the news of Bassel's death reached Damascus, it was first reported to the Syrian Army chief of staff, Hikmat al-Shihabi. He gathered a few of his officers and debated how they would inform the president. Shihabi decided to go tell the president on his own but asked two officers to join him so he wouldn't be the sole target of Hafez's wrath. When they walked into the presidential bedroom—the accident had taken place before dawn—Assad sat up, looked at the military officers and immediately asked who was trying to overthrow him. An authoritarian ruler, the survival of the regime was always first and foremost on his mind.

Bashar received the news of his brother's death, which the Syrians later suspected had been orchestrated by the Mossad, in London where he was pursuing a postgraduate degree in ophthalmology from Western Eye Hospital. He immediately returned home to a grieving father who now had to transform his eye-doctor son into a ruthless leader like himself. Over the next six years, Bashar underwent military training and was appointed chairman of the Syrian Computer Society, the country's domain registration authority and a position once held by Bassel. By 2000, before his father died of a heart attack, Bashar had obtained the rank of brigadier general and was in charge of the Lebanon portfolio. Hafez knew he was dying and wanted to give Bashar the best head start possible.

For Michael Hayden, the head of the CIA, the Assads were like the Corleone family from the *Godfather* trilogy. Bassel, Hayden explained, was like Sonny, the son who was gunned down at the Long Beach Causeway toll plaza. To replace Sonny, Michael returned from exile in Sicily to lead the family, similar to the way Bashar returned to Damascus from London. But unlike in *The Godfather*, in which Vito Corleone was able to rely on his talented youngest son, Michael, to lead the family, "in many ways, Hafez had to settle for Fredo," Hayden said, in reference to Vito Corleone's weaker and unsuccessful second son.

The day after his father's death, on June 11, 2000, Bashar Assad was unanimously nominated by the Baath Party as president. The parliament amended Article 83 of the Syrian constitution, which required that the president be at least 40 years old, to 34, Bashar's exact age at the time. Three days later, in a national referendum, Bashar received 97.29 percent of the vote. It didn't hurt that he was the only candidate.[1]

In Israel, Mossad and Aman were keeping a careful eye on Syria. In the mid-1990s, Israel and Syria had held a number of rounds of peace talks but they all had failed. Consecutive Israeli prime ministers—Yitzhak Rabin, Shimon Peres, Benjamin Netanyahu and Ehud Barak—had all tried to reach a peace deal with Syria but none had gotten very far.

The model was supposed to be similar to the deals reached with Egypt in 1979 and Jordan in 1994. With Jordan, Israel settled land disputes and border disagreements. For Egypt, Israel withdrew from the Sinai Peninsula. And for Syria, it was supposed to return the Golan Heights. Rabin, for example, preferred peace with Syria over advancing the Oslo process with the Palestinians since, in his view, it had the potential to be a bigger game changer for the region. Peace with Syria, he thought, would disconnect Damascus from Iran and isolate Hezbollah in Lebanon.

Israel already had three wars with Syria under its belt and Rabin wanted to avoid a fourth. Syria was the last country with a conventional military that had the ability to really threaten Israel and conquer territory. Its mobilized armored divisions had already once come close to retaking the Golan and Rabin wanted to prevent that from ever happening.

Not much was known about Bashar when he returned to Syria after Bassel's death. In the West, small dossiers had been compiled on each of Assad's children but with very little detail. What was known about Bashar was that he had been raised in a predominantly Christian part of Damascus and most of his friends were Christian. He wasn't overly religious and if anything, he wasn't expected to be any different than his father. At the most, just a weaker version.

Even though Bashar had returned to Syria and was being considered as a possible successor, in Israel, Aman and the Mossad thought there would be other candidates the older Assad would prefer to see succeed him. Hafez's brother Rifaat had served as vice president in the 1980s, and even though he had tried to seize control from Hafez after the leader's first heart attack in 1983, he was seen as a viable candidate. But within a few months it became clear that Hafez had made up his mind. The eye-doctor son was being groomed to rule Syria.

"We didn't ignore Bashar but he was not at the top of our priorities," explained Danny Yatom, who served as head of the Mossad between 1996 and 1998. "He got a low score since he didn't appear to be built to lead the country. He wasn't trained for it, he was a doctor and he had spent some time in Western countries. He was supposed to be more modern."[2]

Yatom had some experience working with Syria. During his term as Mossad chief, he was sent by then prime minister Benjamin Netanyahu to Washington to try to launch peace negotiations with the Syrians. Yatom stayed in a hotel downtown, while Walid Muallem, the Syrian ambassador to Washington, remained in his embassy.

The talks were indirect, which meant that the Americans would cross the street every hour or so with a message from one side to the other. They would then return with the other side's response. Yatom stayed in town for a few days, and when he returned to Israel, he met with Netanyahu and pushed to move forward on the Syrian track.

"Then, it seemed like something could work," he said.

When Bashar took over, at least in the beginning, it seemed like what Yatom had felt in the late nineties was actually going to happen. A new era seemed to have dawned in Syria. The young Assad was perceived as a reformer and some people were calling him "The Hope," a demonstration of just how much the public was yearning for change. In his inaugural address on July 17, Bashar called on the Syrian people to work together to "modernize" their country. "I find it absolutely necessary to call upon every single citizen to participate in the process of development and modernization if we are truly honest and serious in attaining the desired results in the very near future," he said.[3]

Bashar initiated economic reforms, a first step in what people thought would be a whole new direction for their country. The political environment seemed more open. Political prisoners were released, private newspapers received government licensing and, for the first time, criticism against the regime was allowed to be voiced publicly. It was the "Damascus Spring."

But it didn't last long. David Lesch, an expert on Syria who spent countless hours interviewing Assad, told how members of the old guard came to see Assad shortly after he took office and warned him of the repercussions of his reforms. "Probably some of the tough guys in the regime came to Bashar and essentially said, 'Hey kid, this is not how we do things here,'" Lesch wrote.[4]

In 2001, when America declared its war on terror after the 9/11 attacks, Assad initially decided to cooperate. But when the invasion of Iraq came two years later and he saw the deployment of over 150,000 American soldiers on his country's eastern doorstep, he started to fear that Syria was next and that the US was on its way to do to him what it was working to achieve with Saddam Hussein.

Slowly, as Assad gained confidence, he began to turn a blind eye to insurgents passing through his country on their way to fight American troops in Iraq. Publicly he declared his support for America's war, but privately he prayed that the US would fail in Iraq and that the so-called Bush Doctrine, of spreading democracy throughout the Middle East, would fail. He was worried about his own future and if America met failure in Iraq, there was little chance anyone would have an appetite to try and force a regime change in Syria.

At the time, he worked to strengthen his relationship with Hezbollah and its charismatic leader, Sheikh Hassan Nasrallah. Hafez, Bashar's late father, rarely met with Nasrallah and if he did, it was usually after the Lebanese guerrilla chief had been kept waiting for an hour or two. Hafez would let the Iranians fly weapons shipments to Damascus and then truck them across the border into Lebanon. But he didn't work with Hezbollah. They were good to have as an instrument that could be used every once in a while to preoccupy the Israelis, but nothing more.

The younger Assad saw far more potential in Hezbollah. He was impressed by the way it had managed to push Israel out of Lebanon and decided to open up his own weapon warehouses to the Shiite guerrilla group, giving it access to advanced Russian-made weapons, like the guided anti-tank missiles that would wreak havoc on Israeli armor during the Second Lebanon War in 2006.

"Bashar Assad rolled out the red carpet for Nasrallah," one former senior Israeli intelligence officer explained. "He gave him the keys to all his military warehouses and access to his most advanced weapons. He was taken in by Nasrallah and nothing was off limits."

By 2000, when Assad became president, there was a new head of Mossad in Israel. In 1998, Yatom was forced to step down after Mossad agents botched an assassination attempt against a top Hamas leader in Jordan. The agents had sprayed a slow-acting poison into Khaled Mashal's ear but the operation went wrong and two of the assassins were captured. Israel negotiated a deal: Jordan released the captured Israelis and, in exchange, Israel delivered the antidote to save Mashal's life and released Hamas's wheelchair-bound spiritual leader, Sheikh Ahmed Yassin, from Israeli prison.

In the fallout, Yatom was replaced by Efraim Halevy, who was born in London in 1934 and moved with his family to Israel after the establishment of the State of Israel in 1948. In 1961 he was recruited into the Mossad as an intelligence analyst. Within a short time, he moved over to operations.

Halevy devoted much of his career to cultivating covert relationships and ties for Israel. He spent vast periods of time overseas—in the US and throughout Europe—working his way up to deputy head of the spy organization. While Halevy wasn't a spy in the James Bond way, he was often compared to George

Smiley of John le Carré's novels. During the 1990s, he became a special envoy to Jordan's King Hussein and choreographed the secret diplomacy that culminated in a peace treaty with Israel in 1994.

He then left the service and went to Brussels to serve as Israel's ambassador to the European Union. After the botched assassination attempt in Amman, he was called back to lead the Mossad. The man with the British accent was now Israel's top spymaster.

It was a turbulent time for Israel. Ehud Barak's term as prime minister was coming to a premature end but in a last-ditch effort he went to Camp David to try and reach a peace deal with Palestinian leader Yasser Arafat. The talks failed and in September the Second Intifada erupted in the West Bank and the Gaza Strip. In the following four years, more than 3,000 Palestinians and 1,000 Israelis would be killed.

In June 2000, Hafez Assad passed away and it was up to Halevy to monitor and analyze the change in leadership in Syria. The Mossad had already prepared a dossier on the young Assad but Halevy wasn't a big believer in psychological profiles. When he was admitted to the Mossad in 1961, like every new recruit, he had to undergo a psychological assessment by a therapist in Tel Aviv.

When he became head of the espionage organization 37 years later, he asked to see his personal file. In it he found the psychologist's assessment, which praised his intellect and predicted that he would make a superb analyst but concluded that he was not "command material" and would not climb the organization's ranks.

Halevy was a strong proponent of peace with Syria, which he believed was key to stability in the Middle East. He pushed to relaunch peace talks with Hafez Assad just a few months before the Syrian leader died. The first round of talks was held in Shepherdstown, West Virginia, and for several months American mediation helped the sides work through most of the key issues.

"Syria is the fulcrum of Arab and Islamic nationalism in the entire Middle East," he would tell his Mossad subordinates. Damascus, he explained, was one of the world's most ancient cities, referred to in the book of Genesis. It was the city that gave birth to Arab secular political movements like the Baath Party, which later became the dominant movement in Iraq and brought the likes of Saddam Hussein to power.

From Halevy's perspective, Assad and Hussein were dangerous leaders of enemy states. But they also represented a type of secular Islam that he thought Israel needed to encourage more of in the Middle East. Secularists, he believed, were easier to reconcile with than the religious Muslim zealots.

But when Hafez Assad died, that dream seemed to die with him. Bashar was too weak, Halevy assessed, to engage in peace talks with Israel. Before he could sit down with Israel, he would need to spend his first few years in office solidifying his regime. Working toward a peace with Israel that would include compromises and concessions was not the way to do that.

Hafez Assad seemed to ultimately believe the same. His decision to walk away from the Shepherdstown talks appeared to be out of fear that a peace deal with Israel shortly before he died would undermine his son's future. He needed to focus on ensuring a smooth transfer of power to his son, not on trying to make peace with Israel.

For Israeli intelligence, Syria was always one of its most important targets. Over the years, Israel's efforts varied but the focus remained the same: understanding Syria's intentions and ensuring that it was always one step ahead in the event that war broke out. In 1962, for example, the Mossad carried out one of its most daring missions known to date in Syria: infiltrating a spy, Eli Cohen, deep inside Damascus.

Cohen's cover was as a Syrian businessman who had made a small fortune in Argentina, and had returned to his homeland to help it grow and prosper. When the Baath Party took over Syria in 1963, Cohen was already strategically entrenched in Syrian high society and had become the confidant of several top government officials. Every few days he transmitted information back to Israel via a radio transmitter he hid in his room.

His connections gained him access to the Golan Heights, which Israel would conquer in 1967. On one known trip there, Cohen visited a massive Soviet-built military base on the outskirts of the Syrian city of Quneitra. Inside was a three-floor building, at the time one of the more impressive buildings in Syria. There was a hospital in one wing as well as offices for the top Syrian military command. A long winding staircase greeted visitors in the lobby.

During the visit, Cohen was briefed on the fortifications the Syrians had built ahead of a future war with Israel. He looked around and noticed that there were no trees within the base.

"Plant eucalyptus trees," Cohen told the Syrian officers. Due to their relatively large size and long branches, he said, eucalyptuses were ideal for providing shade.

The Syrians liked Cohen's idea and adopted it for all of their bases on the Golan. They didn't know that Cohen wasn't really interested in shade for Syrian soldiers. He had another reason for suggesting the trees. When the Six Day War broke out in 1967, Israel knew exactly where Syrian military bases were located. All they had to do was look for the tall eucalyptus trees.

After the Yom Kippur War in 1973 and its second defeat by Israel, Syria searched for a way to even the playing field. While its Soviet-supplied armored divisions matched up in numbers and quality to Israel's American Patton tanks, it found itself almost helpless against the Israeli Air Force. Lacking the capability to overpower Israel's American-supplied F-4 Phantom aircraft—and later the F-15s Israel received in 1976—Syria decided to invest in two different tracks: chemical weapons and long-range ballistic missiles.

"The 1973 war was the trigger," Yehoshua Saguy, the head of Israel's Military Intelligence from 1979 to 1983, explained. "They started with the idea for chemical weapons in the 1950s but they didn't have the industry or the plans to produce it for the first few decades."

Israel was closely paying attention. By 1975, Syria was hard at work on the construction of a new chemical weapons facility it would later give the academic-sounding name Scientific Studies and Research Center.

"They would regularly send scientists abroad to search for

supplies," Saguy said. Israel shared the intelligence with its American and European allies. Saguy, for example, traveled once a year to Langley, Virginia, for brainstorming sessions with the CIA over the different options for stopping Syria's chemical weapons program.

"It was tons and tons of material that was gathered over years and simply was too much to destroy," he said. "We knew that there were huge amounts and that it was being made to be capable of being used in airborne bombs and artillery shells."

By 1983, US intelligence agencies began to pay more attention. In a special National Intelligence Estimate, the US wrote that Syria is a "major recipient of Soviet CW [chemical weapons] assistance [and] probably has the most advanced chemical warfare capability in the Arab world."[5]

The two countries cited by the Americans as supplying the chemical agents, the delivery systems and the training were Czechoslovakia and the Soviet Union. "As long as this support is forthcoming," the 1983 document continued, "there is no need for Syria to develop an indigenous capability to produce CW agents or materiel."

In another CIA report, the US speculated about the motivation behind the Soviet export of chemical weapons to countries like Syria. The Kremlin, the report stated, saw gas as useful in quelling insurgencies and "breaking the will and resistance of stubborn guerrilla forces operating from relatively inaccessible protected sanctuaries. These weapons offer substantial advantages over conventional weapons."[6] As Hafez Assad had showed a year earlier in Hama, he knew how to put down popular uprisings.

Germany was also complicit in sending scientists and dual-use material to Syria to help advance its CW program. At the end of 1984, for example, Israel's ambassador to Germany met with a top Foreign Ministry official in Berlin and warned of "intelligence service findings" which indicated that since the mid-1970s, German scientists had been helping Syria's chemical weapons program under the disguise of "agricultural and medical research."

The ambassador told the German officials that according to Israel's estimates, Syria had the ability to produce 700 kilograms of sarin gas, enough to kill millions of people.[7] The German government promised to launch an investigation.

Chemical weapons though were not Israel's only concern when it came to Syria's military buildup. There were also missiles—not just any, but long-range ballistic ones, capable of striking anywhere within the small and narrow Jewish state.

In 1974, Hafez Assad flew to North Korea for talks with Kim Il Sung, leader of the communist country from its founding in 1948 until his death in 1994. During the four days he spent in North Korea, Assad joined Kim on visits to some factories, on a leisure boat ride as well as for discussions on military cooperation.

Within a few years, North Korea had become one of Syria's main weapons suppliers, with a focus on ballistic missiles. Israeli intelligence was carefully following the growing alliance between the two countries being built with the Soviet Union's support and blessing. Soon, North Korean airplanes were landing regularly at Damascus International Airport and North Korean engineers were starting to spend long periods of time in Syria helping to build munitions plants and weapon assembly lines.

North Korea, Israel discovered, had succeeded in reverse-engineering Soviet Scud-B ballistic missiles and was supplying them, for a hefty fee, to its allies in the Middle East. Syria's most advanced ballistic missile, the Scud-D—with a range of nearly 500 miles, it is one of the ballistic missiles Israel fears could carry a nuclear or chemical warhead—was copied from North Korea's Rodong missile.

By the early 1990s, Syria had dozens of Scud missiles and launchers deployed throughout the country. North Korea had helped the Syrians establish factories to independently manufacture the missiles. Syria's chemical weapons program had also progressed significantly and it now had the ability to assemble a nonconventional warhead on the Scuds. Israel's northern neighbor was quickly turning into a threat of unimaginable consequences.

At the time, Halevy was deputy head of the Mossad and he felt that something needed to be done. Through connections in Europe, he made contacts with a few high-level members of the regime in Pyongyang.

In September 1992, he met with Yitzhak Rabin, the Israeli war hero and past prime minister, who had once again returned to lead the government just three months before. Halevy proposed an innovative plan: let him go to Pyongyang and see if it might be possible to reach a deal that would put an end to the North Korean–Syrian alliance. It was out of the box but also had its dangers. Israel and North Korea did not have diplomatic ties, let alone relations between intelligence agencies. There was a gamble in sending a high-level Mossad operative like Halevy to a rogue state that was already in bed with Israel's enemies. But Halevy persisted and Rabin gave the green light.

The deputy Mossad chief flew from Tel Aviv to Berlin and there, together with another Mossad official, boarded a North Korean government jet that had been sent to pick them up. Halevy and his associate were the only two passengers on the plane when it took off from Berlin for Moscow, where it stopped so boxes could be loaded onto the empty seats. Due to the freezing temperatures, the plane got stuck on the ground for almost an entire day.

The plane finally took off and flew to Novosibirsk, a city in Siberia. Halevy would never forget the flight. Due to heavy turbulence, the boxes bounced around the cabin the entire time. After picking up North Korean workers stationed in the mines there, it took off again and 10 hours later—after over 48 hours of travel—Halevy was finally on the ground in Pyongyang.

Though he was the deputy head of the Mossad, Halevy came without any security. The North Koreans had vouched for his safety and he had no reason not to trust them. The North Koreans had promised Halevy he was their official guest, but they did not stamp his passport.

Halevy spent the next three days in North Korea in talks with senior members of the Workers' Party, the ruling political party in the country, as well as with officials from the Foreign Ministry. During the first day of discussions, Halevy got straight to the point. "Your supply of Scud missiles to Syria threatens Israel," he told the North Koreans, who claimed they didn't know what he was talking about. They denied even having a relationship with Syria. "We are not giving them anything," they told Halevy.

The deputy Mossad chief refused to accept the denial. "No problem," he said. "If that is the case, then I will leave tomorrow morning for Israel."

The North Koreans believed Halevy was serious and asked him to stay the night. In the morning, they promised, they would talk more openly. The next day, the sides gathered again. This time, they admitted to having a relationship with Syria and to supplying it with weapons, including missile technology. Halevy asked what it would take for North Korea to stop the supply. The answer was impossible for Israel to deliver on— free oil for the entire nation of 20 million people for the next 10 years.

"I don't think it will work but I will take it to my superiors," Halevy told his hosts. After returning to his hotel room to pack up his belongings, he was driven to the airport for a flight to Beijing, the first leg of his journey back to Israel. On the plane, Halevy was surprised to run into Eytan Bentsur, the director general of Israel's Foreign Ministry, who had just wrapped up his own visit to Pyongyang for talks with the North Koreans on a similar topic.

It was a classic case of uncoordinated Israeli bureaucracy. Bentsur's visit was about a gold mine the North Koreans were looking for help to reopen. They needed money plus mining expertise and the Israeli Foreign Ministry pooled together a few businessmen who were willing to put up the necessary funds. In exchange, Bentsur thought, it might be possible to get North Korea to reconsider its relationship with Syria and Iran.

When the two groups returned to Israel, they were summoned to a meeting with Foreign Minister Shimon Peres, who
wanted to try and make some order of the *balagan*, the Hebrew
word for chaos. While Bentsur spoke favorably of his visit and
the chances that the mining deal could be reached, Halevy was
skeptical. First, he said, the North Korean–Syrian missile deals
were far more lucrative than whatever might come from the
mine deal. Second, Israel needed to consider how the Americans would react. North Korea was a known adversary of the
US, and Israel, a close American ally, needed to tread carefully
when wading into complicated diplomatic waters.

Peres agreed. He decided to dispatch both men to Washington, DC, for talks at the State Department. Bill Clinton had
been elected president but George H. W. Bush still had a few
months left in office and Peres wanted to get a sense of what
would be possible. When they returned, the group again met
to update Peres.

Bentsur said that the Americans were not happy with Israel formalizing ties with North Korea but that they "did not
officially object." Halevy, who had been in the same meetings,
walked away with a completely different impression. "The
Americans said we should not play on their back door and in
their area of national interest," the deputy Mossad chief said.
"They expect us not to do anything concerning Korea that is
not first approved by them."

Due to the conflicting reports, Peres decided to get a clearer
answer on his own. In June 1993 he flew to Vienna for talks with
Warren Christopher, the new secretary of state, who confirmed
Halevy's report. While the deals that both Halevy and Bentsur

were trying to advance with North Korea did not succeed, they did demonstrate the extent to which Israel was willing to go to try to cut off Syria's missile supply line. Israel's northern front was a constant worry and Jerusalem was on the lookout for ways to change that.

Nuclear weapons were supposed to be off limits and out of Syria's reach. While the Scud missiles, the chemical weapons and Syria's conventional army were of concern for Israel, they were all threats Israel felt confident it could handle on its own.

For the Scud missiles, it had developed the Arrow missile defense system that was supposed to be able to intercept ballistic missiles. For the chemical weapons, Israel had distributed gas mask kits to its citizens ahead of the First Gulf War with Iraq in 1990. The kits were updated over the years and Israelis were experienced at sealing a room in their homes with plastic sheets and duct tape whenever there was fear of a possible nonconventional attack. And last, for all of the Syrian army's numbers and sophistication, the IDF was believed to be superior in technology, training and weaponry.

Syria, Israeli intelligence believed, had decided after the Yom Kippur War in 1973 to focus its investments on chemical and biological weapons but stopped short of nuclear bombs. Hafez Assad seemed to have decided back then not to follow in the footsteps of the Iranians or Saddam Hussein. Hafez Assad, Israeli intelligence understood, saw nuclear weapons as crossing a red line.

Part of this assessment was based on different reports that came out over the years about Hafez Assad's contacts with the Pakistanis. A. Q. Khan, the notorious rogue Pakistani scientist who led one of the most extensive black market nuclear rings and had helped North Korea, Iran and Libya, had also offered Assad nuclear blueprints in the early nineties but was turned down. Israel let out a sigh of relief when it heard that Assad had turned Khan away. At least one of its enemies, it thought, was not trying to get its hands on nukes.

A few years later, though, Israeli intelligence learned about a Syrian general who had been tasked by Hafez Assad to explore the possibility of obtaining a nuclear capability for Syria, information that went against all of Israel's previous assessments.

Despite a top-secret report summarizing the new and hot intelligence, no one paid attention. The report was ignored by the intelligence community as well as by Israel's political echelon. Israel was in the middle of peace talks with the Palestinians and with Assad. Nuclear suspicions did not fit into the narrative of the new Middle East that the government was working hard to create.

In April 2007 the intelligence officer who wrote the report, by then retired, received a phone call from one of Israel's intelligence agencies and was asked to come in for a meeting a few days later. The agency wanted to know as much as possible about the nearly 10-year-old report. Who had the information come from? What more could the retired operative reveal? Had he left out any details?

When the retired operative asked why, after all these years, they wanted to know, he received a vague reply. "Nothing special," the official he met said. "We are just reviewing some old files."

Months later, the retired operative would get the real answer when reports emerged of Israel's strike on the al-Kibar nuclear reactor.

One other person who warned for years of Syria's nuclear ambitions was John Bolton, the former US ambassador to the United Nations who was appointed as President Donald Trump's national security adviser in 2018. A former assistant secretary of state for weapons nonproliferation, Bolton was considered a world expert in nonconventional weapons and was an avid supporter of George W. Bush's "Axis of Evil" doctrine that singled out Iran, Iraq and North Korea for their development of nonconventional weapons. But he took it a step further and added Syria to the notorious list.

During his confirmation hearings in the Senate Foreign Relations Committee in the spring of 2005, a mini scandal broke out after some of the senators accused Bolton of warmongering and manipulating intelligence. Why, the senators demanded to know, was he warning that Syria might be developing nuclear weapons?

For Bolton, Syria was something like a "junior varsity" evil power. It didn't yet have a full-fledged nuclear program like Iran but his analysis of the intelligence he was seeing, as well as the close alliance between Damascus and Pyongyang, led him to believe that "Syria was demonstrating an interest in nuclear weapons."[8]

The senators blasted him. John Kerry, the senator from Massachusetts who would later become secretary of state under President Barack Obama, accused Bolton of stretching intelligence. Bolton, he said, tried to "inflate language" about Syria's nuclear activities, beyond what intelligence analysts saw. "This is a man who's going to speak for America with credibility about Syria?" Kerry warned.[9]

Joe Biden, the senator from Delaware who would become Obama's vice president, said Bolton's appointment as ambassador to the UN would undermine America's global credibility.

"Is it in the national interest to have someone who has a reputation for exaggerating intelligence, seeking and speaking for the UN when the next crisis arises, whether it's Iran or Syria?" Biden asked. "We have already lost a lot of credibility at home and abroad after the fiasco over the intelligence on Iraq, and Mr. Bolton is not the man to help us to rebuild it."

But Bolton stood by what he believed. He didn't know at the time about the reactor that was already being built along the Euphrates River, but he had suspicions that something was going on in Syria. In the end, Bush insisted on Bolton's appointment, using his right as president to push it through when the Senate was in recess.

Years later, Bolton said that his suspicions about Syria stemmed from a steady flow of news about different components for a nuclear program that he saw coming together in the Arab republic. It was equipment, he said, that was needed "not just for public utility or electrical power generation, but for nuclear weapon objectives."

Despite the years that have passed since the discovery of

al-Kibar and its destruction, one mystery that remains is who exactly started the nuclear reactor project. On this, opinions diverge.

Michael Hayden, the head of the CIA, was convinced that Hafez Assad had started work on the reactor before his death in 2000, something like a parting gift from a father determined to ensure that his weak son would carry the mantle and remain in power.

Danny Yatom, the former head of the Mossad, believes Bashar started the project with the regime's survival on his mind. "He wanted to solidify his power and regime," Yatom explained. "Assad learned that he can rule a rogue state, but if he has nuclear weapons or is close to getting them, he has an insurance card that Syria will never be attacked."

Ehud Barak, Israel's defense minister at the time of the strike, agreed. "It was Bashar who invested in it," he said. "I don't think the father was involved."

Yadlin also believes it was Bashar. The late Hafez Assad, Yadlin said, had met with A. Q. Khan and turned down his offer. Bashar, however, wanted "to create a balance of power with Israel and to be a leader in the Arab world."

Eliot Cohen, Rice's representative on the Drafting Group, never gave much thought to why Assad was even trying to build a nuclear reactor. "They wanted nukes because they wanted nukes," he said, admitting that a lot of mystery still remains.

Was this, he asked, simply North Korea proliferating nuclear technology in exchange for cash or was there something collaborative about the project? Another mystery never solved has to do with Iran—did the Iranians know about the project? Did they give Assad some of the money to pay for it, in what Bolton called a "three-way nuclear venture"? And was it even possible that Iran hoped to use the reactor for its own plutonium purposes?

Dick Cheney, vice president at the time, always assumed that the North Korean–Syrian relationship was simply about money. North Korea lacked real sources of cash and was known at the time to ship its people out of the country to work as slave laborers and then collect their wages for the state. "To be able to peddle that technology to the Syrians and be compensated for it was not insignificant," he said.

Years have passed and for most of the residents of the Middle East, the destroyed reactor is a long-forgotten memory, just another bump in the winding road that turned Syria into a bloodbath where over 500,000 people have been killed since 2011. Even without nuclear weapons, Assad has demonstrated a cruelty no one ever expected. Whether gassing his own people or dropping barrel bombs from helicopters onto civilian areas, he invalidated all of the intelligence assessments written about him. The images of children gasping for air after a chemical attack in Idlib in April 2017 demonstrated exactly what Assad was willing to do to ensure his survival.

"We can only imagine what would have happened had he been allowed to have a nuclear reactor," Yatom said.

8

WAG THE DOG

On Wednesday night, after the cabinet had dispersed in Jerusalem and just hours before the planes were set to take off, IDF chief of staff Lieutenant General Gabi Ashkenazi left his office on the fourteenth floor of the Kirya Military Headquarters overlooking the Tel Aviv expressway and drove to a wedding in a small agricultural town some 30 miles to the south.

With a possible war on the horizon, going to a wedding was the last thing Ashkenazi wanted to do. But he didn't have a choice. The bride, Liron, was his secretary and she was marrying another IDF officer—Oron, the spokesman for the Central Command, the IDF regional command responsible for the West Bank.

Ashkenazi showed up in uniform and stayed for the duration of the chuppah, the traditional Jewish wedding ceremony. He was all smiles. He greeted some old friends, patted others on the back and embraced the bride and groom. People around him were listening to the music and drinking from the generously stocked bar.

Had he not showed up, too many questions would have been asked, and questions were the last thing Ashkenazi needed on the night he was about to oversee what would be one of the most sensitive operations of his military career. Already, the IDF was getting inquiries from a few newspapers about rumors of an impending strike against Syria.

Journalists, he knew, often stake out the Prime Minister's Office to see who comes and goes. If something seemed out of the ordinary—like him not showing up at his secretary's wedding—it would be confirmation that something was amiss. During the wedding, military reporters, who were hearing rumors of a pending large-scale operation, called IDF spokesman Brigadier General Avi Benayahu and asked where he was.

"I am at a wedding," he said. The reporters then asked where Ashkenazi was. "Here next to me," Benayahu replied. "He's enjoying some chicken skewers. I'll put him on so you can wish him bon appetit."

The chuppah was overseen by Rabbi Shmuel Rabinowitz, the rabbi in charge of the Western Wall in Jerusalem. After it ended, Ashkenazi took him aside and asked that he go directly to the Western Wall to pray for the IDF, its soldiers and commanders. Rabinowitz asked why but Ashkenazi just smiled and, like the military officer he was, said: "Learn to follow orders."

As the chief of staff, Ashkenazi was one of only a handful of people in the country who knew what was scheduled for later that night and from the wedding hall, he had a view of the Tel Aviv skyline to the north and the Ashkelon power plant to the south.

By tomorrow, Ashkenazi knew, all of this could be destroyed in an unprecedented barrage of long-range Scud missiles. After the airstrike in Syria that night, what happened next would be completely in Assad's hands.

A former deputy chief of staff and head of the Northern Command, Ashkenazi wasn't even supposed to have been the IDF chief of staff. In 2005, he lost the top job to Dan Halutz, the former commander of the IAF. Frustrated and disappointed, Ashkenazi bit his tongue and after nearly 40 years of service, hung up his uniform and retired from the military he had served and loved. He took a few months of leave, and then decided to try his hand at business.

But then came the Second Lebanon War against Hezbollah and everything changed. Ashkenazi was called by Defense Minister Amir Peretz to serve as the director-general of the Defense Ministry, the highest-ranking civilian post in Israel's defense establishment. Ashkenazi accepted the job and got straight to work. During the war, he spent most of his days in the north with the residents whose safety he used to be responsible for when he was in charge of military forces along Israel's borders with Lebanon and Syria.

In his new position, Ashkenazi fought with the Treasury and succeeded in getting a new and increased budget for the IDF. He allocated large portions to the Home Front Command, the military branch in charge of civil defense, which had been caught unprepared for the Hezbollah missile onslaught.

When the war finally ended after 34 days, Ashkenazi began the tough job of rebuilding the IDF. He worked hand in hand with the military until January 2007 when, amid growing public criticism, Halutz announced his resignation. Peretz had to appoint a new chief of staff and who was better positioned to take over and rehabilitate the IDF than Ashkenazi? The man who had been passed over to lead the military was now getting a second chance.

Ashkenazi returned to uniform in February and was soon updated on Aman's suspicions regarding Syria's nuclear activity. It was described to him as a "suspicion," not a "threat," meaning that it wasn't something that needed his direct attention. Anyhow, Ashkenazi had more immediate challenges. Israel had come out of the Lebanon war bruised and lacking confidence. With new conflicts potentially brewing with Hamas in the Gaza Strip and Hezbollah in the north, he needed to get the IDF ready for war.

In April, once the intelligence on the nuclear reactor was verified, Ashkenazi began overseeing preparations for a strike, honing the options that would later be presented to the cabinet. As chief of staff, he also had another mission possibly even more complicated than the actual strike: preparing the military and the country for a war without being able to explain why. Very few people in Israel's security establishment knew of the existence of the reactor and, due to the sensitivity of the operation, it had to stay that way.

This meant that Ashkenazi had to prepare for war with Syria while creating an elaborate excuse for why it might happen. For this, there was no rulebook. Militaries are always preparing for war but usually the soldiers are given a reason why they are training to fight a specific enemy. In this case, the reason couldn't be revealed so Ashkenazi tasked Yadlin, the head of Aman, to come up with a creative and realistic excuse for war with Syria.

It was like *Wag the Dog*, the 1997 film featuring Dustin Hoffman and Robert De Niro about a spin doctor and Hollywood movie producer who team up to invent a war to cover up a presidential sex scandal. There was one big difference—this time, the threat was real and if Ashkenazi didn't move fast, Israel could be facing a disaster.

The F-16s flew in low and dropped their 500-pound bombs with amazing precision. The explosion of dust and metal could be seen before the sound was heard. On battlefields, where it takes time for sound to travel, destruction at first seems silent.

Next, it was the turn of the artillery batteries, which pounded the enemy battlefield with 155-millimeter shells to clear a path for the infantry troops and tanks that were waiting below in a nearby ravine. As their rotors chopped the air, Cobra attack helicopters scrambled to provide air support and cover for the ground forces while the Engineering Corps laid down makeshift bridges to enable armored personnel carriers and Merkava Mk-4 tanks to advance on their target—a Syrian village— kicking up a storm of sand and dust.

With their guns cocked and ready, the soldiers from the infantry battalion advanced just behind the tanks. On the slope of one of the nearby hills, helicopters landed two companies of paratroopers and immediately took off again to pick up another company.

From a distance, it looked like the grass had come alive. Elite reconnaissance soldiers, dressed in specially designed camouflage suits, popped out of the ground and opened fire as fighter jets broke the sound barrier and launched their missiles at targets invisible to the naked eye.

It was June 2007 and the IDF was waging "war" against the Syrian Army at the Armored Corps' Shizafon training base just north of the Red Sea resort town of Eilat in southern Israel. It was the IDF's annual Joint Forces Exercise, held for the first time since the war against Hezbollah had ended 10 months earlier. And for the first time in years, the mock war was against Syria and not the Palestinians.

Part of the IDF's strategy for a future war was apparent in the way it conducted the exercise. First was the emphasis commanders put on the "joint battle"—jargon for interoperability and coordination between different branches like infantry, armor and the air force as well as the integration of new drones.

The ground soldiers had spent the previous night hiking some 30 miles while carrying kits on their backs with the equivalent of about half their weight.

Behind this requirement was the understanding that in the next war, the IDF would need to be able to move fast if it wanted to stand a chance at suppressing Hezbollah's rocket and missile fire. It would not have time to rely on the air force to bomb enemy targets; it would need to conquer territory. The only way to do that would be with boots on the ground—and lots of them.

At the forward base, a number of tents were pitched next to armored personnel carriers. Inside, one of the brigades had established its war room. Large plasma screens showed a satellite map of the exact locations of friendly and enemy forces. Officers from Aman, the air force, the navy and other branches of the IDF sat around tables discussing planned strikes and attack modes.

It was the exact opposite of the way the IDF waged war the previous summer. Then, different branches didn't even talk to one another, let alone share a tent. The "Ashkenazi Way"—as it was being called throughout the military—was already having its effect.

Four months earlier, in February, Ashkenazi had returned to uniform and found a military still traumatized from the war that had ended in a fragile cease-fire the previous summer. Hezbollah finished the war battered but strong simply by the fact that it survived. In the year that had passed, Hezbollah had already restored most of its capabilities. Its rocket arsenal was almost double what it had been on the eve of the 2006 war and its guerrillas were undergoing new training under Iranian and Syrian instructors.

Peretz gave Ashkenazi a simple-to-articulate but complicated-to-achieve assignment: restore the IDF's confidence, prepare the military for a future war and boost Israel's deterrence. If there was anyone built for the task, it was believed to be Ashkenazi.

While Halutz had come to the top job from the air force, Ashkenazi was a regular infantry grunt. He was drafted in 1972 into the tough Golani Brigade, one of the IDF's elite infantry units known for its frontline battles in Israel's consecutive wars with its Arab neighbors.

The two couldn't have been more different. Typical of the stereotype about Israeli pilots, Halutz was perceived by the public and his subordinates as being aloof. In one of his first statements to the press during the Lebanon war, for example, he refused to take off his aviator sunglasses even though he was speaking on live television.

Ashkenazi never wore sunglasses. He cultivated an image as a simple officer, down to earth, connected to the regular soldiers, someone who understood the battlefield from the ground, not the clouds. Where Halutz frequently met and spoke to the press, Ashkenazi shied away. He stayed focused on ensuring that Israel would win the next war.

For Ashkenazi, the military was a way of life. At the age of 13 he had already decided to become a career soldier, attending a military academy for high school.

Memories of his Holocaust survivor father carrying an old Czech rifle while guarding the family's farm from Arab infiltrators, combined with the stories his mother told of how she escaped her birthplace in Syria and covertly crossed the border into Israel, were always in the back of his mind. When he graduated the academy, he was given the opportunity to choose where he would serve. It was a no brainer—Ashkenazi wanted Golani.

There wasn't a position he didn't hold in the brigade. Ashkenazi participated in Israel's rescue operation to save Air France hostages from Entebbe, Uganda; he got injured during an operation in Lebanon in the late 1970s; and he watched his closest friend get killed during the First Lebanon War in 1982.

Ashkenazi's appointment carried a message: the IDF was going back to basics. A tough infantry veteran, Ashkenazi believed in victory through direct contact with the enemy while utilizing strong and mobile ground forces who knew how to work together to achieve one single goal: conquer enemy territory.

After taking up the post, Ashkenazi started making changes immediately. He worked around the clock. Most nights he simply slept in his office. If he made it home, it was for a quick break and then back to work.

Ashkenazi's version of weapons development and procurement included better armor, advanced command-and-control systems and improved firepower for troops on the ground. What had happened in Lebanon in the summer of 2006 could not be allowed to happen again.

At the Shizafon exercise, Ashkenazi sat at a table hunched over a pile of maps. Every couple of minutes he lifted binoculars strapped around his neck to his eyes. Images from miles away came into sharp focus as he zoomed in on the soldiers waging war in the field below.

"The IDF is preparing for an escalation on both the Palestinian and the northern fronts," he said, as he watched the tanks cross over makeshift bridges to invade the mock Syrian village. "The display seen here today is quite impressive. Only one element is lacking—a real enemy."

Even before the Winograd Commission—established by the government to investigate the Second Lebanon War—had presented its findings, the IDF was in the throes of a self-imposed rehabilitation. Until the war, the IDF had basically operated under the assumption that Hezbollah could be contained and that if something happened, it could be dealt with by the air force or small groups of special forces.

The prevalent assessment in Israel at the time was that the era of conventional wars was over. The days when two nations of similar strength lined up their tanks on two sides of a battlefield in a place like the Golan Heights were not coming back. Since the Yom Kippur War of 1973, all of Israel's conflicts had been asymmetrical, whether in the West Bank or the Gaza Strip. Even the war against Hezbollah was unbalanced. Israel had tanks, artillery batteries and F-16s. Hezbollah had guerrilla fighters who were experts at hiding in forests and firing short-range Katyusha rockets.

Syria was not believed to be a serious threat. While the countries were technically still in a state of war, the border along the Golan Heights was Israel's quietest. Yes, Israel had peace with Jordan and Egypt but both of those borders were constantly busy due to terror and criminal infiltrations. In Syria, there was almost nothing. IDF officers would often joke how the border with the most potent enemy was Israel's calmest.

As a result, starting in the early 2000s, training for conventional wars was canceled. Tank personnel were otherwise preoccupied guarding bases and manning checkpoints throughout the West Bank and participating in operations to stem the Palestinian Second Intifada. The IDF had retaken some of the Palestinian cities it had vacated a few years earlier under the Oslo Accords and the operations were constant.

The military was focused on late-night raids into the West Bank to apprehend suicide bombers, and soldiers were being trained almost exclusively for urban warfare. Battalion-level operations—let alone of a brigade or a division—were unheard of.

And then there were the reserve units, what Israel's founding father David Ben-Gurion had referred to as the backbone of the IDF. They were barely called up and if they were, it was to do guard duty or border patrol. When the Second Lebanon War erupted in 2006, reservists admitted they hadn't been inside their tanks in years.

This approach came with budgetary implications. The Ground Forces Command's budget was slashed by 25 percent while the air force continued to grow. Decisive airstrikes were the new answer to almost every challenge that Israel saw looming on the horizon.

For Ashkenazi this sophisticated talk was nonsense. Victory for him was far simpler to define. "It is when, after the war, no one needs to ask who won," he would often tell his men.

One of the problems brought up during the postwar inquiries was the lack of coordination between the IDF's various branches—the infantry corps and the armored corps, and of course with the air force. Maps that soldiers went into battle with were outdated and did not match the electronic ones loaded into Israeli F-15 or F-16 cockpits. This meant that ground forces couldn't even rely on air support if they encountered resistance, for the simple reason that there was no real way to explain to pilots where they were located and where the enemy was.

On August 14, 2006, when the cease-fire went into effect after a monthlong war with Hezbollah, it wasn't only the fighting that ended. So did Halutz's doctrine that overly relied on the air force. The IDF embarked on a process of going back to basics, retraining its ground forces and preparing for the next war that everyone feared could break out as soon as the following summer.

A few months later, IDF surveillance teams began spotting Hezbollah guerrillas back along the border, although this time dressed in civilian clothing and driving Land Rover jeeps and Mercedes sedans. On rare occasions, IDF cameras caught a familiar face. Military Intelligence officers then ran the pictures through databases of known Hezbollah operatives and commanders stored on IDF computers.

Clearly, Hezbollah was still there but something had changed. Due to the increased presence of UN peacekeepers in southern Lebanon, Hezbollah could no longer base itself inside the "nature preserves"—a name the IDF gave for the guerrilla positions the Iranian-backed group had built in forests—where it had stored its missiles and rockets ahead of the summer of 2006. It quickly adapted and instead settled inside the villages themselves, setting up command posts and rocket launchers in schools, homes and hospitals.

The assessment within Israel was that in a new war with Hezbollah the IDF would face the same challenges it had in 2006, although they would be more significant. Hezbollah, in 2006, fired an average of 150 rockets a day. By 2007, the assessment was that in a future conflict the number would likely be double and possibly even triple. The same was believed to apply to the number of advanced anti-tank missiles that Hezbollah would fire at IDF tanks in a future war. And then there were reports of Hezbollah efforts to get its hands on advanced anti-aircraft systems, which it planned to use to try and undermine the IAF's ability to fly freely over Lebanon.

And finally, the IDF believed that war with Hezbollah would not be isolated to Lebanon but would likely also include Syria, leading the military to coin the phrase "war on two borders but one front."

Ashkenazi sent every unit back to training. Reservists were called up to hold down the line in the West Bank while the standing army was sent to the field to train. For some soldiers it was the first time they had participated in a large-scale exercise in their entire service. For others, it had been years.

Meanwhile, the IDF's different branches had to learn how to work together. One day, for example, Ashkenazi visited a Paratroopers Brigade drill in southern Israel. As he stood on a hill watching the soldiers below, a group of pilots came over to introduce themselves to the chief of staff. As they were talking, a large explosion went off somewhere in the distance.

"What was that?" one of the pilots asked. Ashkenazi rolled his eyes. "That's what we call a 155-milimeter artillery shell," the chief of staff snapped at the pilot. Getting the military to the place it needed to be, Ashkenazi knew, was going to be a long process.

The rehabilitation of the IDF wasn't just in training. Immediately after the war, the government approved about $500 million in aid for the sole purpose of replenishing supplies for reservists and purchasing new equipment like bulletproof vests, lightweight helmets and kits for carrying ammunition and other supplies.

The reservists who had finished the war with little faith in the military were invited to their bases and shown the new kits filled with brand-new equipment—night-vision goggles, assault rifles and ammo—all with name tags on them. They were finally getting what they needed.

Additionally, Ashkenazi oversaw a rewrite and update of all IDF operational commands. Soldiers needed to know what was expected of them and what would happen if war broke out on a specific front. Orders needed to be simplified and clarified. There was no more room for sophisticated but unclear military jargon.

Budgets were also redistributed with an emphasis on upgrading the ground forces. The Armored Corps ordered hundreds of Trophy active protection systems for its Merkava tanks. Developed by an Israeli defense company, the Trophy creates a hemispheric protected zone around armored vehicles by detecting and intercepting rocket-propelled grenades or anti-tank missiles.

In addition, the IDF fast-tracked the installation of Tzayad, a revolutionary command-and-control system. Hebrew for "hunter," Tzayad works like a GPS navigation system in a car, but in this case displays the exact location of all forces in the area, while differentiating between friendly and enemy forces. If a soldier spots an enemy position, all he has to do is tap the location on the digital map and it will appear, immediately, on the screens of all other Tzayad users. This dramatically shortens the time it takes to find the enemy and lay down fire.

All the changes had one common goal: war was coming and Israel needed to be ready.

When Yadlin came to present the new intelligence revelations on Syria to Ashkenazi in March, the chief of staff was shocked. In his wildest dreams he wouldn't have imagined that Syria—a country he knew well from his term as head of the Northern Command—was building a nuclear reactor. His most immediate threat at the time was the Gaza Strip, where, almost daily, Hamas was firing rockets into Israel. These were the days before Iron Dome, meaning Israel had no way to defend itself and every rocket had the potential to turn into a strategic nightmare.

Even then, Ashkenazi knew that Israel would not be able to tolerate a nuclear Syria and would likely need to destroy the reactor. But, it also needed to do everything possible to avoid war, which meant that the army needed to be quiet and discreet. Nothing about the mission could get out.

The problem was that Syria was not Hezbollah. It was a far more serious and potent adversary. Syria was a country with a full-fledged conventional military. It had armor divisions, elite infantry forces and an old but still capable air force. It also had hundreds of Scud missiles capable of paralyzing Israeli cities and airfields. While Israel's Arrow missile system was operational, it had not yet been battle-tested; and anyhow, in the first few days of a war, Ashkenazi knew that it would be virtually impossible to stop all of the missiles that would rain down on Israel.

But even before considering how Israel would defeat Syria in a future war, Ashkenazi had to explain why the IDF was suddenly preparing for a war with Syria, a country that it had barely had an exchange of fire with—let alone a full-fledged war—in 25 years. He also needed to find an excuse for why the IDF would again be training in the Golan Heights, something it hadn't done in years.

It was one thing to hype up a threat for the public, but it was another to have to explain to military commanders why their training regimens were suddenly being changed and the war scenarios they were used to practicing were being modified. This was made even more complicated by the fact that almost no one in the IDF knew what was really happening. Even in the Northern Command, which would lead a future war against Syria, only the commander and his top intelligence officer knew the truth.

Commanders needed to be prepared. They needed to know where they would cross the border, what their initial targets would be and what type of resistance they should expect. Obviously, the air force would play a prominent role in trying to neutralize Syria's missile capability, but the ground forces would be needed to take over territory and they would have to move fast.

Ashkenazi and Yadlin convened a series of top-secret discussions to brainstorm. In the end, they came up with a strategy summarized by one word: "miscalculation."

The idea went something like this: Syria had closely followed the Second Lebanon War and was impressed by Hezbollah's effective use of rockets and guerrilla tactics, which at times seemed to undermine Israel's conventional but powerful and technologically advanced military. It too was now contemplating taking on the IDF.

As a result, the IDF spread stories of how the Syrians were investing in new guerrilla tactics, were expanding their commando units, were purchasing motorbikes for anti-tank squads and were building ghost towns along the border that could be used as death traps in the event that the IDF tried to maneuver into Syrian territory. Some of these stories were based on reality. Others were hyped up to help shape the narrative.

At the time, Syria had a massive military made up of 12 divisions totaling close to 400,000 soldiers at full mobilization, compared to just over 200,000 active personnel in Israel. One of the Syrian divisions consisted of some 10,000 elite commandos, a formidable force that would serve as the first line in an offensive against the IDF.

Aman used these stories to warn of the possibility of a "miscalculation," a small border incident between Syria and Israel that could quickly escalate, due to a misunderstanding between troops on both sides, into a full-blown war.

The misunderstanding could happen in a number of ways. A terror attack could take place along the Lebanese border, Hezbollah would renew rocket fire, and, in response, the IDF would bomb southern Lebanon and hit a target near the Syrian border. The Syrians would view the attack as an excuse to open a second front and invade the Golan Heights. From there the path to war would be pretty simple.

There was also the possibility that Syria would launch its

own terror attack along the border with Israel. The IDF would likely respond, one thing would lead to another and in this case, as well, a full-fledged war could follow.

Particularly concerning for Israel was the increase in Syrian missile production. The facts were stark. In 2006, Syria had perhaps 500 missiles capable of hitting Tel Aviv. By 2007, Syria's arsenal of long-range missiles had doubled. By 2010, it would jump again, to an estimated 2,300 missiles.

As the weeks went by, Ashkenazi began to see the fruits of his labor. One summer day he was up in the Golan Heights watching the Paratroopers Brigade complete a weeklong exercise that included two days of hiking, during which the soldiers went without sleep and carried loads sometimes close to twice their own weight.

Ashkenazi joined the soldiers as they made their final ascent of one of the Golan's steepest hills, mimicking the assault on an enemy base. Most of the soldiers didn't recognize the older man running alongside them. When they reached the top, Ashkenazi turned to one of the soldiers and asked him what it felt like to have completed the drill. "I feel that I now have confidence," the soldier replied. "Like I can accomplish what I need to get done."

The possibility of war with Syria was a fairly easy sale to the public. Everybody in Israel believed that after the Second Lebanon War it was better to be safe than sorry.

"An army is always in one of two states of mind," Ashkenazi would often tell his soldiers. "Either it is fighting or it is training so it will be ready for the next fight to come."

• • •

Miscalculations had almost led to war once before. In 1996, Yehuda Gil, an admired veteran Mossad operative, had fabricated intelligence reports alleging that Syrian president Hafez Assad was planning to attack Israel.

Gil was a master spy and legendary Mossad case officer. Born in Libya in the 1930s, Gil spoke fluent Spanish, Italian, French and Arabic. He immigrated to Israel just months after the country was established in 1948. In 1970, he joined the Mossad and became a "Katsa," the Hebrew acronym the spy agency uses for case officers.

Gil's personality and language skills made him a top recruiter of agents. He could switch easily between identities and was one of the Mossad's most skilled operatives. Some called him the "man with a thousand faces."[1]

He traveled frequently and was one of a handful of spies sent by the agency to "target countries," Mossad lingo for hostile Arab states. At the end of 1973, shortly after the bloody Yom Kippur War, Gil was given a new target, a Syrian general who was stationed in Europe and whom Israel thought could be turned against his country. His code name was "Red Falcon."

Gil met the general a number of times but failed to recruit him as an Israeli agent or informant. Nevertheless, and to avoid admitting failure, he told his superiors that he succeeded in turning the general. He then began fabricating intelligence and wrote fake reports based on information purported to have come from the Syrian mole.

In the summer of 1996, the IDF detected strange but significant Syrian troop movements. A division of Syrian commandos, the IDF learned, was planning to move from Lebanon to just below the Syrian side of Mount Hermon, not far from the border with Israel.

The IDF asked the Mossad to have Gil contact Red Falcon to get a clearer picture of what the deployment meant. Both men had retired from their respective services but Gil had actually kept in touch with the general, who was still plugged in to the Syrian leadership. Within a few days, he returned from a meeting with the general and claimed that Syria was preparing for an assault on the Golan Heights.

Panic broke out within the top echelons of the defense establishment. The Security Cabinet convened immediately to decide what to do. One of the first steps considered was to call up the reserves. It was a tricky call. A draft on that scale would easily be detected by the Syrians and could itself lead to a war neither side intended or wanted. So instead, the cabinet decided to play it safe and ordered the IDF to discreetly bolster border defenses and make the necessary preparations to call up the reserves when and if a decision to do so was made.

While war was ultimately averted—Gil was caught in his lies and admitted under interrogation to having passed on false information to the Mossad for over 20 years—senior officers in the IDF were quietly retelling the Red Falcon story in the summer of 2007 to describe the tension along Israel's northern border and why they believed a miscalculation could lead to war.

This time, though, war was not being instigated by a rogue Mossad agent. If it happened, it would be the result of the government's own actions.

What helped the IDF's spin was Assad himself, who kept sending mixed messages to Israel and the world. On the one hand, after the war in Lebanon, he spoke about freeing the Golan Heights by force, and then a month later called on Israel to sit down and negotiate peace. He placed his military on high alert and embarked on the largest-ever weapons shopping spree in Syrian history but, at the same time, claimed that it was actually Israel that was planning to attack his country.

For those who knew about the reactor, there was concern that Assad really was planning to attack. Not only did he have the chutzpah to build a nuclear reactor and try to pursue a nuclear weapon, but he also thought that he could take on the IDF.

Adding to the concern was Assad's decision to remove his father's old cabinet members and replace them with new advisers whom Israel perceived as more radical, like his brother-in-law, Assef Shawkat, a notorious Syrian intelligence chief who within a few years would be promoted to deputy chief of staff. All of the moderates who had served his father had disappeared: Farouk al-Sharaa had been removed from the Foreign Ministry and Abdul Halim Khaddam, the former vice president, was sent into exile in Europe. Some Israeli intelligence officials genuinely thought that Assad was preparing for war.

Even though the IDF was actively pushing these stories to get the military prepared, in Israel people had difficulty believing that Syria would really launch an attack without a clear provocation. The discrepancy in strength between the two countries was too obvious. Yes, Syria had a significant number of tanks and infantry soldiers but the IDF was believed to be better trained and to have more advanced weaponry. Syria's air force was outdated. It was incomparable to the IAF.

That's how the IDF came up with the "Opportunist Approach."

According to this theory, Syria lacked the military capability to defeat the IDF on the battlefield and conquer significant territory. Nevertheless, it could potentially use its commando forces to quickly and covertly sneak into Israel and capture a small kibbutz or moshav along the border even though it wouldn't be able to do real damage. The objective, these officers warned, would be to plant a Syrian flag inside Israel and thus raise awareness of the Israeli occupation of the Golan and to transmit a message of strength to the world.

Olmert oversaw all of the preparations from above. He was nervous about the possibility of war but he also didn't want to give Syria a reason to believe Israel knew about the reactor.

"If we aren't careful, the Syrians will know that we know and think that there actually is going to be a war and then they will try to preempt it," the prime minister said.

Before there could be war, Israel first needed to desperately replenish its armory, which was drained during the Second Lebanon War. This meant making weapons orders as well as getting local companies—like Israel Military Industries—to keep their tank and artillery shell assembly lines open seven days a week.

During the last war, the IDF had fired over 200,000 artillery shells into Lebanon with little effect. It needed a new supply alongside anti-tank missiles, mortar shells and grenade rounds. The home front also needed to get ready since civilians could quickly find themselves once again sitting in bomb shelters for extended periods of time.

Most critical was restocking the IAF's supply of JDAMs, kits that turn regular bombs into precision-guided weapons. Once the bomb is launched, a satellite guides it to its target, enabling the pilots to quickly leave enemy territory.

During the first five days of the Lebanon war, the IAF depleted a large percentage of its JDAM inventory, prompting the US to expedite—in the middle of the war—a delivery of JDAMs as well as Hellfire anti-armor missiles for Israel's fleet of Cobra and Apache attack helicopters. In one case, when the IAF bombed the Dahieh—Hezbollah's stronghold in Beirut—it dropped over 500 precision-guided munitions in just one aerial raid. Overall, precision-guided munitions were used in almost half of all combat sorties during the war.

What this meant was that if a new war broke out, Israel would quickly find itself out of smart bombs. It needed them fast.

That is why just months after the war in Lebanon—even before the discovery of the Syrian reactor—the IDF started to place new orders for JDAMs from the US government. One order came out to over $100 million worth of JDAMs, the largest weapons sale to Israel since the war had ended.

"There is no way for us to know for certain if war will break out," Defense Minister Ehud Barak told his staff one day. "All we can do is be as best prepared as possible."

As he had told the cabinet, Ashkenazi genuinely believed that there was a 50 percent chance—and possibly more—that war would erupt after Israel attacked the reactor. Following the last war in Lebanon, Hezbollah and Syria had dramatically tightened their cooperation and coordination. A war with one would almost definitely mean a war with the other.

As the clock ticked down toward the airstrike, Ashkenazi knew he had done all he could to prepare his country for war. What would happen next was out of his hands.

9

WHAT'S NEXT?

Back in the Bor, all eyes turned to Yadlin. The Israeli planes had bombed the reactor and were making their way back to their bases. Now, the waiting game began.

The air in the Bor was tense.

But Yadlin was confident that his men, who had come up with the "deniability zone," were right. Assad would let this slide just like he had done after other Israeli aerial incursions over the years. If he decided to go to war, he would have to explain why to his people. Why, in response to a mysterious bombing in the early hours of September 6, had he decided to drag his country into a massive war with Israel, the largest since the Yom Kippur War in 1973?

With an already failing economy, Syrians would wonder why their country was being dragged into a war they were almost certain to lose. What good would come of it? When the Syrian people later learned that Assad had been secretly building a nuclear reactor—at the cost of hundreds of millions of dollars, if not billions—they might turn on him. Why was he wasting the country's money on nuclear reactors at a time when his own people didn't have enough to eat?

On the other hand, the Aman analysts knew that there was nothing quite like a war to unite a fragmented and disgruntled people behind their leader. If Assad decided to retaliate and spark a war with Israel, he would run the risk of defeat but he would have a compelling argument to make to his people. I tried building a capability that would have turned Syria into a world superpower, he would have been able to say. The Zionists took it away from us and therefore I went to war.

But then there was the fact that besides a few officials from Assad's innermost circle, almost no one in the Syrian government knew about the existence of the reactor.

As a result, the IDF's Northern Command was on standby. If war broke out, the infantry and armored brigades deployed along the border would have to hold the front line until backup could arrive.

The pilots who had flown the mission to bomb the reactor were told before takeoff to expect to land, refuel, rearm and then take off again into a warzone. No one knew what Assad would ultimately do.

Ashkenazi was prepared for a wide-range of scenarios. Hours before the strike, he gathered all of the General Staff and briefed his generals on what was about to happen. Some of the officers already knew about the reactor but most didn't.

What would Israel do, for example, if Assad fired just a few short-range rockets at IDF bases in the Golan Heights? Would it need to retaliate? Or, how would the country respond if Assad fired long-range Scud missiles into open areas near Tel Aviv? One thing was for certain: if Assad launched a massive attack, Israel would respond like never before and Syria would never look the same.

Israel's response would have to be something like the opening salvo to the Six Day War all over again. Then, the Israeli Air Force surprised the Egyptian, Jordanian and Syrian air forces and destroyed over 450 of their aircraft in a matter of hours. Israel could not afford another war with an unclear ending like the one against Hezbollah the previous summer.

In the days before the bombing, Olmert considered the idea of transmitting a covert message to Assad immediately after the attack. The purpose would be to tell Syria that while Israel had destroyed the reactor it was not planning any additional operations. "If you stay quiet, we will also stay quiet," the message would have said.

There were several theoretical options for how to do this. The message could have been passed through the United Nations, which had forces stationed along the Israeli-Syrian border since 1974, or via Turkey, which had an active embassy in Damascus. There was also a third option, one that was a bit more complicated but had been tested and could also potentially work.

In July, two Jewish Canadian businessmen with strong ties to Israel and the Likud Party had traveled to Damascus to meet with Assad, reportedly with Olmert and Dagan's blessings. Israel wanted to get a sense of Assad's mood ahead of the strike and, at the same time, establish a channel of communication that, if needed, could be used as the situation progressed.

The businessmen flew to Syria from Israel via a neighboring country, then spent a couple of days on the ground, including an almost-three-hour meeting with Assad, which focused mostly on ways to renew peace talks with the Jewish state.

During the meeting, Assad asked the businessmen what food Olmert liked eating. "Hummus," they answered. The next day, a courier brought a box of hummus to their hotel room. The businessmen flew back to Israel and went to see Olmert to update him on their talk with Assad. They brought the hummus with them for everyone to enjoy.[1]

In the end, Olmert decided not to contact Assad. There was no need, he felt, to help the Syrian president piece together what had just happened.

In the Bor, Yadlin was getting regular updates from his men. Assad had apparently put his mobile missile systems on high alert but decided not to fire them, a decision that Olmert would later comment "took discipline."[2]

Within a few hours, Yadlin had confirmation that Aman's "deniability zone" had worked. Syrian activity was not out of the ordinary. Troops were not being mobilized, the air force was not being scrambled and the Syrian Scuds were not being loaded onto launchers. Someone, it seemed, had woken up the Syrian president in the middle of the night to tell him that his prized possession had been destroyed but he went right back to sleep. War was not going to break out that morning.

Later that day, Israel received further confirmation that its gamble had worked. Assad was making up stories to cover up what had happened. At around noon, the Syrian news agency, SANA, released a short and laconic statement claiming that its air defense systems had chased away Israeli warplanes the night before. "Air-defense units confronted them and forced them to leave after they dropped some ammunition in deserted areas without causing any human or material damage," the statement read.[3]

A Reuters report quoted a Western diplomat based in Damascus saying that the Israeli planes had been on a reconnaissance mission but had been caught by Syrian air defense systems and had to drop their bombs and extra fuel tanks to escape.

Yadlin finally relaxed. Assad seemed to be comfortably within his deniability zone.

After receiving an update from his military aide, Olmert asked his staff to immediately connect him to President Bush. By this time, he was back in the Prime Minister's Office in Jerusalem. His staff called the White House Situation Room and was told that the president wasn't near a secure line. "Call back in an hour," the Americans said.

A week earlier, as the attack date drew near, Olmert used a random excuse to call Bush and ask him where he'd be next week. "I might need to speak to you," Olmert said. Bush, who was familiar with the plan and the countdown to the strike, had an idea what Olmert was referring to and told the prime minister that he would be in Australia for a meeting of APEC, the Asia-Pacific Economic Cooperation. If you need me, Bush said, I'll make sure to be available.

After an hour, the White House called back. Even though they were on a secure line, Olmert was still concerned there might be people near the president who could hear what he said and potentially compromise Israel, which needed to maintain complete silence about the strike.

"Mr. President, how are you?" Olmert asked. "Fine," Bush said.

"How are you enjoying Australia?" Olmert continued. "It's a great country. Sydney, it's very nice."

"Yes," Bush said, with a slight rise of agitation in his voice. Olmert figured that the president was wondering why the Israeli prime minister was wasting his time calling him to talk about sightseeing Down Under.

"By the way, Mr. President, remember there was something in the north that we didn't like?" Olmert asked.

"Yes," Bush said.

"I just wanted to let you know that it does not exist anymore," Olmert said.

Bush was careful. "Oh, that is very interesting," he said. "Do you expect any response or have a feeling about a possible response?"

Olmert replied, "No. For the time being, it seems that all indications are that there will be no response." Olmert thought that would be the end of the conversation but then Bush said something that took the prime minister completely by surprise.

"Okay," Bush said. "I just want you to know that if there

will be a response, you can count on all of America being behind you."

Olmert shook with emotion. It was a statement he would never forget, one that gave him confidence and assurance that he had made the right decision.

With a huge smile on his face and Bush clearly on his side, Olmert put down the receiver and turned to his staff. "Now, I can go and rest."

A few days later, Bush called again. He was back in the Oval Office and this time he was ecstatic. "Ehud, my buddy!" he yelled into the phone. In Australia he had to be reserved, he said, but what Israel had done was the right move—it had successfully eliminated a threat it viewed to be of an existential nature.

In the meantime, back on September 6, Foreign Minister Tzipi Livni was bombarded with phone calls from her foreign counterparts. Russian foreign minister Sergey Lavrov called, as did Javier Solana, the European Union representative for foreign affairs. She read each of them a version of the vague text her staff had prepared before the bombing and promised to update as more information became available.

With the attack over, the order was given to activate the "Premier League," the code name for the countries Olmert and the cabinet had pre-approved to be updated about the strike and what Israel had taken out. The Mossad had stored top-secret dossiers, including the original pictures of the reactor, in Israeli embassies in Berlin, Moscow and Paris. It was time to send them out.

Special emissaries were dispatched to each country. Olmert's chief of staff, Turbowicz, was sent to Paris where he met President Nicolas Sarkozy and briefed him on what had happened.

Olmert went on with business as usual. The night after the bombing he attended a Kadima Party event in honor of Rosh Hashanah, the upcoming Jewish New Year. All of the press was there, hoping to learn something about the mysterious bombing, but Olmert disappointed them all. He didn't say a word. In Israel, it was as if nothing had happened.

But even with the success, there were some glitches. Two days after the strike, the Turkish press published pictures of fuel tanks it said the Israeli fighter jets had jettisoned after the bombing, likely as they hit their boosters to return home. The fuel tanks had landed in an open field on the Turkish side of the border. Ankara was furious that its airspace had been violated by Israel.

The Turkish chief of staff, General Yasar Buyukanit, called Ashkenazi to get an explanation but Ashkenazi avoided taking the call. He simply didn't know what to say. A day later, Turkish prime minister Recep Tayyip Erdogan called Olmert. He was furious. "How come my chief of staff is calling your chief of staff and he is not answering the phone?" Erdogan asked, adding some words about the violation of sovereignty.

Olmert played it stupid. "Mr. Prime Minister, I am not familiar with this, but I can imagine that they were training and that the planes lost direction and that in order to help themselves, the pilots had to throw the tanks," Olmert said.

Erdogan pushed back. This was before he turned into one

of Israel's most virulent critics. He told Olmert that he
needed an official and public apology that he could use to save
face, at least in the eyes of his people. The two agreed to meet
in a couple of weeks in London.

In the meantime, Ashkenazi received permission to update
his Turkish counterpart. In 2007, the IDF and the Turkish
military were the closest of allies. Ashkenazi placed the call to
Ankara and admitted to Buyukanit that Israel had been behind
the bombing. "It was us and it was a nuclear reactor," he told
his Turkish counterpart. "I am trusting that you will keep this
information to yourself."

Another problem Olmert faced was surprisingly from back
home and from none other than a former Israeli prime minister. While Olmert and his ministers were maintaining a strict
policy of silence, some politicians couldn't help themselves. On
September 19, less than two weeks after the attack, Netanyahu,
the former prime minister and current head of the opposition,
went on the evening news.

"I was a partner to the operation from the beginning," Netanyahu said about the bombing that no one even knew had
been carried out by Israel. He then confirmed that he had already personally congratulated Olmert. Even though he was
head of the opposition, Netanyahu said: "When a prime minister does something that I think is important and necessary, I
give my support," he said.

Olmert was furious but knew better than to respond. Even
if minimal, there was still a chance that Assad would try something. Israel needed to stick to its policy of silence.

A month later, on October 14, Eric Edelman, the US under

secretary of defense and a member of the Drafting Group, was dispatched to Turkey. He was on a visit to Moscow to talk about Iran but Bush had called and asked him to head to Ankara. Edelman had formerly served as ambassador to Turkey and the president hoped he would be able to ease concern there about a resolution moving through Congress to recognize the 1915–23 Armenian genocide, something vehemently opposed by the Turks.

During his meetings, though, all the Turks wanted to talk about was the recent Israeli airstrike. Edelman met with the deputy chief of staff and deputy defense minister, who quizzed him on what he knew about the mysterious operation.

It was one of the more awkward conversations Edelman had to conduct in his career as a US diplomat. Even though he had been in the know since the beginning, he was under direct orders—like all other Drafting Group members—to remain silent.

"We've been asked not to comment on this but you should ask your Israeli counterparts," Edelman told them. "I think when you understand all the facts, which I'm not really at liberty to discuss, you will understand that this is a matter of common concern to all of us and that even if there was a violation of Turkish airspace, it was in a good cause."

A few days later, Turkey finally got its official explanation when Olmert flew to London to meet with Erdogan on October 23. He showed the Turkish leader the dossier and briefed him on the reactor. Erdogan said he understood why Israel had needed to act but asked Olmert to issue a public apology for violating Turkey's airspace.

A few days later, at the regular Sunday cabinet meeting, Olmert took advantage of the presence of news teams in the room and spoke to the cameras. "In my conversation with the Turkish prime minister, I told him that if Israeli planes indeed penetrated Turkish airspace, then there was no intention thereby, either in advance or in any case, to—in any way—violate or undermine Turkish sovereignty, which we respect," Olmert said, adding that he had expressed Israel's apology to the Turkish government and to the Turkish people for any violation that may have occurred.

Olmert then had his staff make a DVD of the on-camera statement, which he immediately sent by courier to Ankara. Later that evening he received a phone call from Erdogan, who said that now Israeli-Turkish ties were back to normal.

What Olmert didn't tell the public was the other message he had conveyed to Erdogan, one he asked the Turkish prime minister to be sure to pass on to Assad. "Tell Assad," Olmert said, "that the next time something of this nature will happen in Syria, the post-strike picture will not be of the reactor but of his palace."

A few days later, he dispatched Yadlin to Ankara to give General Buyukanit a more detailed briefing. The Turks put up a façade of anger but after they saw the evidence, they too let out a sigh of relief. Israel, they understood, had saved them from a regional Armageddon.

Olmert also personally visited Russia. A few days before his meeting with Erdogan in London, Bush called Olmert and told him that Rice and Gates were in Moscow for meetings with President Vladimir Putin. The two were there to try and defuse growing tension over a NATO plan to deploy missile defense systems in Poland and the Czech Republic.

Bush asked Olmert if it was okay for Rice and Gates to update Putin on the reactor. Olmert pushed back. He wanted to be the one to speak with Putin about Syria, as well as about the Russian leader's personal relationship with Assad.[4]

While Bush respected Olmert's decision, the Israeli prime minister was still nervous that the topic would come up during Gates and Rice's visit. To prevent that from happening, Olmert called the Kremlin right after getting off the phone with Bush and told Putin that he needed to meet with him urgently.

"Come tomorrow," Putin replied. Olmert said that he would love to but that it would be impossible to arrange a flight and the necessary security detail in such a short timeframe. In that case, Putin said, the visit would have to wait a few more days since he was scheduled to fly to Iran the day after. The two agreed that the visit would take place once Putin had returned from Iran. Olmert, though, was not done. If he already had Putin on the phone on the eve of his meeting with Iran's Supreme Leader Ayatollah Ali Khamenei, there were other issues to discuss.

At the time, Israel was extremely concerned with Russia's growing relationship with Iran. Moscow seemed prepared to supply Iran with the vaunted S-300 surface-to-air missile system as well as fuel it needed to activate its nuclear reactor. The S-300 was the Israeli Air Force's nightmare. It is one of the most advanced multitarget anti-aircraft missile systems in the world, with the reported ability to track up to 100 targets simultaneously while engaging up to 12 at the same time.

The IAF was urging Olmert to do everything possible to stop the delivery of the S-300. If it arrived in Iran, officers warned at the time, it could severely undermine a future Israeli operation to destroy Iran's nuclear facilities. Other officials, including Olmert, were less concerned and claimed that if and when the S-300 was delivered to Iran, Israel would develop an electronic warfare system capable of neutralizing it. But he still had to try.

A state in possession of these kind of missiles, he told Putin, would feel like it is immune to international pressure and would become more aggressive toward other countries. In addition, Olmert said, while the nuclear fuel was designated for Iran's civilian nuclear reactor at Bushehr, its delivery would also boost the Islamic Republic's covert nuclear weapons program. Putin promised Olmert to give careful thought to both issues.

It turned out that Putin had taken Olmert's call from his dacha, just outside Moscow. Olmert had no way of knowing that Gates and Rice were already there and that, due to his call, Putin kept them waiting for about 20 minutes. The American press was oblivious to the phone call with Olmert and later reported that Putin's unpunctuality was a diplomatic slight aimed at insulting the Bush administration. When he finally came in and the press had left the room, Putin apologized and explained that he had been on the phone with Olmert, talking about Iran's nuclear program.

A few days later, on the eve of his trip to Moscow, Olmert received another phone call from Bush. "You succeeded with Putin," the president said. Olmert had no clue what the US president was talking about. Bush went on to explain that Putin had called to tell him that he would not be supplying Iran with the fuel or the S-300. Bush asked what had changed his mind and Putin answered simply: Olmert. He convinced me.

Olmert explained to Bush that Putin was misleading him. What actually happened, the Israeli prime minister said, was that Putin had succumbed to pressure from the US but couldn't admit to that being the case so he used Olmert as his excuse. It was a nice attempt by Olmert to score points with Bush but it didn't make a difference. The result was a positive one for Israel.

Days after the bombing, Olmert met with a group of Russian reporters at his residence in Jerusalem. Israel, he said, was interested in renewing peace talks with Syria. "We want to make peace . . . we are willing to make peace with Syria unconditionally and without demands," Olmert said, adding, "I have a lot of respect for the Syrian leader."[5]

What Olmert didn't reveal was that already before the bombing, back in April, he had spoken to Erdogan about having the Turkish leader serve as a mediator for peace talks between Jerusalem and Damascus. While Israel purposely stalled in starting the talks in the months leading up to the airstrike, Olmert felt that now was the time to get the ball rolling.

A few weeks later the talks kicked off in Ankara. The Israeli side sat in one hotel and the Syrian negotiators in another one not too far away. As a first step, the Turkish mediators shuffled between the suites in an attempt to see if there was even a basis for peace talks. It would take some time but by mid-2008, Israel and Syria felt confident enough to issue a joint press statement revealing the existence of the indirect negotiations.

Olmert's interest in the talks stemmed from a belief that peace with Syria could break up its alliance with Hezbollah and Iran, whose nuclear program was the primary threat Israel faced at the time. Further isolating the Islamic regime in Tehran, he thought, was a goal for which it was worth making concessions, even a potential withdrawal from the Golan Heights. According to members of his party, Olmert also thought a big diplomatic win like a deal with Syria would help him score some political points in the wake of the criminal investigations against him.

But even as the talks moved ahead, Olmert was not yet ready to stop his battle against Hezbollah and Assad. If anything, Israel's success in discovering and destroying the nuclear reactor had given the CIA and the Pentagon newfound appreciation and respect for Israel's intelligence and military capabilities. Whatever stain the Second Lebanon War had left on Israel's image, it now seemed to be gone.

The cooperation between the CIA and the Mossad on al-Kibar helped establish new lines of communication between the agencies, allowing for joint operations that in the past would not have been possible. One of them was about to be as big a blow to Hezbollah as the destruction of the nuclear reactor had been to Syria.

This time, the target was a man by the name of Imad Mughniyeh, Hezbollah's 45-year-old chief of operations and Iran's primary terror emissary in the Middle East. In his short life, Mughniyeh personified a nexus of terrorism and served as a link between Hezbollah, Iran, Syria, Hamas and Islamic Jihad. Israel and the US had been hunting him for decades.[6] He was on the FBI's most-wanted list with a $5 million reward on his head for his involvement in the 1983 bombings of the US embassy and Marine barracks in Beirut that killed over 300, as well as the 1985 hijacking of a TWA airliner. Israel wanted him for his direct involvement in the 1994 bombing of a Buenos Aires Jewish community center that killed 85, the bombing of the Israeli embassy in the city two years earlier that killed 29 people, and for masterminding the abduction of IDF reservists Eldad Regev and Ehud Goldwasser, which sparked the Second Lebanon War.

"He was very slippery," former Mossad chief Danny Yatom said. "He never gave interviews and there were only a few pictures of him . . . He had special capabilities—a satanic and creative mind and he never left tracks behind him. He was the mastermind of every major Hezbollah attack."

Born in 1962 in southern Lebanon, Mughniyeh joined Fatah as a teenager and quickly climbed the ranks, eventually becoming a member of Force 17, the terrorist group's elite force. One of Mughniyeh's first missions was to protect Abu Jihad, a Fatah operative whom Israeli commandos later assassinated in Tunis in 1988.

"It was unusual for the Palestinians to give such a senior position to a Shiite like Mughniyeh," said Brigadier General Shimon Shapira, one of the first Israeli intelligence officers to hear the name Mughniyeh. "This was a clear indication of Mughniyeh's skill, talent and looming greatness."

In 1982, after Yasser Arafat fled Lebanon, Mughniyeh

decided to leave Fatah. He did not remain unemployed for long. A few months later, Iran hired him as a bodyguard for Sheikh Fadlallah, the Shia community's spiritual leader.

Hezbollah was growing fast at the time and was gaining strength as a ruthless terrorist group. In 1983, it carried out one of its greatest attacks ever, against the American embassy and Marine barracks in Beirut. Two years later, Mughniyeh's name came up again, as one of the planners of the hijacking of a TWA airliner.

In 1994, Israel decided to try to strike back, but since the Mossad didn't know where Mughniyeh was, they had to lure him out into the open. To do that, Lebanese agents, reportedly working for Israel, detonated a 50-kilogram car bomb outside a store owned by his brother Fouad.[7]

Israel hoped that Mughniyeh would attend the funeral so they could assassinate him there, but the top Hezbollah terrorist sensed the trap and stayed away. Another attempt to capture him, this time by the Americans, was made in 1995 but it too failed.

After Israel's unilateral withdrawal from Lebanon in 2000, Mughniyeh traveled to Iran and offered to let the Revolutionary Guard Corps turn Lebanon into its forward base against Israel. Hezbollah, he told the Iranians, will be a sword on Israel's neck.

"This was when Iran decided to turn Hezbollah into a real strategic asset and began deploying thousands of missiles in Lebanon," Shapira said. "Mughniyeh was responsible for all of this."

After years of evading capture, he was killed on February 12, 2008, in a meticulously planned joint CIA-Mossad operation. Israel helped provide the initial intelligence on Mughniyeh's location but needed help from the CIA's infrastructure in Damascus—safe houses and spotters—to track him over a period of several months.[8] The operation was personally approved by Bush, who, following the discovery and successful strike against Syria's reactor, gained a better appreciation for Dagan and the Mossad.

Dagan flew to Langley and met with CIA director Michael Hayden. The plan they came up with was like out of a Hollywood movie. The Americans manufactured a special bomb that could be installed in the spare tire compartment on the back of Mughniyeh's Mitsubishi Pajero SUV.

The Mossad's Kidon Unit, an elite group of expert assassins, was tasked with the actual mission. Not much is known about this mysterious unit, which operates outside the Mossad's regular framework. Kidon means "spear" and unit members are taught to be stealthy, lethal and precise like a spear. It was Kidon that installed the bomb on Mughniyeh's SUV and pressed the detonator at the right time.

Mughniyeh's assassination was a major blow to Hezbollah operations. He was not only the commander of its military forces but also served as the group's liaison to the Iranians, the Syrians, Hamas and Islamic Jihad. Shortly before he was killed, he met with Qasem Soleimani, head of Iran's Quds Force, the Revolutionary Guards unit responsible for all of Iran's overseas activities.

The assassins' success in infiltrating Hezbollah's top echelons shocked Assad. Coming on the heels of the bombing of
the reactor, there was a clear message being sent: this shadow
war would continue as long as Iran, Syria and Hezbollah threatened Israel. No one and no thing was out of reach. If the
Mossad could get its hands on Mughniyeh in the heart of Damascus, they could get their hands on anyone.

Olmert was not yet done. Israel reportedly still had one more
score to settle in Syria.

It was August 2008 and, this time, the target was in the ancient Syrian city of Tartus, a coastal town perched on the sandy
shores of the Mediterranean. The former fiefdom of the County
of Tripoli, Tartus was the last of the Crusader states established
in the twelfth century immediately after the church's first attempt to conquer the Holy Land.

Tartus's strategic military significance was well known. In
the 1970s, the Soviet Union signed an agreement with Syria that
allowed it to establish a military port in the city and in 2017,
the agreement was updated to allow Russia to dredge and
deepen the port so even more ships, including nuclear-powered
submarines, could dock there.

But on this August weekend, Israel's sights were on al-Rimal
al-Zahabieh, also called Golden Sands and known as one of the
most luxurious and prestigious seaside resorts in Syria. Opened
in the 1980s, the resort sits on a stretch of about 30 kilometers
of sandy beaches, lined with private homes, apartment build-

ings, lounge chairs and sun umbrellas. During the summer season, some 20,000 people call the gated community home.

As on most summer nights, the waters were calm and a few yachts were anchored off the coast, not far from the home of Mohammed Suleiman, a Syrian general, who might have been barely known to the general Syrian public but was quite popular in CIA and Mossad headquarters. Suleiman was one of the closest men to Assad and was in charge of the Syrian president's "special projects." He oversaw the nuclear portfolio, including the construction of al-Kibar as well as keeping up Syrian support for Hezbollah in Lebanon and other terrorist proxies under Damascus's umbrella.

Suleiman was surrounded by bodyguards wherever he went—to the beach, the pool or the market. But this night, he was relaxing outside his home, sipping a cocktail on a lounge chair when two men, dressed in black wet suits, came out of the water and shot him at close range, riddling his body with bullets. Before the bodyguards could react, the men had disappeared back in the water like ghosts. They belonged to Flotilla 13, Israel's equivalent to the US Navy SEALs.[9]

Suleiman was not like Mughniyeh. He wasn't a terrorist working for a terror organization but was a general in a foreign—albeit—enemy military. The NSA would later catalog the assassination as the first known instance of Israel killing a legitimate foreign government official.[10]

It was a strange time for Israel to be carrying out an assassination against a senior Syrian official. Just months earlier, in May, Israel and Syria jointly announced that they were engaging in indirect peace talks in Ankara with Turkish mediation. This kind of operation ran the risk of derailing those reconciliation efforts. Despite the risks, it needed to be done. Suleiman presented a clear and immediate danger to the State of Israel.

Suleiman was not just any Syrian general. He was one of Assad's closest advisers. He had known the president for years, since he studied engineering at Damascus University with Assad's older brother, Bassel. Suleiman knew all of Assad's most intimate secrets. His office was located in the Presidential Palace, down the hall from the president, whom he reported to directly, bypassing the military's regular chain of command. He ran Assad's shadow army.

In 2007, the US Treasury identified Suleiman as a candidate for sanctions. In a diplomatic cable, Suleiman was referred to as a "Special Presidential Advisor for Arms Procurement and Strategic Weapons." In the end, the US embassy in Damascus wrote that Suleiman was a "low-payoff target" and wasn't really known by the Syrian people. As a result, the embassy staff said, imposing sanctions on him would have little domestic or regional impact. Instead, the Treasury Department decided to focus on people and issues ordinary Syrians cared about—corruption and the suppression of basic human rights.[11]

The assassination shocked Assad. He ordered his men to bury the body immediately. While the government officially remained silent, after a day, reports of the assassination started to leak out on Arab websites. The US embassy in Damascus reported back to Washington that, according to one of its sources, Suleiman's entire family had been killed. The source was wrong but it didn't make much of a difference. The government imposed a strict blackout on any news about the assassination.[12]

America's initial concern was focused on security. It feared that the Syrian government would accuse the US of involvement in the assassination and retaliate by launching staged protests outside American interests in Syria or even target US installations via terrorist proxies funded by the government.

Loss of the reactor as well as Mughniyeh's assassination were supposed to be isolated incidents. They clearly weren't. When authorities searched one of the homes owned by Suleiman near the Syrian-Lebanese border and discovered $80 million hidden in a bag in the basement, Assad became even more agitated, concerned that Suleiman had betrayed him. He immediately ordered an investigation to uncover how the general had gotten his hands on so much cash.[13]

In the meantime, Assad had to keep up appearances. He sent his younger brother Maher to attend the funeral while he himself left for a scheduled state visit to Tehran.

Back in Israel, Olmert understood that his political fate was sealed. Just days before Suleiman's assassination, Olmert held a press conference in Jerusalem and announced that he would be stepping down as Israel's prime minister. The police investigations that would ultimately send him to prison were closing in. He told the country that he needed to leave office to fight for his innocence. Someone else would need to continue leading Israel's shadow war against Iran, Syria and Hezbollah.

Olmert left office in March 2009 after general elections brought Benjamin Netanyahu back to power. It was the end of a tumultuous three years as prime minister that included a war in Lebanon, an operation in Gaza, the bombing of a nuclear reactor in Syria and multiple covert operations throughout the region.

Olmert would go down in history as the first Israeli prime minister to be sent to prison. But he would also be remembered as a man of action. When presented with a threat, Olmert never shied away from tough decisions.

10

CONCLUSION

T his is fake," said Kim Kye Gwan, a senior North Korean
diplomat and the regime's top nuclear negotiator. "It's Pho-
toShopped. All of it."

Kim was sitting across from Christopher Hill, an assistant
secretary of state and head of the US delegation to the Six Party
Talks. They were meeting in Beijing on the eve of another round
of nuclear negotiations with North Korea.

Israel's bombing of al-Kibar had taken place three weeks before and Hill had come to China with a top-secret dossier,
filled with the original photos the Mossad had obtained in the
operation that had set off the hunt for Syria's reactor. He pulled
the photos out one by one and showed them to Kim, who didn't
bat an eye.

But Hill saved the best for last. He took one last photo out,
of two men—one Syrian and one North Korean—standing
next to a Mazda sedan with a Syrian license plate in front of

the now destroyed reactor. The Syrian was Ibrahim Othman, head of Syria's Atomic Energy Commission. The other man, wearing the blue tracksuit, was Chon Chibu, one of the scientists in charge of the Yongbyon nuclear reactor.

"That would take a lot of PhotoShopping, don't you think?" Hill said to Kim without expecting a response. Hill wasn't even sure that Kim, who maintained a poker face throughout the interaction, knew about the Syrian project. But it didn't make a difference. After months of negotiations, Hill had learned that whatever he said around the negotiating table made its way back to the Supreme Leader in Pyongyang, and this time he wanted to make sure he was being heard.

"The point we were making was that you can't hide things from us because we find out about things," Hill explained years later.

A few weeks earlier, after finishing the phone call with Olmert during which he received an update about the successful strike, Bush had asked to see Hill in his Sydney hotel room. A veteran diplomat, Hill had joined the president in Australia to help ease the concerns of some of America's Asian allies. Hill had visited North Korea for the first time in June and, with the negotiations gaining momentum, he seemed on the verge of a major breakthrough. Pyongyang had expressed a willingness to open its nuclear facilities to international inspectors and looked like it might soon agree to dismantle its entire nuclear weapons program.

But then, the intelligence from Israel came in. While North Korea was negotiating with Hill, not only was it not dismantling its own nuclear program, it was proliferating weapons of mass destruction to another rogue country. This wasn't just a violation of trust within the Six Party Talks. It was a potential justification for an all-out war.

Bush updated Hill about his call with Olmert, telling him how the Syrian reactor had been bombed. "None of this can get out," Bush warned. Hill already knew about the existence of the reactor. He had been read in on the intelligence by Condoleezza Rice a few weeks earlier but, like the rest of the US officials in the know, he was sworn to secrecy. Now that the reactor was destroyed, Bush wanted Hill to bring it up with the North Koreans, if not in public, then at least at the next round of the Six Party Talks. He wanted to see how they would react.

Hill had spent hundreds of hours with the North Koreans and had gotten to know them quite well. He was aware of their military relationship with Iran and Syria but nuclear cooperation was supposed to be off limits. Nevertheless, when he learned about the reactor the North Koreans were building in Syria, he wasn't overly surprised. "They would sell their own grandmothers for the right price," Hill would tell people.

But after the dinner with Kim, the reactor wasn't mentioned again. The photos were put away. Hill embarrassed North Korea but not much more. There were other, seemingly more pressing issues that needed to be discussed.

Back in Washington, a debate was raging over the future of the negotiations with North Korea and whether America needed to pull out of the Six Party Talks, or at the very least extract a price from Pyongyang for what had happened in Syria, now a publicly known nuclear violation. It was similar to the debate that would take place in 2018 before Donald Trump's historic summit with Kim Jong Un: should America negotiate with Pyongyang without preconditions or should it expect concessions before proceeding?

Hill was of the opinion that what happened in Syria was the exact reason why the talks needed to continue. It didn't seem like North Korea was working with Syria due to an ideological kinship, he said, but rather out of pure financial gain. America, he argued, already knew that North Korea was a rogue and violent regime. The sale of a nuclear reactor to Syria and the assistance it provided in constructing it only reinforced what was already known. It also highlighted the urgency of the negotiations and why they needed to continue.

"Were we surprised? Were we shocked that they would engage in such activities? No," Hill explained years later. "To know the North Koreans is not to be surprised by anything."

Hill's position was not overly popular. While it had the support of Rice, other top Bush administration officials thought something needed to be done and that North Korea and Syria both needed to pay a price for their violations. Some members of Bush's staff—like Cheney—reminded the president that he had threatened to take action if North Korea was caught proliferating nuclear technology. It had. So now, what was he going to do about it?

But Israel's insistence, due to fear of war with Syria, that everyone remain silent tied the administration's hands. Bush and his staff couldn't just come out and accuse North Korea of building a nuclear reactor in Syria after the president had promised Olmert that everyone on the American side would keep quiet.

Eliot Cohen, Rice's assistant who had served on the Drafting Group, tried to push back. Now that the reactor has been destroyed, he told his boss, the chance of a regional war breaking out was slim. To Cohen it seemed that Israel's insistence on silence was more out of self-interest than anything else. Israel, he explained, needed to restore the image damaged during the Second Lebanon War in 2006. Staying quiet created an aura of mystery and myth around what had happened in northeast Syria on September 6 and Israel liked it that way.

"The Israeli military establishment sort of saw this as an opportunity to restore the kind of picture of a steel hand that reaches out in the middle of the night," he recalled years later. The problem was that while this might have benefited Israel's image of deterrence, "it did not serve American interests because the North Koreans would pay absolutely no penalty," he said.

Rice gave Cohen permission to review all of the intelligence the US had collected on North Korea's nuclear program. He spent weeks going through the material and discovered that Pyongyang had been lying about its plutonium program and likely had a whole separate secret nuclear program hidden in unknown and undeclared facilities.

Cohen took his findings to Rice and urged her to act. Combined with what North Korea was discovered to have done in Syria, Cohen argued that there was justification to "throw the heaviest possible sanctions onto them and isolate them to the extent that is possible internationally."

Cohen found an ally in Cheney, who agreed that something needed to be done to punish and "out" North Korea and Syria.

Despite their best arguments, Bush, toward the end of his presidency, was hesitant, showing greater restraint than in his first
term when he went to war in Iraq and Afghanistan.

Cheney and Cohen came up against resistance from Hill and
Rice, although each for a different reason. Hill, who Cheney
regularly knocked heads with, convinced the president that it
didn't make sense to upset the North Koreans in a way that
would compel them to pull out of the talks. America had a real
chance to stop North Korea's nuclear program once and for all,
he said. Why waste it all on something that was already in the
past?

Rice agreed but had an additional reason. She wanted to
keep quiet to prevent Syria from pulling out of a summit she
was trying to organize in November to restart the Israeli-
Palestinian peace process. Assad ended up sending his deputy
foreign minister to the summit, but when Olmert arrived no one
said a word about the reactor. It was as if nothing had happened
two months earlier along the Euphrates River.

Hadley, the president's national security adviser, also joined
the Rice-Hill camp. He questioned the claim that Syria and
North Korea had not been punished. Israel had destroyed their
reactor and their investment went down the drain. If that was
not a punishment, what was?

Hadley warned that more sanctions on North Korea, as
Cheney was advocating, would ultimately backfire. They might,
he said, enforce the ban on proliferation, but Pyongyang
would bolt from the talks and the source of the real threat to
the world—North Korea's ongoing nuclear program—would
remain. "Reinforcing the norm of proliferation would not have

solved the source of the problem that North Korea had a nuclear program that upset the balance in the Far East," he explained. Japan and South Korea, he told people, were already
contemplating the development of their own nuclear programs.
The only way to stop this from happening, Hadley concluded,
was exactly what the administration was trying to do—negotiate
a deal.

Administration officials came up with other excuses as well.
The Syria nuclear reactor, some said, had been started years before President Bush announced—after Pyongyang's first nuclear test in 2006—that the US would consider the transfer of
nuclear technology to other states a "grave threat." He didn't
know about the Syrian reactor when he made that speech and
therefore, these officials claimed, it did not need to apply.

The excuses didn't satisfy everyone. Some people were not
happy with the US agreement to remain silent. Two of them
were prominent members of Bush's own party: Pete Hoekstra,
the senior Republican congressman on the Permanent Select
Committee on Intelligence, and Ileana Ros-Lehtinen, the senior
Republican on the House Foreign Affairs Committee.

Hoekstra had been briefed with the rest of the Gang of Eight
shortly after Dagan's visit to Washington, DC, in April. Sworn
to secrecy, he remained silent and never spoke about the reactor. A week before the strike, he received a phone call from the
office of the director of National Intelligence updating him that
it was likely to happen soon. He was sure that once the reactor
was destroyed the US would immediately go public with what

had happened and use the story to up the pressure on Pyong-yang. But weeks went by and nothing happened.

Congress, though, wanted a detailed report and Hoekstra started feeling pressure from his committee. Media reports were coming out with details of what had happened, claiming that the Bush administration had known about the existence of the reactor from the beginning. Some in Congress were shocked. If the reports were true, how could Bush continue ne-gotiating with North Korea without punishing the regime?

Members of Congress were demanding an official briefing from the administration. Some had different motivations but, for the hawks, one interest was clear—a desire to unmask North Korea and prove that it could not be trusted. In the meantime, Syria had quietly destroyed what was left of the reactor, paving it over with concrete and what looked like, in satellite imagery, an empty metal warehouse.

At around the same time, the CIA learned of a visit by top North Korean engineers to the site, leading some analysts to suspect that the reactor might have been a North Korean facil-ity meant to produce and then ship plutonium back to North Korea. According to this theory, it was possible that Syria was simply hosting the reactor and in exchange was to be given a finished weapon at a later date. The evidence was scarce but it was enough to push the CIA to scour the world for other possi-ble North Korean nuclear plants. Even after the operation, there were still a lot of unanswered questions.

In late October, and after numerous requests to the admin-istration went ignored, Hoekstra and Ros-Lehtinen's patience ran out. The two penned an op-ed in the *Wall Street Journal* titled "What Happened in Syria?," in which they threatened to torpedo the administration's efforts to finalize a deal with North Korea. "The proposed deals with North Korea will involve substantial expenditures of US funds to pay for heavy fuel oil deliveries," Ros-Lehtinen and Hoekstra wrote. "Congress will be asked to approve the authorization of funds for this expenditure. We cannot carry out our duties when we are being denied information about these critical national security matters."[1]

It took some time but the pressure eventually paid off, partially because Hayden, the CIA director, agreed with Hoekstra and saw value in giving the congressional committees what they wanted. Hayden thought it was important to share news of a successful mission.

CIA veterans remembered how former director George Tenet had sat behind Colin Powell during his 2003 speech about Iraq's weapons of mass destructions that were never found. That experience was a stain on the agency's record. Now, there was an opportunity to pocket a win and show the world that sometimes intelligence agencies get it right.

There was also the deal Christopher Hill was working on with the North Koreans. Hayden believed that Hoekstra and Ros-Lehtinen were right. North Korea had been caught red-handed proliferating nuclear technology and gotten away with it.

"My country was getting close to getting a deal with the North Koreans, and we hadn't told many people the North Koreans had just committed the biggest proliferation crime in history," Hayden explained. Congress, the CIA director felt, needed to know what really happened.

At a series of meetings in the White House, he pushed hard

to get approval to brief Congress. It took some convincing but after a while, Hadley came around, albeit with one condition: the CIA had to make a movie that would include all of the visual evidence. Only this way, he said, "can we show that we got this one right."[2]

The CIA produced a film about the reactor using some of the photos Dagan had brought to the White House a year earlier alongside America's own satellite imagery. The idea was to prevent anyone from accusing the administration of falsifying intelligence. The 11-minute movie laid out in chronological order the sequence of events and, most important, how the US intelligence community had arrived at the conclusion that Syria was covertly building a nuclear reactor.

A few weeks later, in April 2008, almost exactly a year after Dagan's initial visit to the White House, Hadley, Hayden and Director of National Intelligence Mike McConnell went to Capitol Hill to brief six congressional committees. They then drove to Langley, where they held a similar briefing for the press.

Bush updated Olmert ahead of time about the planned disclosure, explaining that due to congressional pressure he didn't have a choice. While the US revelations could have been Olmert's opportunity to bask in the glory of the successful operation, the Israeli prime minister stuck by his vow of silence and instructed everyone in Israel to follow suit. Despite the year that had passed, Israel still feared that if it flaunted the successful strike, Assad would retaliate. Even after the entire world media reported on the strike, Israel refused to officially confirm or deny its involvement.

• • •

With the briefings on Capitol Hill over, it was now Condoleezza Rice's turn to update her staff. In an encrypted diplomatic cable sent to US embassies around the world, Rice explained the administration's strategy on the reactor as well as its decision to remain in the Six Party Talks. She wanted diplomats to be prepared for any questions they might encounter in their respective host countries.[3]

Rice went chronologically through the entire affair: how the US had detected the building that housed the reactor in 2006 but had not known what it was, and how Israel had come to the US in the spring of 2007 with conclusive evidence of a reactor. She explained the policy debate within the administration in general terms and how Israel had eventually decided—without US consent, she stressed—to attack.

In what seemed like an attempt to stave off future claims that the US green-lighted Israel's operation, Rice said that Israel did not seek American consent. "Nonetheless, we understand Israel's decision," she wrote. "Israel saw this reactor, and what Syria may have intended to do with it, as an existential threat that required it to act to defend itself."

She explained why the US was continuing to talk to North Korea and to participate in the Six Party Talks. The US, Rice said, had "made our concerns known to North Korea in a frank and comprehensive way." North Korea, she added, "acknowledged" those concerns. Rice added that the US intelligence community was closely following North Korea's "interactions" with Syria and that it was no longer at the level that it had been before the Israeli airstrike.

In conclusion, Rice said, the world needed to continue working together to stop the proliferation of nuclear technology. "This episode reminds us of the dangers of proliferation and that we must rededicate ourselves and act cooperatively to prevent the spread of weapons of mass destruction," she wrote.

While Rice's commitment to nonproliferation seemed sincere, it didn't really matter. North Korea and Syria continued to deny that they had engaged in illicit nuclear activity. After months of pressure, in June, Syria felt confident enough that it had destroyed any remaining proof to allow a group of inspectors from the International Atomic Energy Agency to visit the site.

The small team of inspectors was given one day to visit the site where the al-Kibar reactor had once stood. The inspectors took soil samples and conducted other environmental tests, which came back showing particles of man-made uranium. Syria, of course, rejected the findings and said that if they were real, it was because Israel used missiles with uranium. It went on to demand an international investigation into Israel's use of such weapons.

At the same time that the IAEA inspectors were heading to Syria, the US intelligence community made a shocking discovery of its own. Traces of highly enriched uranium were found on documents North Korea had provided the US as part of its commitment to come clean on its past nuclear activity. The uranium particles were not supposed to have been there. Pyongyang, which had consistently denied having a program to enrich uranium, was again lying to the world.

Not even this was enough to stop Bush and Rice from trying to get a deal done with North Korea. In October, they went a step further and removed North Korea—after 20 years—from the State Department's list of countries that sponsor terrorism. Practically, this meant that sanctions and other restrictions the US had imposed on North Korea could now be lifted. (The decision would be overturned in 2017 by President Donald Trump.)

But even that couldn't get North Korea to agree to a nuclear deal. By the end of Bush's presidency, the talks had completely fallen apart. North Korea had failed to reach a satisfactory verification protocol with the West on opening its nuclear facilities and had restarted its nuclear program, kicking out inspectors and barring them from the country. If that wasn't enough, in May 2009, just four months after Barack Obama entered the White House, North Korea tested a new nuclear weapon. Over the next few years it would test four more nuclear devices. Years would go by and Pyongyang would continue to provoke the world.

Did the al-Kibar affair and the Syrian experience teach Pyongyang that it could do whatever it wanted? Did the fact that it did not pay a price for proliferating nuclear technology to another rogue regime give it the confidence to keep working on its own nuclear program and test-fire ballistic missiles throughout the region?

While more than a decade has passed since the events of 2007, to many of the people who participated in the deliberations in Jerusalem and Washington it seems that what happened then emboldened Pyongyang. North Korea and Syria learned a bad lesson in September 2007: that America was more talk than action and they could do whatever they wanted. If the US was not prepared to take action against Syria, why would it ever use military force to stop Pyongyang?

What happened in 2007 should serve as a lesson in humility. The nuclear reactor being built in Syria was the greatest known act of state-sponsored nuclear proliferation. It is true that Syria and North Korea's investment went down the drain, but the world saw that sometimes crimes even on this scale can go unpunished.

For Israel there were also lessons that needed to be learned, but it didn't have much time for them. It had to shift its focus to the greater threat that loomed over everything—what was it going to do now about Iran?

Before the Syrian reactor was discovered, Olmert was sure that Bush would stop Iran's pursuit of a nuclear weapon. He was not alone. Other Israeli government and intelligence officials believed that Bush—the president who had gone to war in Iraq and Afghanistan—would not leave office with Iran still on track to obtaining a nuclear capability.

That assessment changed after al-Kibar. When Bush called Olmert in July 2007 to inform him of his decision not to attack Syria, the Israeli prime minister immediately understood that this applied to Iran as well. If Bush was not willing to approve an attack against a single facility in Syria that would have little fallout, there was no way he would one day order a large-scale multitargeted attack against Iran that could lead to a regional war. Israel, Olmert understood, would always be alone.

That understanding was reinforced just a few months after the bombing, when in December 2007 the US intelligence community published an updated National Intelligence Estimate (NIE) on Iran.[4] Titled "Iran: Nuclear Intentions and Capabilities," the lengthy report claimed that Iran had stopped its efforts to manufacture a nuclear bomb in 2003, around the same time as the American invasion of Iraq. While enrichment of uranium had since been renewed, the report claimed that as of mid-2007, Iran "had not restarted its nuclear weapons program."

The Israeli intelligence community was furious. In essence, the report meant that there was no need for a military strike against Iran's nuclear facilities and possibly not even sanctions.

Dagan and Yadlin gathered their top experts on Iran to review all previously obtained intelligence to see if, somehow, they had missed something along the way. The answer was no. Yes, Iran had frozen its military program back in 2003 but it had restarted it a few years later. How America had reached a different conclusion was unclear.

The report had originally been written with the intention of staying internal. Once word got out that there was a new NIE on Iran, Congress and the public demanded to see it. The administration couldn't stop its release. Otherwise, it would have seemed that the Bush administration was manipulating intelligence to advance its policies, just like some people believed it did with Iraq.

Some Israeli government officials believed that the US intelligence community had politicized the report to prevent Bush from embarking on another war. Basically, they claimed, America not only refused to attack Syria, it was now trying to stop anyone from attacking Iran. The CIA, some Israeli officials said, should really be called the CPIA—the "Central Political Intelligence Agency."

Yuval Steinitz, a future cabinet minister who at the time served as head of the Knesset's prestigious and discreet Intelligence Subcommittee, claimed that US intelligence services were suffering from the "Pendulum Syndrome." The US, he explained, was influenced by the trauma it suffered after the intelligence failure with Iraq's weapons of mass destruction and did not want to be caught crying wolf again. Israel, on the other hand, was traumatized by its failure to learn of Libya's nuclear program before it was abandoned in the deal Gaddafi had struck with the US in 2003.

As a result of these traumas, the countries interpreted the situation a little differently and both swung, like a pendulum, in the opposite direction. Israel took the more stringent approach since it was closer to Iran and would ultimately face the brunt of its missile attacks. America, on the other hand, took the laxer approach so it wouldn't find itself again in an unjustifiable war. Iraq was a mistake of overestimating; now with Iran, it seemed, the US intelligence community was making a mistake of underestimating.

It didn't help that a few months later, in early 2008, Bush rejected an Israeli request to receive overfly rights over Iraq and to purchase advanced bunker-buster bombs and new aerial refueling tankers. The US understood that Israel was contemplating an attack against Iran. The only system it was prepared to give Israel at the time was the X-Band radar, a sensitive early detection system that would increase the warning time Israel would have after Iranian missiles were launched its way.

The delivery of the radar sent a clear message to Israel— while America was willing to invest in Israel's defense, it was not willing to provide capabilities that could be used to attack Iran.

Israel was not ready to simply give up just yet. Six months later, in June 2008, 100 aircraft took off from multiple air force bases in Israel and began flying west. There were F-15s, F-16s, reconnaissance planes and helicopters. With Stars of David emblazoned on their wings, the planes flew 900 miles, all the way to Greece and back, the same distance it would take to fly from Israel to Natanz, Iran's main uranium enrichment facility.

Israel was again telling the world: we might be alone, but we are always prepared.

Mossad headquarters are located just north of Tel Aviv, near a movie theater and an aging army base. Old eucalyptus trees line the road leading up to the highly protected compound where some of Israel's greatest secrets remain hidden from the world for eternity.

Beyond serving as headquarters for Israel's foreign espionage agency, the compound is also a favorite venue for Israeli prime ministers interested in holding long off-the-books meetings far from the inquisitive eye of the public and particularly the media. In the summer of 2010, Prime Minister Benjamin Netanyahu convened a series of Security Cabinet meetings there.

One of the meetings focused on Iran and ways to combat its nuclear program. As it ended, Netanyahu turned to Ashkenazi and Dagan and ordered them to activate "P Plus," code for placing the IDF on high alert and ready for an imminent attack.[5]

There was silence. "P Plus" was the order given to the military for it to be prepared for a war within days. Both men were completely surprised. While the IDF had been preparing for years for a long-range airstrike against Iran's scattered nuclear facilities, it seemed that there was still time to allow sanctions and diplomacy to have their full effect. Iran had not yet broken out and enriched uranium to military levels. It was close to a bomb but not yet there.

Ashkenazi, who would have to oversee such a strike and the war that would follow, tried to explain that if the military fast-tracked its preparations, Iran and the rest of the world would notice. To meet the new schedule, the IDF would need to call up reserves, amass troops on the northern border and prepare the home front for the expected retaliatory missile onslaught from Iran and Hezbollah.

It's impossible, Ashkenazi said, to hide that kind of activity. Iran, he warned, would detect what is happening, fear that Israel is planning an attack and then potentially launch a preemptive strike of its own against Israel. To put the military on high alert, he said, meant that war would eventually come. "This is not something you do unless you are prepared to act," the chief of staff warned. "This accordion makes music when you play with it."[6]

Dagan, the Mossad chief, went a step further. "This order is illegal," he snapped at Netanyahu and Ehud Barak. According to Israeli law, Dagan reminded the two, a decision to go to war can only be made in a vote of the entire Security Cabinet, which at the time consisted of seven ministers. "What you are telling us means we are de facto starting a war with Iran. Get it first through the cabinet," Dagan said.

Netanyahu and Barak were furious. They felt like they had just experienced something of a rebellion. But Dagan and Ashkenazi were completely united in their opposition to a strike. They also had the support of some of the Security Cabinet members, including Moshe Ya'alon, a former IDF chief of staff, and Dan Meridor, the intelligence minister and author of Israel's defense doctrine.

Netanyahu learned that day that without his security chiefs' support, he had no way of getting an attack approved by the cabinet. Still today, it remains a mystery whether he and Barak were really planning on attacking Iran or were simply bluffing, a ploy to get the world to ratchet up sanctions. If it was a bluff, it was one of the greatest diplomatic ruses in recent times.

Genuine or deceptive, Israel scared the world. It created a credible military option and convinced the US that it was prepared to use it. Fearing that an Israeli attack would spark a regional war that would draw in the US, the Obama administration decided to increase its own efforts to find a solution, culminating in 2015 with the controversial nuclear deal with Iran.

This was a far cry from how Israel had stopped Syria's and

Iraq's nuclear ambitions. In 2007, everything was done in secret. Barely anyone in the government or the IDF knew that Israel was planning to bomb a nuclear reactor. Iran is a completely different story. For nearly 20 years, Israeli leaders have openly spoken about the possibility that one day they will attack Iran.

In addition, in contrast to what happened in 2010, Olmert succeeded in getting all of the security chiefs and almost his entire cabinet to agree that the reactor needed to be destroyed. From the beginning, there was a consensus that an Israeli attack would be needed if the Americans refused to act on their own.

While that hot summer day in 2010 was the closest Israel is known to have come to giving the attack order against Iran, it might not be the last time. In the coming years, Israel might again need to convene its cabinet and contemplate a unilateral strike against Iran's nuclear facilities.

But can Israel even take on Iran? Is the Begin Doctrine—according to which Israel will take preemptive action against nuclear threats—even relevant in the case of Iran, which has scattered its nuclear sites across the country, burying some of them in deep and fortified bunkers?

In addition, at what point, if at all, does Israel come to terms with the possibility that other countries will obtain nuclear weapons? The Islamic Republic of Pakistan, for example, has a significant nuclear arsenal but Israel does not consider the possibility of launching an attack there. Why?

Meridor, one of the participants in that fateful 2010 Security Cabinet meeting, told me that for Israel to consider preemptive action against another country's nuclear program, two criteria first have to be met: the country has to be one of Israel's enemies and also have the potential to one day consider using a nuclear weapon against it. Syria fit both. Pakistan does not.

For Meridor, the Syrian reactor story is a lesson in humility. Syria has always been one of Israel's primary intelligence targets. But despite Aman and Mossad's focus on the country, it took several years to learn about the existence of the al-Kibar reactor. The Israeli intelligence community faced a similar situation just four years earlier in 2003, when it learned of Libya's nuclear program only after Gaddafi announced that it was being dismantled.

These limitations will always exist, and leaders will only be able to make decisions based on the information they have before them. They will also always be informed by their life experiences. Menachem Begin faced global opposition and was on the eve of reelection when he sent the air force on an unprecedented mission in 1981 to bomb Saddam Hussein's reactor. Olmert was under criminal investigation and was facing calls to resign due to the outcome of the Second Lebanon War. Both might have been excused for agreeing to plans to use diplomacy, and not force, to stop Hussein and Assad.

But they didn't back down. Would other politicians have done the same? It is difficult to know. Like any politician or statesman, Begin and Olmert both had their flaws. But they also understood their place in history and the need for action. That is what leaders do. They don't take the popular route, go with the safe bet or look for the easy way out.

The story of Syria's nuclear reactor took place more than a

decade ago, but the lessons learned from it resonate more than ever as Israel and Iran remain locked in a game of brinkmanship that could easily evolve into an all-out conflict. It is a story that combines the stuff of legends and is on par with Israel's most memorable operations: the Sayeret Matkal raid on Entebbe, Uganda, in 1976 to free Israeli hostages; the bombing of Saddam Hussein's nuclear reactor; and the destruction of the Egyptian and Syrian air forces in the opening salvo of what became known as the Six Day War.

While years have passed since the bombing along the Euphrates River, the Middle East is far from becoming a safe place. As work on this book progressed, Israel was continuing to carry out mysterious bombings in Syria while combating Hamas terrorists in the Gaza Strip. Trump had pulled out of the nuclear deal with Iran and held a historic summit with Kim Jong Un, just months after threatening to destroy North Korea.

The way Begin and Olmert handled the Iraqi and Syrian reactors showed the world that there is no such thing as an "international community" when it comes to one's national security. Three times Israel tried to get the world to act—in 1981, in 2007 and in more recent years against Iran—and in all of the cases it ended up feeling isolated and on its own.

Concerns about a future war with Iran are real and legitimate. Its proxy Hezbollah has missiles today that can carry warheads with half a ton of explosives and strike anywhere inside Israel with amazing precision. Some experts fear that preemptive action is simply not worth it.

This book shows how, if needed, it can still be done. What happened in 2007 is a playbook for how one country neutralized an existential threat. How it diligently and secretly gathered intelligence, cooperated with its close allies, readied its military and launched an attack without any guarantees of how it all would end. But most of all it is about decision making.

This book is not about who was right or who was wrong. The US had legitimate concerns that a strike against Syria would destabilize Iraq and escalate into a regional conflagration. Israel, on the other hand, felt an urgency that the US simply did not share.

More important, in this story, we are given a glimpse into what makes Israel unique. It is a complicated country, threatened like no one else. But it takes its role—the preservation of the Jewish people—seriously.

As the ancient Jewish sage Hillel asked some 2,000 years ago: If I am not for myself, who will be for me?

Acknowledgments

The morning of September 6, 2007, I arrived at an IDF base in central Israel together with a group of Israeli military reporters. We had been invited for a briefing with the commander of the IDF Medical Corps, an officer with the rank of brigadier general. He told us about some new developments within his corps and how it was applying some of the lessons learned from the Lebanon war a year earlier.

Then our phones started to buzz with some mysterious news. The Syrian government's news agency, SANA, had released a short statement claiming that its air defense systems had chased away Israeli warplanes the night before.

We asked the general sitting before us what had happened. He mumbled something about how if it was Israel it was probably important. It seemed that he had no idea either.

As the days went by and the true story of what happened

that night came out, it became clear that we had been played. The IDF Spokesperson's Unit had intentionally set up a briefing for us reporters on a matter as mundane as the Medical Corps to try and keep us busy with other news. It was all part of the overall military strategy—stay quiet and divert attention away from what really happened in northeast Syria.

Ever since that day, this story has fascinated me. As more details emerged over the years, it became clear that this was a story of huge significance, not just for Israel but for the entire world. It had all the ingredients of a blockbuster movie—an existential threat discovered by master spies, a vaunted air force called into action, nonstop nail-biting debates in the war cabinet and a perfectly executed plan to distract the world.

This book would not have been possible if the people who were involved had not agreed to share their stories with me. They are the men and women from Israel and the US who worked—sometimes together—to eliminate what Israel perceived to be a threat of an existential nature. Some of these people I met with numerous times. Others sat with me for hours, patiently helping me piece together this complicated puzzle.

I thank my agents, Peter and Amy Bernstein, who helped me craft the idea into a book from the day I first proposed it over breakfast at their New York apartment, and of course, Elisabeth Dyssegaard, my editor at St. Martin's Press, who believed in this book and me from when the proposal first landed on her desk. Her comments were invaluable in making this book better. I also thank the *Jerusalem Post*, where I serve as editor in chief and which has provided me with a platform to share

Israel's amazing stories with the world. A special thanks as well to Carolyn Hessel for her wise counsel. Thank you all.

I finished this book at a time of great personal trial. Our second daughter, Miki, was diagnosed with a rare bone cancer and set us on a journey that we never imagined was even possible. Many of these pages were written late at night in a hospital room watching her sleep as bags of chemotherapy drugs dripped slowly into her body. Seeing Miki battle cancer and still smile has taught me how resilient children can be and how despite their pain and suffering, they can still enjoy life and care for others even when it is they who need the care.

The biggest debt of gratitude I owe my wife and partner, Chaya. Without her there wouldn't be this book or any of the others I have written. She has always pushed me to strive for more and to be better. Thank you.

Notes

A note on sources: endnotes are provided for references to material taken from transcripts, books and other written material. Numerous people from Israel, the United States and Europe were interviewed during the work on this book. Some agreed to be quoted on the record; others spoke on background while agreeing that the information they provided me could be used. Conversations described in the book are based on the recollections of participants in those conversations or documented transcripts.

Introduction

1. Jeffrey Heller, "Netanyahu Signals Israel Will Act with Free Hand in Syria," Reuters, November 13, 2007.
2. Ariel Sharon, address, Government Press Office, Jerusalem, December 15, 1981.

1. A Raid in Vienna

1. The exact details of how Israel collected the incriminating evidence that Syria was building a nuclear reactor remain a mystery to this day. Although this chapter relies heavily on previous publications—specifically an article by David Makovsky in the *New Yorker*—it must be noted that Israeli officials have neither confirmed nor denied the accuracy of these claims.

2. Based on interviews with participants at the meeting.

3. Interview with Dick Cheney; and Dick Cheney, *In My Time* (Threshold Editions, 2011), 465–66.

4. Cheney, *In My Time.*

5. See President Bush's Statements on North Korea Nuclear Test, October 9, 2006, https://georgewbush-whitehouse.archives.gov/news/releases/2006/10/20061009.html.

6. "Meir Dagan, Israel Spy Chief—Obituary," *Daily Telegraph*, March 18, 2016, www.telegraph.co.uk/news/obituaries/12196869/Meir-Dagan-Israeli-spy-chief-obituary.html.

7. Man of the Year for 2008, Channel 2 News, September 26, 2008, www.mako.co.il/news-channel2/Friday-Newscast/Article-f1cbeb726ef9c11004.htm (Hebrew).

8. Interview with Michael Hayden in 2017; and Michael Hayden, *Playing to the Edge* (Penguin Press, 2016), 255–56.

9. David Makovsky, "The Silent Strike," *New Yorker*, September 17, 2012.

10. Julian Borger, "Iran's Nuclear Programme: The Holy Grail of the Intelligence World," *Guardian*, December 10, 2012.

11. Nuclear Threat Initiative, August 15, 2012, www.nti.org/learn/facilities/464/.

12. Based on interviews with Israeli officials present at the meeting.

13. Ibrahim Othman and Maha Abdulrahim, "Establishment of a Zone Free of Mass Destruction Weapons in the Region of the Middle East: Requirements and Constraints," UNIDIR, 2004, www.baselpeaceoffice.org/sites/default/files/imce/menwfz/building_a_wmd_free_zone_in_the_middle_east_unidir.pdf.

14. Ronen Bergman, *Rise and Kill First* (Random House, 2018), 588–90.

2. What Do We Do Now?

1. Michael Hayden, *Playing to the Edge* (Penguin Press, 2016), 255.

2. Interview with Michael Hayden in 2017.

3. Interviews with Ehud Olmert throughout 2017 and 2018; and George Bush, *Decision Points* (Broadway Books, 2010), 420–22.

4. Elliott Abrams, *Tested by Zion* (Cambridge University Press, 2013), 236.

5. Hayden, *Playing to the Edge,* 257.

6. See Title 50 U.S. Code 3091—General Congressional Oversight Provisions, www.law.cornell.edu/uscode/text/50/3091#a_1.

7. Condoleezza Rice, *No Higher Honor* (Crown, 2011), 488.

8. Dick Cheney, *In My Time* (Threshold Editions, 2011), 469.

9. Ibid.

10. Ibid.

11. Hayden, *Playing to the Edge,* 250.

12. Robert Gates, *Duty: Memoirs of a Secretary at War* (Alfred Knopf, 2014), 173.

13. Ibid., 174.

3. Nuclear Déjà Vu

1. Roger Claire, *Raid on the Sun* (Broadway Books, 2004), 137.

2. Moshe Nissim, "Leadership and Daring in the Destruction of the Iraqi Reactor," *Israel's Strike Against the Iraqi Nuclear Reactor 7 June, 1981* (Menachem Begin Heritage Center, 2003), 31.

3. Leonard S. Spector and Avner Cohen, "Israel's Airstrike on Syria's Reactor: Implications for the Nonproliferation Regime," *Arms Control Today* 38, no. 6 (2008): 15–21.

4. Ibid.

5. UPI, "Israeli Spy Visited a Plant Where Uranium Vanished," *Los Angeles Times*, June 16, 1986, http://articles.latimes.com/1986-06-16/news/mn-11009_1_israeli -intelligence.

4. Ticking Clock

1. Mark Matthews, *Lost Years: Bush, Sharon and Failure in the Middle East* (Nation Books, 2007), 21.

2. Governor George W. Bush on His Trip to Israel, Jewish Virtual Library, www .jewishvirtuallibrary.org/governor-george-w-bush-on-his-trip-to-israel.

3. Dennis Ross, *Doomed to Succeed* (Farrar, Straus and Giroux, 2015), 302.

4. Israeli Foreign Ministry readout of the meeting, June 19, 2007, www.mfa.gov.il /mfa/pressroom/2007/pages/press%20conference%20pm%20olmert%20 meets%20with%20us%20president%20bush%2019-jun-2007.aspx.

5. Robert Gates, *Duty: Memoirs of a Secretary at War* (Alfred Knopf, 2014), 174.

6. Ibid. 176.

7. Cheney, *In My Time,* 471.

8. Eric Edelman on Al-Kibar and Operation Orchard, Tikvah Fund event, December 28, 2015, https://tikvahfund.org/library/eric-edelman-on-al-kibar-and -operation-orchard/.

9. George Bush, *Decision Points* (Broadway Books, 2010), 421.

10. Gates, *Duty,* 175.

11. David Makovsky, "The Silent Strike," *New Yorker*, September 17, 2012.

12. Yossi Verter, "Three Prime Ministers, One Beating Hatred," *Haaretz,* March 23, 2018, 1 (Hebrew, translated by author).

5. Olmert's War

1. Yossi Verter, "Look Who's Becoming a Ben-Gurionist, Peres Said with Amazement," *Haaretz,* December 3, 2003 (Hebrew, translated by author).

2. Aluf Benn and Yossi Verter, "Olmert Promised: People Will Love Saying They Love the Country," *Haaretz*, March 10, 2006 (Hebrew, translated by author).

3. Ewan MacAskill, "Blair Refuses to Back Olmert's Go-It-Alone West Bank Plan," *Guardian*, June 12, 2006.

4. Amos Harel and Avi Issacharoff, *34 Days: Israel, Hezbollah and the War in Lebanon* (St. Martin's Press, 2008), 81–83.

5. Poll: Israelis support Lebanon incursion, Associated Press, August 1, 2006.

6. Amos Harel, "The General Who Is Not Ashamed to Storm," *Haaretz* (Hebrew, translated by author), May 11, 2012.

7. Elliott Abrams, *Tested by Zion* (Cambridge University Press, 2013), 190.

6. Time to Attack

1. The following sequence of events is based on interviews with Israeli military planners on how past and similar covert operations took place as well as on previous publications including: Yaakov Katz and Yoaz Hendel, *Israel vs. Iran—The Shadow*

War (Potomac Books, 2012), Michael Bar-Zohar and Nissim Mishal, *Mossad: The Greatest Missions of the Israeli Secret Service* (Ecco, 2014), as well as Erich Follath and Holger Stark, "The Story of 'Operation Orchard,'" *Der Spiegel,* November 2, 2009.

2. The following section is based on interviews with British officials.

7. What Was Assad Thinking?

1. David W. Lesch, *Syria: The Fall of the House of Assad* (Yale University Press, 2012), 3.

2. Interview with Danny Yatom in 2017.

3. Cbsnews.com staff, "Syria's Assad Sworn in as Prez," CBS/AP, July 17, 2000.

4. Lesch, *Syria,* 8.

5. Jannis Bruhl, "Where Did Syria's Chemical Weapons Come From?" ProPublica, September 25, 2003, www.propublica.org/article/where-did-syrias-chemical -weapons-come-from.

6. This link is to a 1982 CIA intelligence report on illicit chemical weapons in Asia and Afghanistan, www.cia.gov/library/readingroom/docs/DOC_0000284013 .pdf.

7. Gunther Latsch, "Did German Companies Aid Syrian Chemical Weapons Program?" *Der Spiegel,* January 23, 2015, www.spiegel.de/international/germany /german-companies-suspected-of-aiding-syrian-chemical-weapons-program-a -1014722.html.

8. Interview with John Bolton in 2017.

9. Transcript from the Senate hearing on May 18, 2005, about the nomination of John Bolton as ambassador to the United Nations, www.congress.gov/congressional -report/109th-congress/executive-report/1/1.

8. Wag the Dog

1. Ronen Bergman, "Red Falcon," *Atavist Magazine,* 2015, https://magazine.atavist .com/operation-red-falcon.

9. What's Next?

1. Bruce Livesey, "The Bizarre Life of Nathan Jacobson," *National Observer*, November 29, 2017, www.nationalobserver.com/2017/11/29/news/rise-and-fall-nathan-jacobson; and Nahum Barnea, "How We Missed North Korea," *Yediot Ahronot* (Hebrew, translated by author), December 24, 2017, www.yediot.co.il/articles/0,7340,L-5018916,00.html.

2. See US cable on meeting of Congressional delegation led by Mike Boehner to Israel, March 28, 2008. https://wikileaks.org/plusd/cables/08TELAVIV738_a.html.

3. Roee Nahmias and AP, "Syria Says Defenses Opened Fire on Israeli Aircraft Overnight," Ynetnews, September 6, 2007.

4. Ehud Olmert, *In Person* (Hebrew, translated by author) (Yedioth Ahronot Books, 2018), 212.

5. Ronny Sofer, Olmert "ready for unconditional peace talks with Syria," Ynetnews, September 18, 2007.

6. While Israel has never formally taken responsibility for the assassination of Imad Mughniyeh, numerous reports have emerged over the years detailing the joint Israeli-US operation.

7. Ronen Bergman, *The Secret War with Iran* (Free Press, 2008), 242.

8. Jeff Stein, "How the CIA Took Down Hezbollah's Top Terrorist, Imad Mughniyah," *Newsweek*, January 31, 2015; and Adam Goldman and Ellen Nakashima, "CIA and Mossad Killed Senior Hezbollah Figure in Car Bombing," *Washington Post*, January 30, 2015.

9. Bergman, *The Secret War with Iran*, 605.

10. See copy of NSA document on Suleiman at www.documentcloud.org/documents/2165140-manhunting-redacted.html#document/p1; and Matthew Cole, "Israeli Special Forces Assassinated Senior Syrian Official," *Intercept*, July 15, 2015.

11. See US cable titled "US Sought Financial Pressure on Top Syrian Officials" at www.theguardian.com/world/us-embassy-cables-documents/100578.

12. See US cable titled "Israel Suspected in Syrian Sniper Killing" at www.theguardian.com/world/us-embassy-cables-documents/164634.

13. See US cable titled "Corruption Investigation Rattles Business Community," April 9, 2009, at www.wikileaks.org/plusd/cables/09DAMASCUS274_a.html.

10. Conclusion

1. Peter Hoekstra and Ileana Ros-Lehtinen, "What Happened in Syria?" *Wall Street Journal,* October 20, 2007.

2. Michael Hayden, *Playing to the Edge* (Penguin Press, 2016), 267.

3. See US cable titled "Syria's Clandestine Nuclear Program," April 25, 2008, https://wikileaks.org/plusd/cables/08STATE43817_a.html.

4. See full report titled "Iran: Nuclear Intentions and Capabilities, National Intelligence Estimate," November 2007, https://www.dni.gov/files/documents/Newsroom/Reports%20and%20Pubs/20071203_release.pdf.

5. See Uvda's broadcast from November 4, 2012. www.mako.co.il/tv-ilana_dayan/2013-e2afde9009f4a310/Article-335511a3cebca31006.htm.

6. Ibid.

Index